Blooms & Baskets

GEMS OF SUMMER

Blooms & Baskets
GEMS OF SUMMER

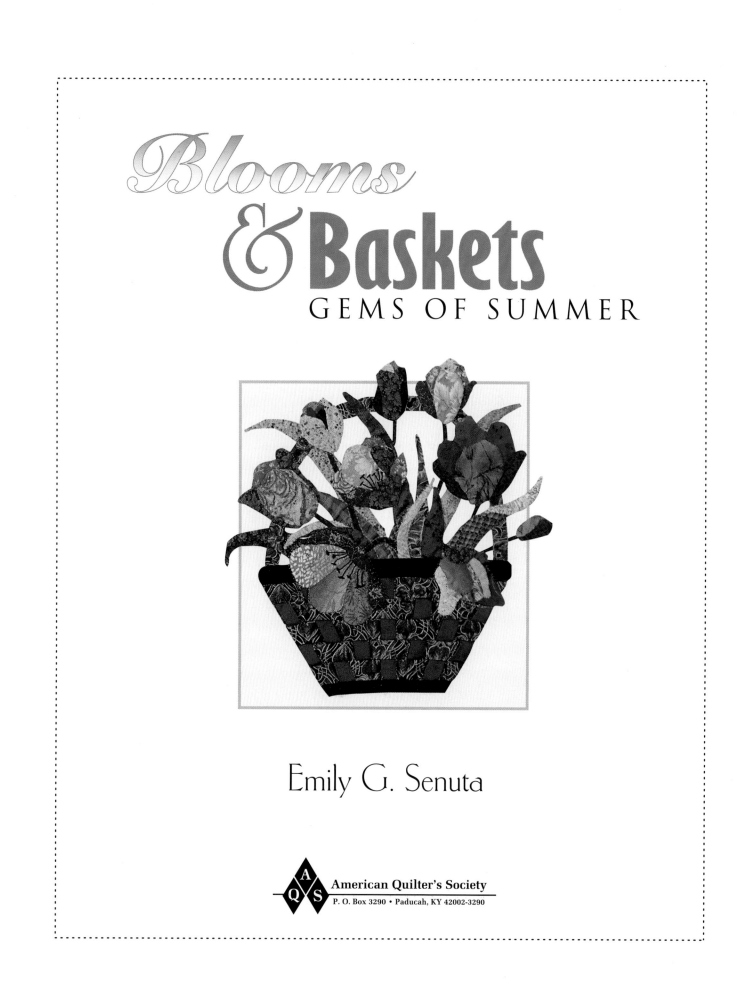

Emily G. Senuta

American Quilter's Society
P. O. Box 3290 • Paducah, KY 42002-3290

Located in Paducah, Kentucky, the American Quilter's Society (AQS) is dedicated to promoting the accomplishments of today's quilters. Through its publications and events, AQS strives to honor today's quiltmakers and their work and to inspire future creativity and innovation in quiltmaking.

EDITOR: BARBARA SMITH
BOOK DESIGN/ILLUSTRATIONS: ELAINE WILSON
COVER DESIGN: MICHAEL BUCKINGHAM
PHOTOGRAPHY: CHARLES R. LYNCH

Library of Congress Cataloging-in-Publication Data

Senuta, Emily G.

Blooms & baskets : gems of summer / Emily G. Senuta

p. cm.

ISBN 1-57432-716-X

1. Quilting--Patterns. 2. Flowers in art 3. Appliqué

I. Title. II. Title: Blooms and baskets.

TT835.S452 1998

746.46'041--dc21 98-40863

CIP

Additional copies of this book may be ordered from: American Quilter's Society, PO Box 3290, Paducah, KY 42002-3290 @ $24.95. Add $2.00 for postage and handling.

Printed in the U.S.A. by Image Graphics, Paducah, KY

Dedication

To…

my friend, Jacquita Ellis, who years ago made me believe I could write a book;

my friend, Doreen Perkins, who made and helped me do it;

my family, Jan, Chad, and Lisa, who understood and supported my endeavor;

and my mom, Margaret Ferguson, for getting me started in quilting and for sharing her love of flowers and much more with me.

EVERLASTING GEMS OF SUMMER (Quilt Setting 4), 60" x 78", by the author. The 12½" blocks are set on point with alternate pieced blocks that create the circular frame around each basket. The baskets in this quilt were made from the original patterns, which were later redesigned slightly.

Acknowledgments

Many people have assisted me in a variety of ways during the production of this book.

The American Quilter's Society, which agreed to publish my patterns.

My friends who contributed samples for my book.

My students who provided me with the basis to perfect the material.

And the following people:

Margaret Berglund
Jinny Beyer
Glenda Bond
Don Brady
Bonnie Browning
Marianne Fons
Pam Fowler
Bev Goebel
Rosie Grinstead
Klaudeen Hansen
Anna Kephart
Jeana Kimball
Dan Larson
LaDonna Marks
Phyllis Miller
Sharon Neuer
Bea Oglesby
Nancy Pearson
Doreen Perkins
Anita Shackelford
Reiko Watanabe

I would like to thank all these people from the bottom of my heart, for without their help and support, this book never would have been created.

Contents

Preface

My love affair with fabric began at an early age. When I was a young girl, my sisters and I would go to town with Mother to shop for groceries. More often than not, we also visited the department store, almost always to look at dress patterns and fabric. I remember wandering down the aisles with my mother and caressing the fabrics as we tried to select one for a dress. I learned to appreciate their beauty, but equally important, was the recognition of quality I gained by comparing the feel of the fabrics. I now know that I was experiencing the "hand" of the fabric. The natural fibers of cotton, wool, and silk were always my favorites.

When I was old enough, I learned embroidery and a little crochet from my grandmother, but I finally found my niche when I learned to sew in home economics class in high school. After that, I had a vested interest in fabric shopping. My early sewing projects were, of course, garments. I learned first-hand which fabrics were good choices and which ones were most compatible with my projects. I had to consider sewability, wearability, and durability. I learned about the special problems of patterned fabrics, directional prints, plaids, and textured and napped fabrics. I considered the drape of the fabric, the thread count, and the weight. I initially selected patterns within my abilities, but quickly branched out, choosing patterns that offered a greater challenge. The more difficult ones forced me to learn about fitting odd shapes together and taught me the importance of accuracy and sewing a straight line, as in topstitching. The pride I felt when wearing a garment that looked professionally made was very satisfying.

During these years, I was aware of quilts since my mother had made several, as did each of my grandmothers. I even cut out the pieces for Sunbonnet Sue and Little Dutch Boy quilts when I was in high school, after seeing one my grandmother was making. It would have been my first appliqué project. But for the lack of time and instruction, the pieces were put away in a box, never to be stitched. I was married with a small son before it again occurred to me to make a quilt. It sounded easy. After all, I was a skilled seamstress, and sewing garments had become a chore. I needed a challenge that would also satisfy my creative urge. After all, how difficult could it be?

I now look back at my early attempts with chagrin. The good news was that I already had a working knowledge of sewing and fabrics, and I was already an accomplished seamstress. The bad news was that much of what I knew did not translate well to quilts. I had a hard time letting go of ⅝" seam allowances, polyester fabrics (double-knits were big then), and easing fullness. But I had the advantage of a good teacher, my mother, who was more than willing to teach me this skill. We still enjoy this common interest.

Soon, making quilts became my method of artistic expression. Before this, I had dabbled in oil painting, but I put my paints away. Fabric, after all, was safer around my small son, I reasoned, even though great care had to be taken with scissors, needles, etc. Because my mother was making a quilt and had the pattern, I started with one made from the Clay's Choice pattern. It was simple enough, and I made two tops, one for my sister Mary and one as a fund raiser for my son's school. (Does any of this sound familiar?)

Then, of course, I had to make a quilt for my sister Madeline. I chose a one-patch pattern, Thousand Pyramids. I had these first three tops quilted by a group of ladies for a nominal sum. But the natural progression was to learn to quilt, so I canvassed my friends until I found eight or nine who also thought quilting would be fun, and with my mother's tutelage, we learned to quilt.

I have always been intrigued with making original designs. Few of my quilts are exact duplicates of something I have seen. But only in the last five years have I limited the majority of my work to original designs. I consider everything I have done a stepping stone, part of the ongoing learning process necessary to master a vast and complex medium. The journey is not complete...I still have much to learn and many more quilts to make.

Introduction

Gems of Summer

These designs are the result of (1) ignorance - I had no idea how much work was involved in designing; (2) ambition - it was important to me to use my own original materials; and (3) faith - a group of lovely quilting friends had enough confidence in me to take a block-a-month class when only three designs existed. What pressure there was each month to develop a new basket pattern, sew it, and write directions. I was always up until the wee hours the night before a class, writing instructions I hoped would make sense. And always before the class, I had to make a last minute trip to copy the pattern and instructions for each class member, praying I would not be late for class. During this process, as I learned what worked best and what I liked, I changed my fabrics three times. Somewhere along the line, the designs took on a life of their own. What started out to be a focus on different-shaped baskets, became a focus on the floral arrangements contained in the baskets. The arrangements became more realistic, more intricate, and more difficult to sew. The number of pieces in each pattern increased, bringing groans from the class as I presented each one.

As I watched the star pupils eagerly attack each pattern, it soon became obvious to me that I would not be the first to finish a quilt with my designs. At the completion of the class, I was also aware that some of the patterns had to be improved or retired. I retired one simply because I didn't like it. (How odd that it is the block many people miss.) Another block was retired because I didn't feel comfortable calling it my design, when in fact, I had copied it (with some changes) from a set of dishes. Completely new floral arrangements were added to two other baskets. While the design process continued, I was sidetracked by other projects, as quilters often are - family, work, guild projects, and challenge quilts. So five years later, I finally finished my Everlasting Gems of Summer quilt, shown on page 6. Because it had become such a part of me, and with the help of my good friend Doreen Perkins (who diligently searched the dictionary and thesaurus for a title while I quilted madly to meet a self-imposed deadline), I gave it a name based on my initials, E. G. S.

After an encouraging response, the desire to publish the patterns emerged. With that desire came the realization of how difficult a project it would be. Instructions given verbally in class must be put to paper in a language that clearly conveys the idea. Illustrations, many illustrations, would be required. And quilts! I would need a lot of quilts to photograph for the book. How fortunate that my students were making beautiful quilts. So I started at the beginning and progressed to the end, just as I would for making a quilt. And with much help, encouragement, and advice, it comes to this. I pass the designs to you with the hope they will provide hours of pleasure in the making and years of enjoyment to follow.

Chapter 1

Before You Begin

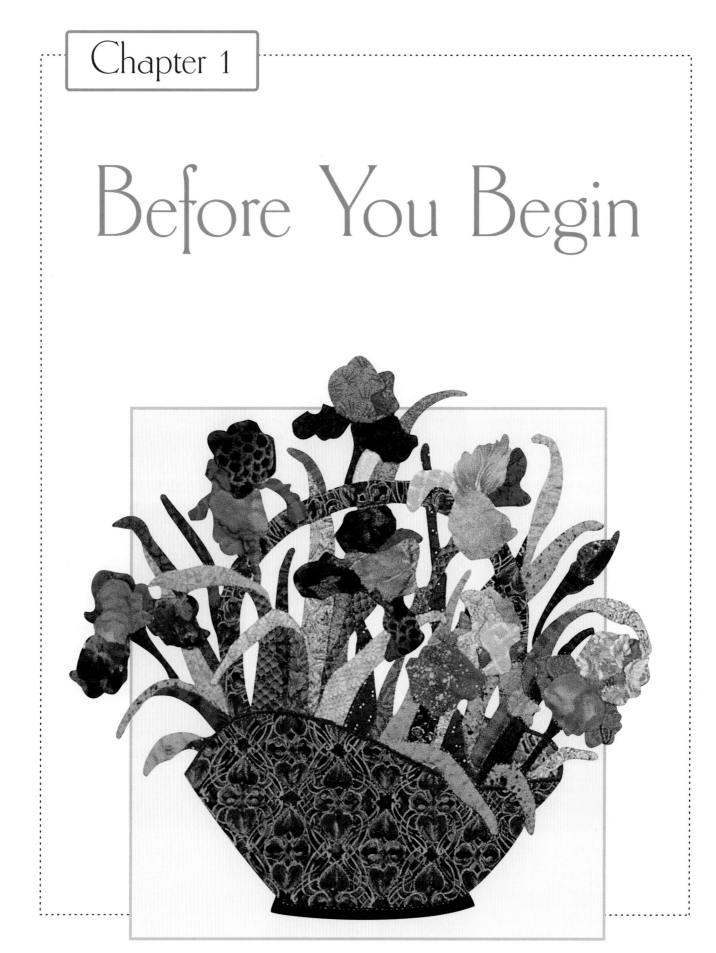

Fabric

To achieve a well-balanced design, it is good to have a general idea of the color scheme and overall look you want to achieve before selecting any of the fabrics. Your fabrics for the patterns in Chapter 3 fall into four distinct categories: background, basket, flowers, and leaves and stems.

Backgrounds

The background fabric provides a canvas for your appliqué art. Choose one that will enhance and complement the designs that will be applied to it. Consider this fabric an investment worthy of the time you will spend on your project. Effective choices include the following:

Hand-dyed cottons and watercolor fabrics. Their subtle shadings add wonderful depth and interest. There are a lot of these available, but if you can't find just the right one for your project, consider having your background fabric custom dyed. Look for high-quality fabrics, such as Pima cotton. The pattern and shading should be subtle (Fig. 1–1). If there is too much variation in color or contrast, your appliqué may tend

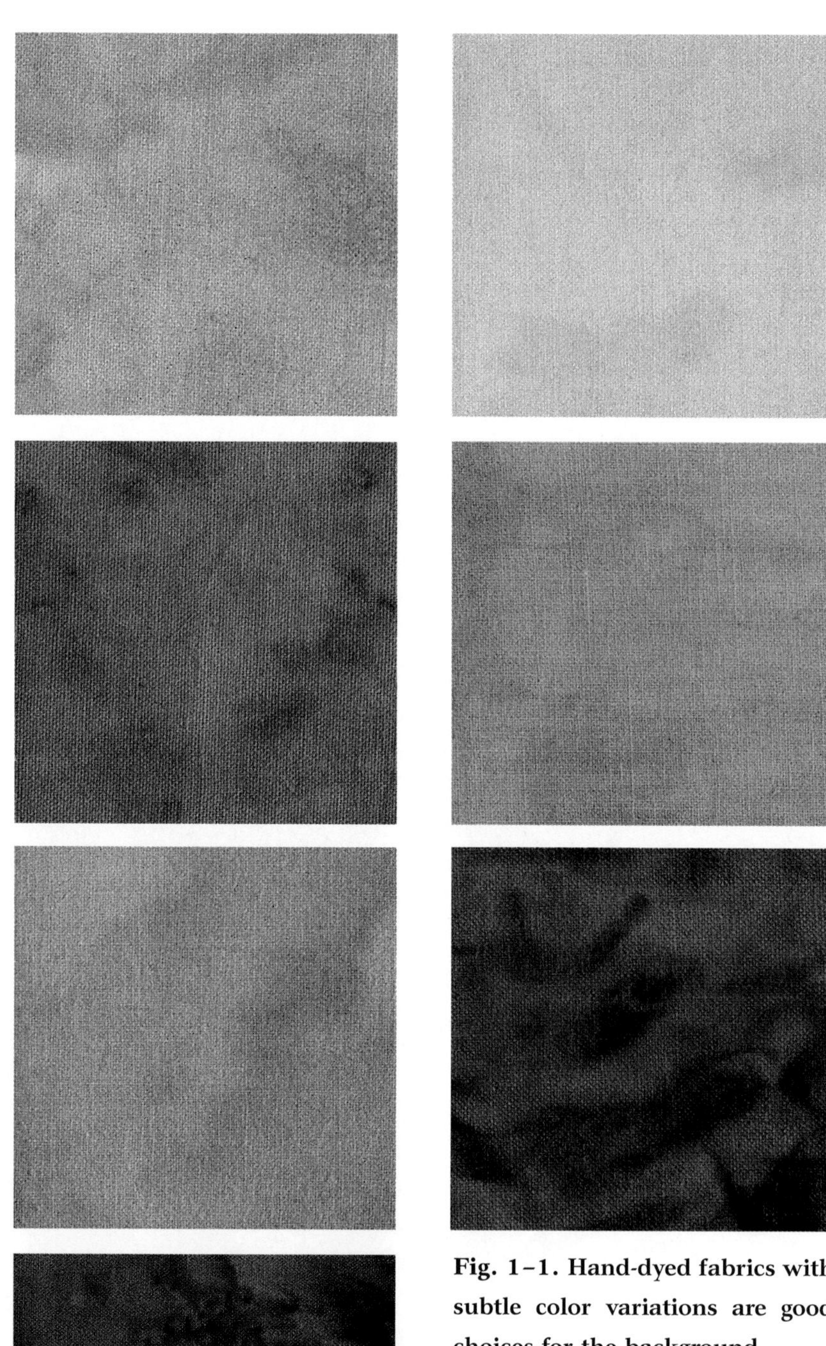

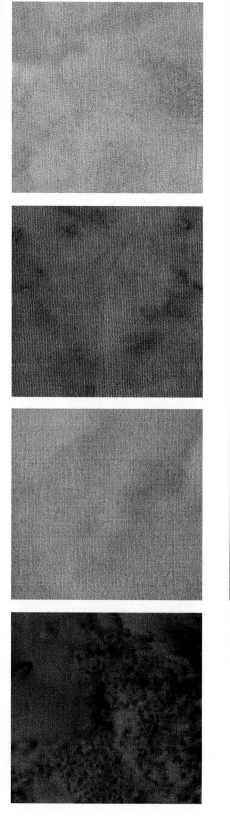

Fig. 1–1. Hand-dyed fabrics with subtle color variations are good choices for the background.

to disappear or lose importance (Fig. 1–2).

Neutral colors with unobtrusive all-over print. There are some lovely printed neutrals available (Fig. 1–3). White-on-white fabric is included in this category, but it is not a first choice because it can be difficult to needle.

Solid-colored Pima cottons. Few quilt shops carry them, and you may have to search to find them. They are more likely to be found at fashion-fabric stores in the spring

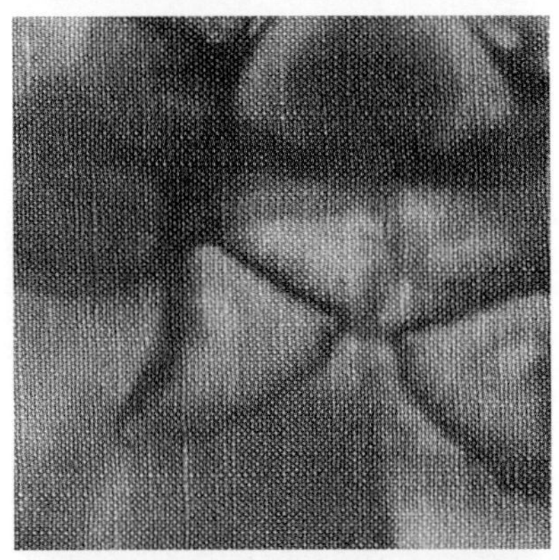

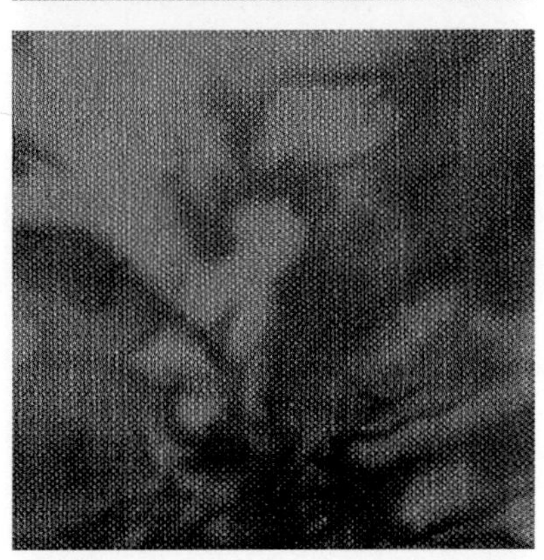

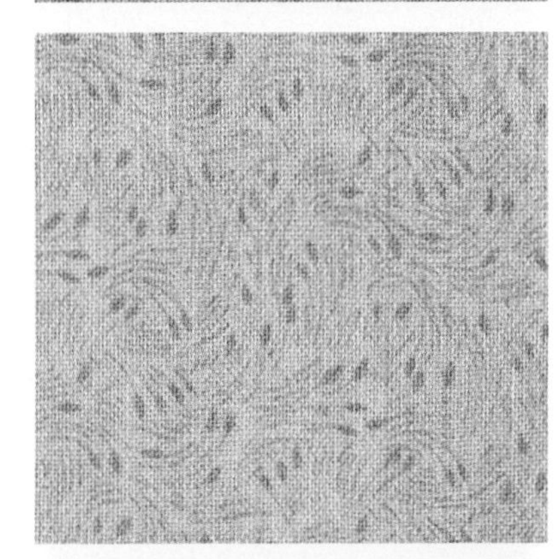

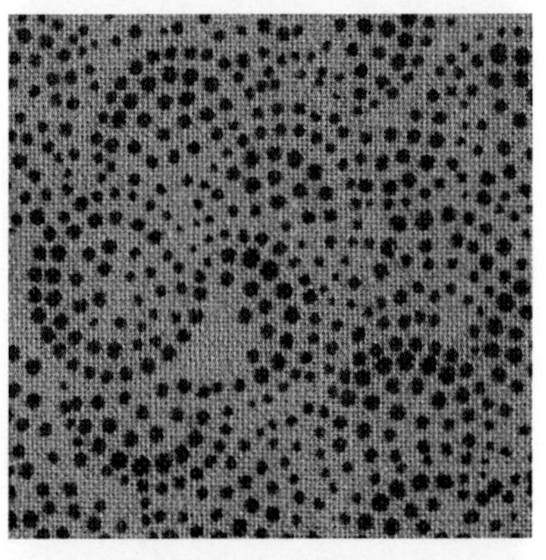

Fig. 1–2. Hand-dyed fabrics with strong color variations will be too distracting to use as backgrounds.

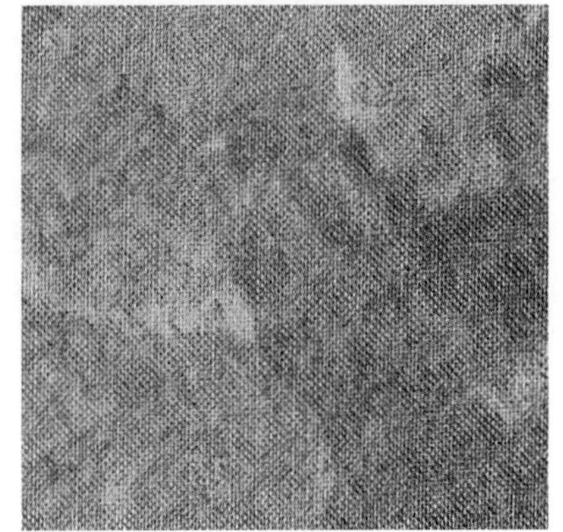

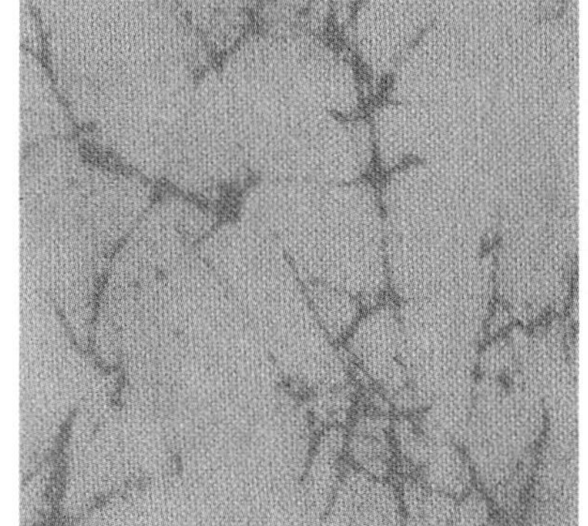

Fig. 1–3. (RIGHT) **Neutral-colored prints make good background fabrics.**

and summer, and they are worth the time and the generally higher price. Pima cottons will give your quilt a luxurious quality, and you will enjoy working with them.

High-quality solids. Several of the better fabric manufacturers produce solids in a wide range of colors. These fabrics are preferable to muslin because of the more elegant look they provide. Before purchasing, check the thread count because some solids are too loosely woven for appliqué.

It is not necessary to limit yourself to neutral colors like white or beige in any of the above categories. Just remember to consider the various aspects of your quilt before making your final selection. A green background, for example, will require you to take greater care in your use of greens for leaves to prevent them from disappearing into the background. The same would happen with red flowers on a red background.

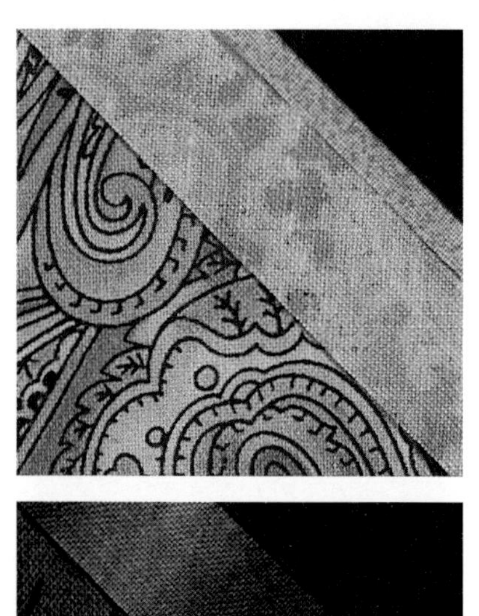

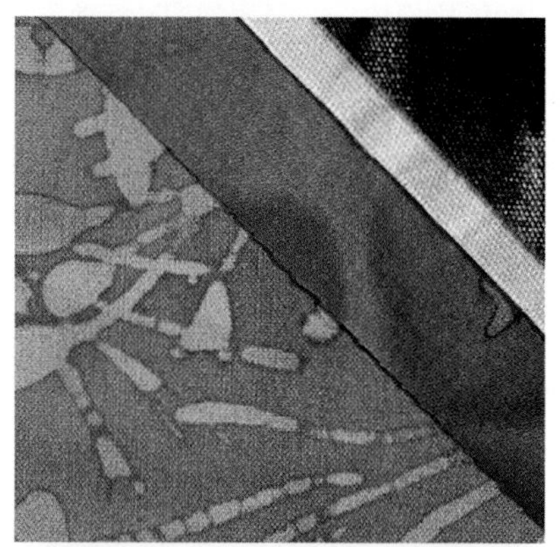

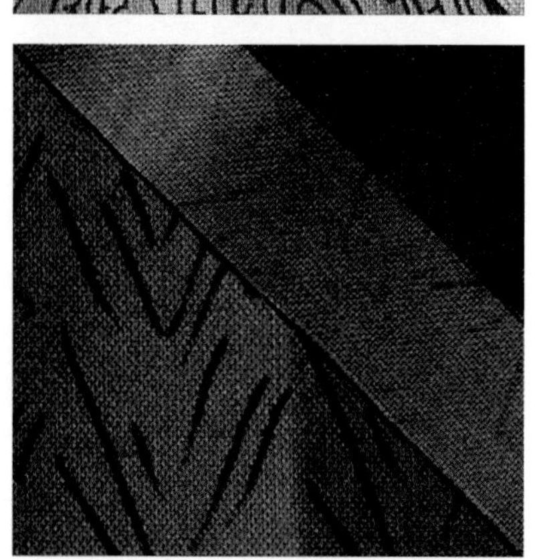

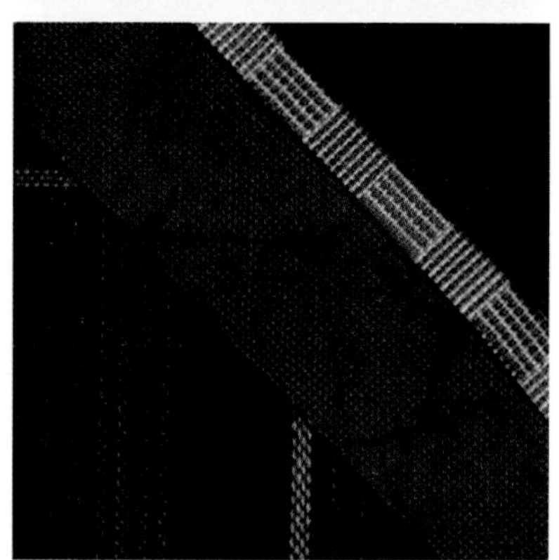

Fig. 1–4. A sampling of good basket fabric combinations.

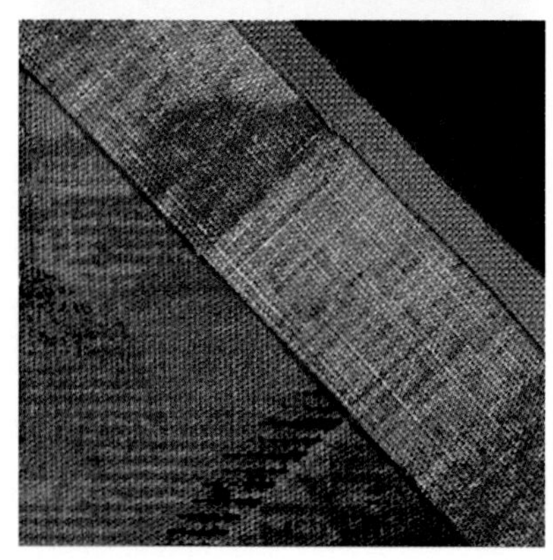

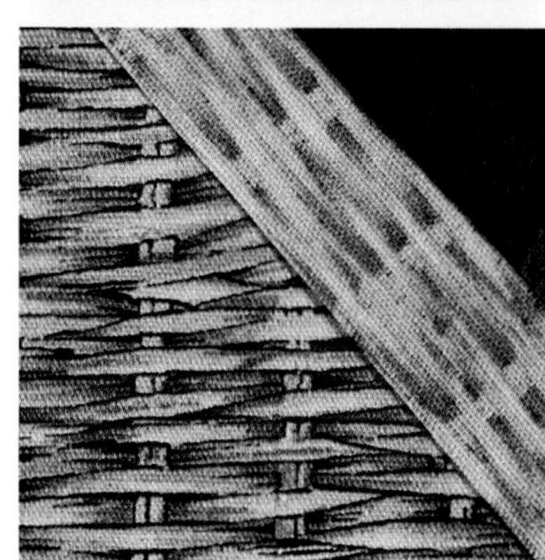

Fig. 1–5. These designs are too prominent for baskets.

Remember that artistic license is allowed. A very pretty quilt, Baskets, Blooms, Butterflies, and Bows, page 118, made from the patterns in this book, has tan leaves. The black background used in Imperial Garden, page 118, is a dramatic color choice. Use your imagination and have fun with your quilt. Choose fabrics you love!

Baskets

You will need two or three fabrics for each basket. The main fabric is the one used for the body of a basket. It can set your color scheme and act as a unifier if you use a small multicolored print or plaid (Fig. 1–4). Or, you may prefer that the basket look more realistic and choose a tan with a basketweave pattern. If you desire a more understated basket treatment, you may want to select a soft and/or neutral colored batik, water-color, or hand-dyed fabric. Avoid large florals and splashy prints because they will confuse the eye and draw attention away from the beautiful flowers (Fig. 1–5). Remember, the basket should not be more prominent than the flowers.

The additional basket fabrics are used for the bases and

the insides of the baskets that are visible behind the flowers. The purpose of the base is to weight and anchor the basket. A dark fabric seems to accomplish this well. For a realistic appearance, the fabric for the inside of the basket should contrast subtly with the main basket fabric. Check the wrong side of the main fabric. It may be just right for the inside of the basket. There should be enough contrast in color and value that, when sewn, the basket fabrics don't all blend together.

The handles can be made from the the main fabric or from one of the coordinating fabrics for contrast. For the decorative trim and other accents, such as the basket rims or the diamonds in the Primrose Basket, it can be effective to use the base fabric, provided there is enough contrast. It would be unfortunate if the trim did not show up after all your work. Study the quilts in this book to see how their makers successfully combined their fabrics.

The basket fabrics should not be used in the flowers or leaves, but they can be repeated in sashings or borders. So, you will want to plan ahead and purchase enough.

Flowers and Leaves

A rather large assortment of generally small monotone prints, ranging from light to dark and bright to dull, will be needed to provide wide color palettes for the flowers and leaves (Figs. 1-6 & 1-7). You will need only small amounts of these fabrics. To get enough, you can trade or collect them, or you can order swatches or fat eighths. You cannot have too many, and you will probably add new fabrics right up to the last basket. Remember, you are essentially painting with fabric, and shading is important. However, don't overmatch. Your arrangements will be flat if you do. Use zingers (unexpected or bright colors) to excite the eye. For example, throw in an orange or a peach petal in a yellow flower. Only small amounts of each fabric will be visible, but the surprise will add life. Think flowers when choosing these fabrics. Walk through your garden. Flowers have bright, clear colors that are luminescent. Look for fabrics that convey this feeling.

A source for leaves and flowers that should not be overlooked is your stash of large florals and novelty print fabrics (Fig. 1-9, page 24). Sometimes,

Flower Fabric Samples

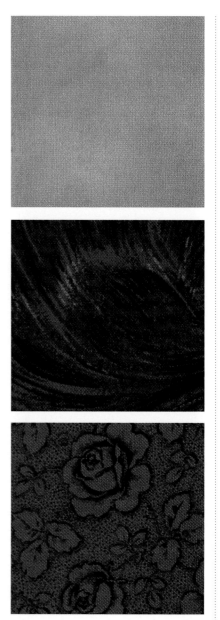

Fig. 1-6. A broad color range is needed in each color family you intend to use in your flowers. Many of these fabrics have the transparent quality that seems to give a more natural look to flowers.

Flower Fabric Samples

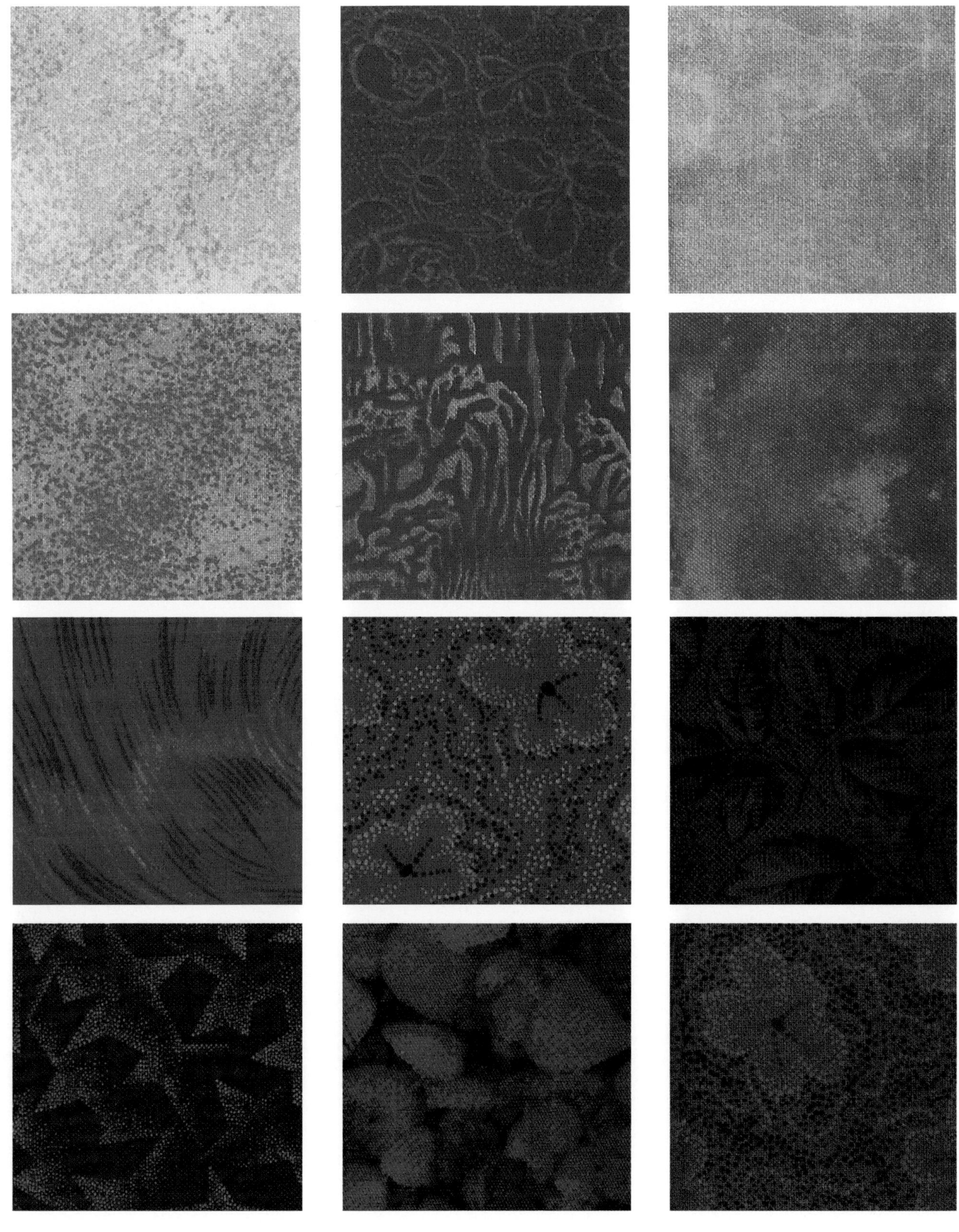

Flower Fabric Samples

Leaf Fabric Samples

Fig. 1–7. You will need a variety of greens for the leaves.

Leaf Fabric Samples

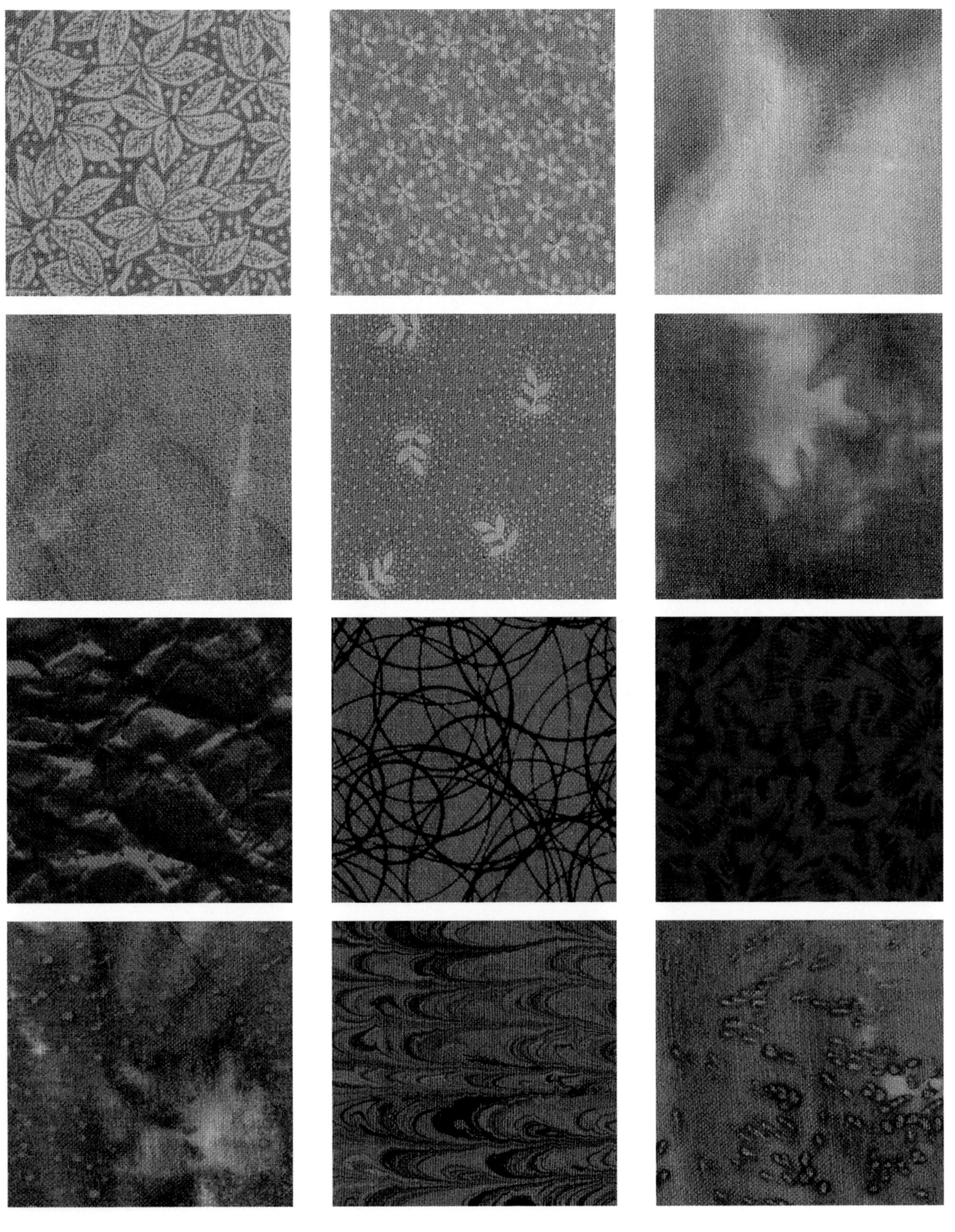

Leaf Fabric Samples

with selective cutting, you can find just the right color and shading that you may have been unable to find anywhere else. Occasionally, a fabric will do double duty, being acceptable for both leaves and flowers (Fig. 1–8).

If you like a realistic look, especially for flowers, an alternative to a large collection of small prints is some well-chosen hand-dyed fabrics or commercial fabrics that have a hand-dyed quality (Fig. 1–10). From these, you can selectively cut petals and leaves to create beautiful, subtle, natural shading (see the Canna Pillow, page 120).

Stems

A small monotone print is the best choice for making stems (Fig. 1–11). As a general rule, this fabric should be darker than any of your leaf fabrics. Don't let a fabric fool you. Sometimes you will perceive a fabric to be very dark because it contains dark areas, when in fact, because of the size of the pattern and variations in color, the fabric is really a medium. Remember, the stems are narrow and sometimes long. To be effective, the stem fabric must remain dark the length of the stem. Choose just one fabric that is used only for stems and that won't disappear among the leaves (Fig. 1–12). You might look for one in a slightly different color family, yellow-green if your leaves are mostly blue-green, or vice versa. A brown, tan, or green-black may be just right. The important thing is that the eye recognize the stems among the leaves and that the stems show up against your background fabric.

Fig. 1–8. With selective cutting, this fabric can be used for leaves or flowers.

Fig. 1–9. (LEFT) **A large floral or novelty print can provide the colors needed for flowers and leaves.**

Fig. 1-10. All the petals for one flower can be cut from a fabric such as one of these to achieve a natural, realistic look.

Fig. 1-11. These fabrics will make good stems.

Fig. 1-12. These fabrics will be less effective for stems because they will tend to fade in and out.

Fabric Preparation

Before you begin, you will want to take time for preparation. Testing fabrics and markers may seem like a waste of time, but if you've ever had a quilt ruined by bleeding dye, you will understand the importance of preparation.

It is important to determine if a fabric's dye will bleed onto other fabrics before using that fabric in a quilt. Pre-wash all of your fabrics before you start. Wash like colors together by hand or machine with a mild soap and cold or warm water. Test dark or intensely colored fabrics for dye-fastness by hand washing them first before washing them with other fabrics. After checking that the rinse water is clear, place fabrics in the dryer on the permanent-press cycle. (It is good to pre-wash your fabrics in a product called Synthrapol, which was designed to deactivate any excess dye remaining in the fabric.) If you remove the fabrics immediately after the dryer stops, you won't have to iron them now. Simply fold them and put them away until you are ready to use them. However, it is important that you press the fabrics before using them, if needed, because wrinkles can cause inaccuracies or distortions in the pieces you cut.

Color

It is not really necessary in making the appliqué patterns in this book for you to be able to identify complementary, split-complementary, analogous, cool, or warm color schemes. You know what colors you like, and given the time involved in making these patterns, it is best to work with those you like. Trust your instincts!

Here are a few points to consider when selecting colors.

Value and Intensity

The value of a color refers to the amount of light it reflects. Think pink (light) versus maroon (dark) (Fig. 1–13). The intensity of a color refers to the amount of true pigment present. Think royal blue (bright) versus slate blue (dull) (Fig. 1–14). Lights and brights come forward, darks and dulls recede. Study each basket

Fig. 1–13. (BELOW) **Color value: Colors change from light to dark with the addition of black or white. Colors with white added, like the ones shown, are called *tints*, and colors with black added are called *shades*.**

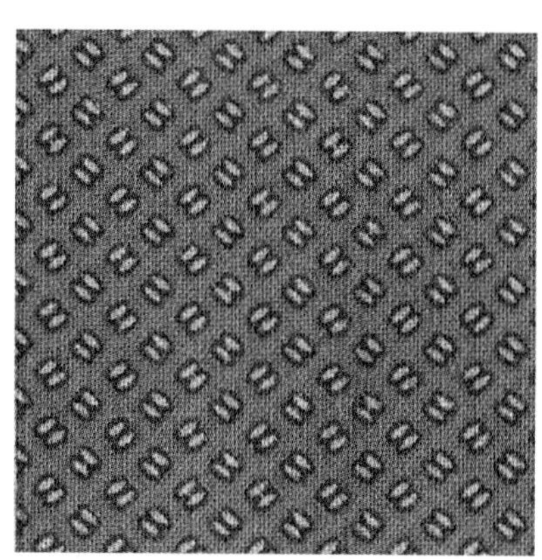

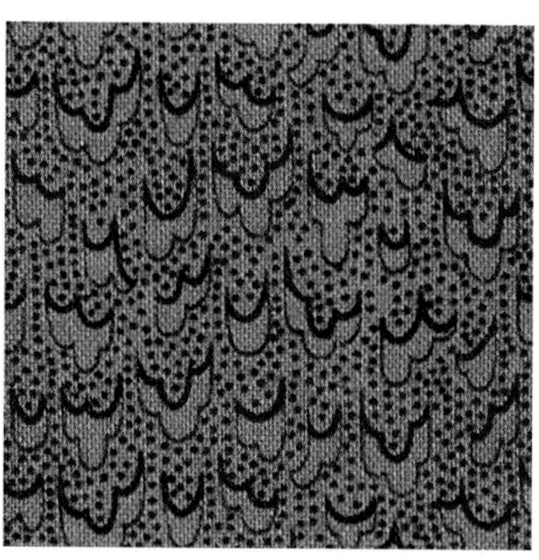

pattern as you choose your fabrics. Try to visualize which leaves and flowers are in the forefront and which are farthest away. In many cases, it will be obvious. Pieces that are lowest in the numbering sequence, which are applied first, are generally the ones that should recede. But this rule does not always hold true. Try to imagine a light shining on an arrangement. It can come from any direction. Then, figure out how the imaginary light source would cause some things to be shaded and some to shine. Let your fabric choices reflect what you imagine.

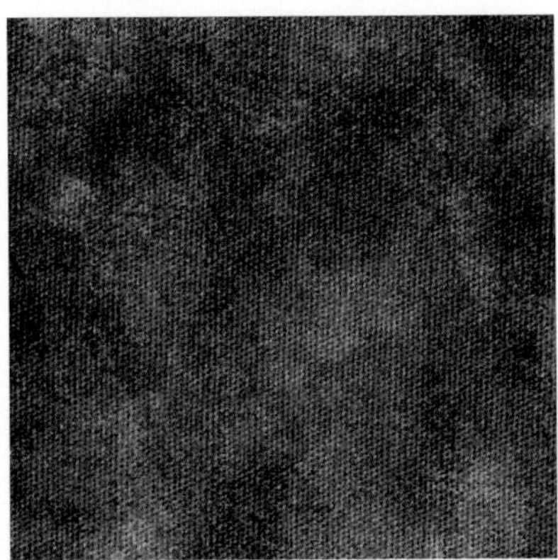

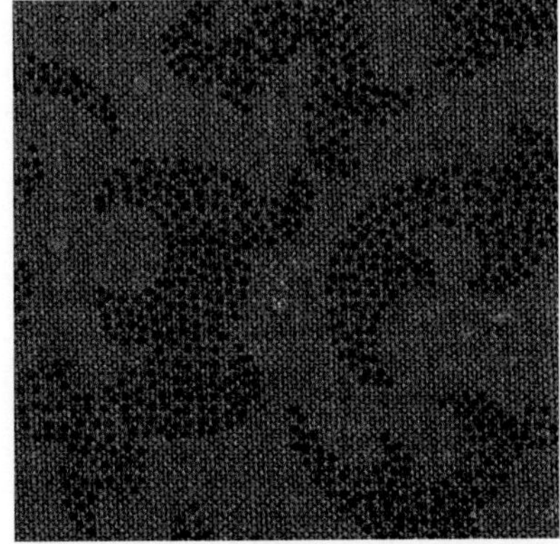

Fig. 1–14. Color intensity: The more true pigment contained in a dye, the brighter the color is, like the green on the top. Adding gray mutes the color and makes it duller or less intense, like the green on the bottom.

Contrast

Consider the fabrics for leaves that are adjacent to each other. From a distance, the eye should be able to distinguish each leaf. Try standing approximately 10 feet away. If you cannot tell where one leaf stops and the other begins, there is probably not enough contrast between the fabrics, and another selection would be wise. You will come to appreciate the necessity of having a wide selection of fabrics.

Conversely, too much contrast may look unnatural in some cases. For example, if a leaf is twisted, requiring two fabrics for one leaf, too much contrast in the fabrics will confuse the eye. You won't be able to tell that they form one leaf. In fact, you might not be able to tell that it is a leaf.

It appears that you will be walking a fine line between too much and too little contrast, doesn't it? Don't worry. You will get the hang of it. Perhaps it will comfort you to know that some good things have happened when my students have "broken the rules." Who says leaves have to be green or daffodils yellow? Do your own thing. Make a statement. Make a beautiful quilt!

Design Transfer

Master Patterns

Because of the size of the patterns, it was necessary to divide them in fourths. To make a master pattern, you will need to photocopy the quadrants and tape them together or redraw the quadrants on one piece of see-through paper (craft paper, freezer paper, or tracing paper).

To prepare paper for tracing, draw two lines perpendicular to each other or fold the paper into fourths. Make certain the lines form a right angle in the center of the master pattern (Fig. 1–15, page 28). Number the quadrants 1 through 4 as shown. (Diamond shape indicates block on point.) Position quadrant 1 of the master pattern over quadrant 1 of the basket pattern. Match the center lines on both. Pin or tape the pattern under the tracing paper to prevent shifting. Trace the first pat-

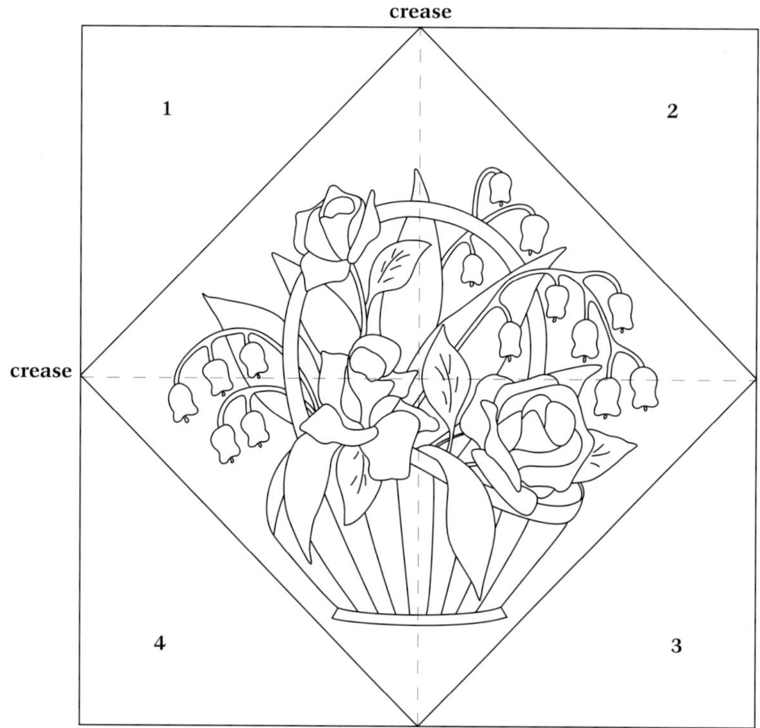

Fig. 1–15. Making a master pattern. Fold a piece of tracing paper, large enough to accommodate the pattern, into fourths. Number the quadrants as shown. Trace by quadrant. Diamond shape indicates 12½" block, which sits on-point.

tern quadrant, including all instructional marks. Repeat for the other three quadrants to complete your master pattern.

Background Squares

To make blocks for one of the quilt settings from Chapter 4, cut either twelve 15" (to be set on point) squares or twelve 20½" (straight-set) squares, depending on the quilt pattern you have chosen. Both of these measurements are oversized because the background squares will be subjected to a lot of wear and tear while you appliqué. By starting out with them oversized, you can trim away the frayed edges when you are ready to assemble the quilt. They will be trimmed to 13" or 18½", respectively.

Many solid-colored fabrics and monotone prints that appear to be the same color front and back may actually have a nap or a pattern that becomes evident only after the blocks have been sewn side by side. To avoid problems, as you cut, mark the right side and the top of each square with a safety pin or tailor's tack. Also mark the remaining fabric that will be used later in setting pieces or borders. Then, when you transfer the appliqué pattern to your background squares and when you assemble the quilt, you will be assured that all the blocks, borders, etc., are turned in the same direction. Marking your pieces is a good habit to form when cutting fabric for any quilt. By doing it, you can be confident that you will have no odd shading and no pattern that runs the wrong way when your quilt is finished.

To transfer one of the basket designs to a light-colored background square, first lightly crease the square diagonally, as shown in Figure 1–15, to divide it into quadrants that correspond with those of your pattern.

Place the background square right side up over the master pattern, carefully line up the creases in your square with the center lines of the pattern, and match the centers. Remember to position all of your squares on the same grain line. Lightly trace just inside the design on the background square and include all the details, such as petals, leaves, and stems. However, it is not necessary to include the numbers or any of the marks or interior lines on your background square.

It is helpful to use a light box for this process, but if you don't have access to one, you can tape the master pattern to a large window, or if you have a glass-top table, you can create a makeshift light box by removing the shade from a small lamp and placing the lamp under the table. Use only pens or pencils that you know will wash out. (If you haven't already done it, take the time now to test every pen or marker you plan to use to make sure the lines can be removed.)

If your fabric is too dark to transfer the design by placing the master pattern behind the square, it will be necessary to reverse the process. Place your square right side up on a hard, flat surface, center the master pattern right side up on top of it, and pin around the edges to prevent shifting. Slide a piece of washable dressmaker's carbon, carbon side down, between the pattern and background fabric and trace the pattern with a medium ball-point pen. If you are using this method to mark your background squares, it is recommended that you make your appliqué templates first or make a duplicate pattern, because tracing over the pattern with a ball-point pen will damage the pattern to some degree.

Appliqué Templates

Templates for the appliqué pieces can be made from freezer paper or a contact-type shelf paper, or you can use a combination of the two for your project. Contact paper stays in place better than freezer paper, but freezer paper templates can be used for the larger pattern pieces, such as the baskets and many of the leaves. For these pieces, you will probably not need to keep the templates in place while you sew, but you can if you want to by pinning them.

Contact paper is recommended for pieces that will be appli-pieced (described on page 43), such as the flowers and the overlapping leaves in the Iris, Tulip, and Daisy Baskets. These pieces can be more accurately sewn with the templates in place, and the freezer paper would detach too easily from the fabric.

Writing on contact paper requires a pen or pencil especially made for marking template plastic. Because there are grid lines on the back of the contact paper, which can make tracing more difficult, you may need to use a light box. A certain amount of dexterity is required to peel the backing off the templates after cutting them out, but no heat is necessary to apply the contact paper to the fabric. In all other ways, the process for making templates from contact paper is the same as for freezer paper.

It is recommended that you experiment with contact and freezer paper templates by appli-piecing a flower with each one. These samples will give you an idea of how each paper performs and will help you decide if you like appliquéing with the template attached.

If you prefer, all the patterns in this book can be made with conventional appliqué methods, for which freezer paper templates will suffice. The following instructions and those in Chapter 2, if followed, will give you the flexibility of sewing with or without attached templates.

For the flower templates,

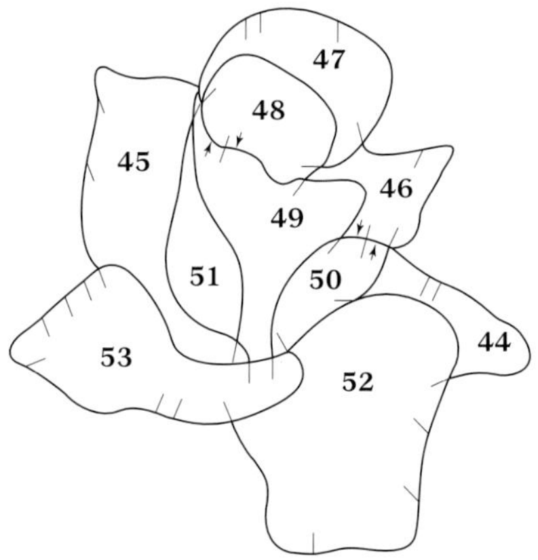

Fig. 1–16. Flower template.

trace each flower in one complete unit on template paper (Fig. 1–16). For pieces such as leaves and stems, trace each template individually, repositioning the paper slightly for each leaf. For pieces overlapped by a flower, another leaf, or a handle, make one template for the entire piece by simply continuing the lines across the overlying appliqué as in pieces #11 and #15 (Fig. 1–17). After you have appliquéd such a piece in place, you can cut out the part that will be covered before appliquéing over it, but be sure to leave an ample allowance to tuck under the overlying piece. To avoid any risk of unsightly shadowing, it is important that unnecessary layers be removed, especially if the top layer is a light color. (Removing excess layers is described on page 81.)

On each template, trace any lines from overlapping pieces (overlay marks, Fig. 1–18) and include the number of the pattern piece for identification. Add any twist (Fig. 1–19), underlay (Fig. 1–20), match-up (Fig. 1–21), and leave-open (Fig. 1–22) marks. Mark *X*'s along the edges of the template where the appliqué will be overlapped by another piece so you will remember not to turn under the allowance in that area (Fig. 1–23). For a complete template, see Fig. 1–24, page 32).

Instead of making bias strips, you can cut templates for the handles and stems just as you did for the flowers and leaves. Place the templates on the bias whenever possible to make it easier to sew the narrow stems. Include all the marks mentioned previously. To avoid losing the small stem

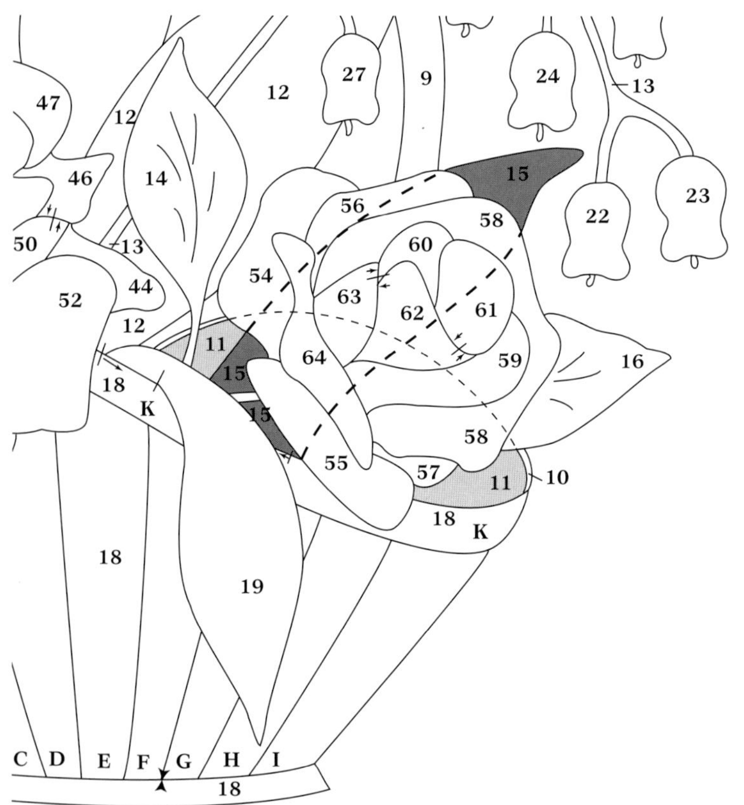

Fig. 1–17. Make one template for a leaf that is overlapped by connecting the lines through the overlapping pieces (dashed lines).

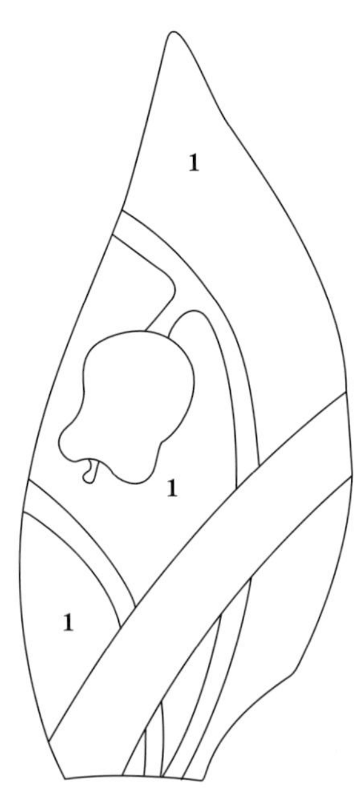

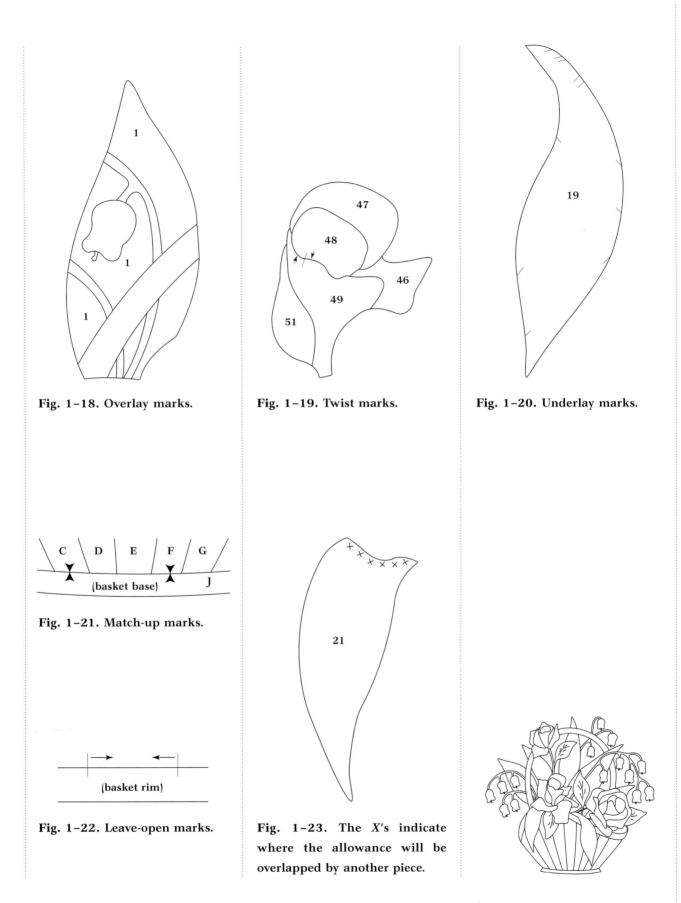

Fig. 1–18. Overlay marks.

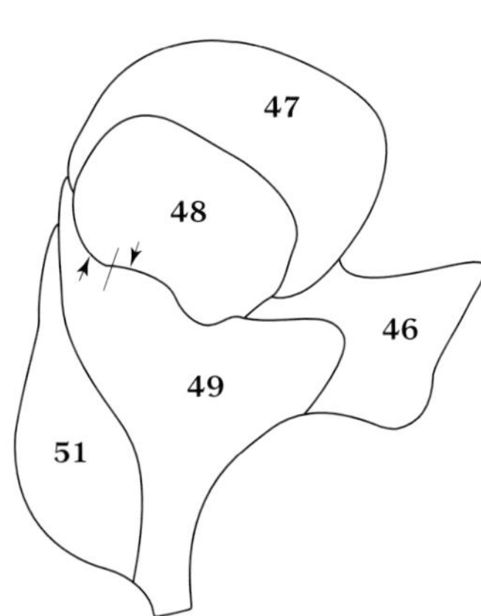

Fig. 1–19. Twist marks.

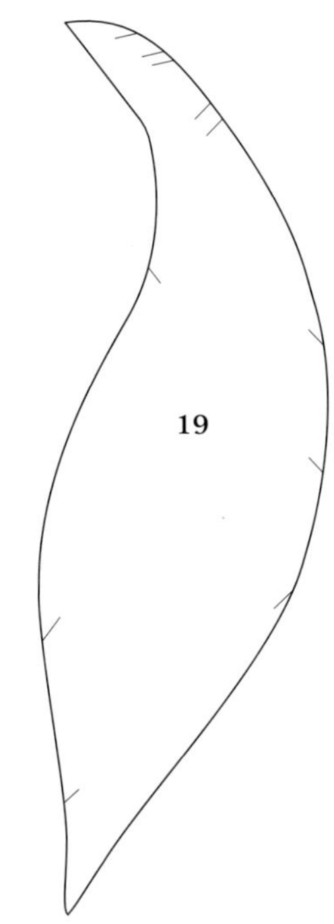

Fig. 1–20. Underlay marks.

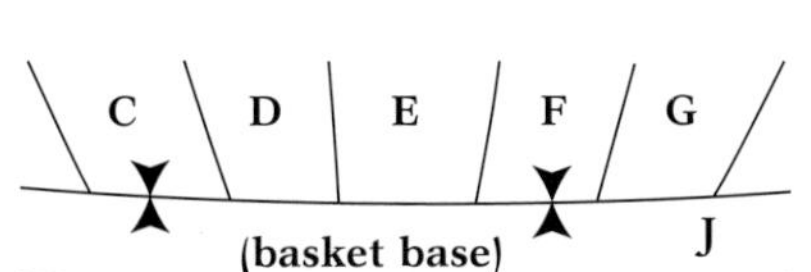

Fig. 1–21. Match-up marks.

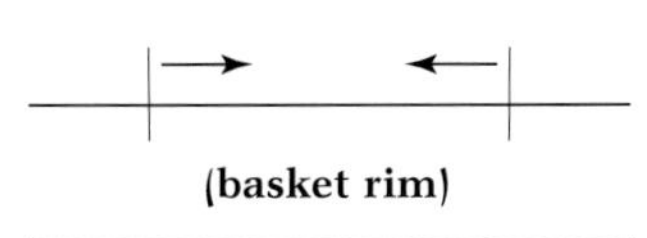

Fig. 1–22. Leave-open marks.

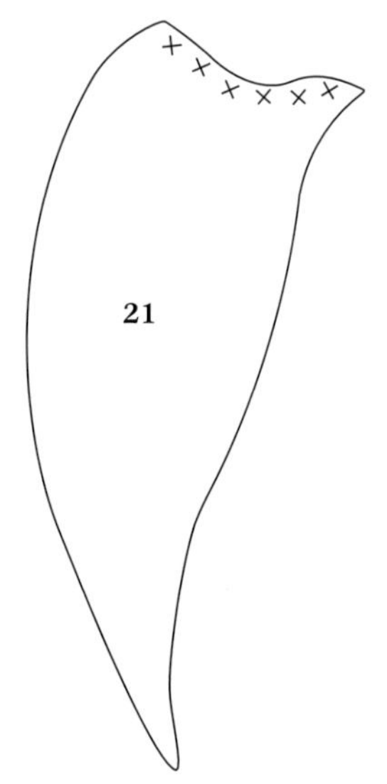

Fig. 1–23. The *X*'s indicate where the allowance will be overlapped by another piece.

templates, it is best to attach them to the fabric and wait to cut them out until you are ready to appliqué.

Trace the basket shapes on template paper and include all the marks mentioned previously. Some baskets have divisions that can be pieced with contrasting fabrics.

Because the basket pieces are large, match-up marks have been added to facilitate placement when you are sewing the pieces together. If you have ever done garment sewing, these marks are equivalent to the match-up notches and dots found on dress patterns. If you find additional marks are needed, just place more at convenient intervals along the edges of the divisions before making your templates. If you prefer, the division marks can be ignored during piecing and used later as quilting lines.

It is important that you include all the described marks on your templates. They will make it possible for you to achieve the precise placement necessary for these patterns. It will be time consuming, as well as annoying, if you have to backtrack to this step. Please note that, as you apply each piece, a portion of the design marked on the background will be hidden from view. The reason for the marks will become clearer once you begin sewing.

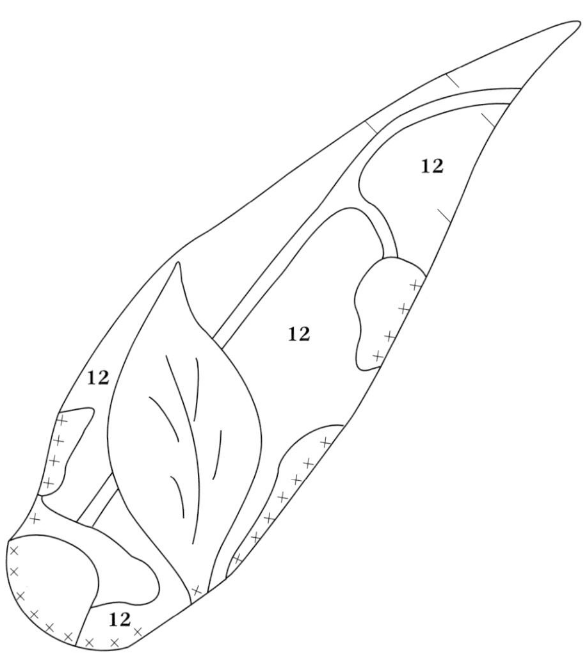

Fig. 1–24. Completed template, with overlay and underlay marks. The *X*'s indicate areas where the allowance will not be turned under.

Chapter 2

Appliqué

Getting Started

The process for selecting just the right fabric for your appliqué pieces is best done in stages. First, select the basket fabrics and attach the appropriate templates. Then do all the leaves, then the stems, and select the flowers last. This way, you won't have to get all your fabrics out at once. Your ironing board or table isn't that big.

Take time to get comfortable, this is going to take a while. First, arrange your ironing board close to a table or counter to provide a larger work surface or, if you have decided to use contact paper templates, just find a nice large, flat work surface. Get a chair or stool and sit down. It helps to pin or tape your pattern to a wall near you for reference.

Some people prefer to prepare and sew one block at a time. Some choose an assembly-line approach, ending up with 12 kits ready to appliqué. It is really nice to get all the preparation work done so you can sit down and enjoy the appliqué. But consider this. Each block will serve as a stepping stone to the next, so that a learning process takes place. You will discover which fabrics work well and which don't, and you are likely to shop for more fabrics along the way. In this respect, preparing and sewing one block at a time is best.

For freezer paper templates, set your iron on medium to hot with no steam. If you have made contact paper templates, you will not need an iron. You will need sharp paper scissors as well as fabric scissors. For freezer paper templates, cut them out, place the shiny side down, and press each template on the *right* side of your chosen fabric. For contact paper templates, cut out the templates, remove the backing, and attach them to the *right* side of the fabric.

After attaching templates to the fabric, cut out each piece, leaving a ⅛" turn-under allowance outside the template as you cut. For needle-turn appliqué, this narrow allowance works best. You may find it helpful to try the pieces out on your background fabric as you cut them out. You can get some idea of the color placement this way, even with the templates attached. Place the pieces for each basket, with the templates attached, in an envelope or a plastic zippered bag labeled with the basket name. This bag can also contain the background block and a copy of the pattern and instructions for that block. Now you have a very portable kit, and you can get on with the fun of sewing.

Pay close attention to the number on each pattern piece. The numbering sequence controls the way the pieces are layered. If pieces #3 and #4, for instance, share a common seam, #4 must be appliquéd on top of #3 to provide the correct appearance. Leaves that tuck behind a basket will have a lower number and must be appliquéd before the basket. While you can deviate from the sequence on occasion, take care in doing so. It is never pleasant to find that you have to remove pieces after they have been attached.

The quality of your work, in large part, will be determined by the invisibility of your stitches. A good, fine, sharp needle is essential for fine appliqué. A #11 or #12 sharp is an excellent choice or, if you prefer a more substantial needle, try a #11 straw needle. A high-quality thread will aid you greatly. Use #60 embroidery-weight, 100-percent cotton thread, or you can try using silk thread. Silk melts into the fabric, so it is easier to make invisible stitches. It also rarely knots, and that is a big plus. Use thread the same color as the piece you are appliquéing in place. Next to needle and thread, good lighting is important, and magnifying glasses are recommended on an as-needed basis.

Start by locating template #1 for the pattern you are making. To mark the fold line for the turn-under allowance, trace closely (on the right side of the fabric) around the edge of the template with one of your marking pens or pencils. Choose one that will be visible on the fabric. To keep the fabric from slipping while you are tracing, place a piece of fine-grain sandpaper under the fabric.

After cutting out the piece, you will find it helpful to crease the fold for the turn-under allowance, especially for the larger pieces. To make a thumbnail crease, fold the allowance under and gently press the fold between your thumbnail and index finger. Use short strokes and gentle pressure with your thumbnail. The natural fiber of the cloth will remember this crease, helping you to get a smoother edge as you sew.

Without removing the template, carefully pin piece #1 to the background. Select two or three places where the overlay lines on the template meet the fold line for the turn-under allowance (Fig. 1–18, page 31). You can use these as matching points. With a pin, pierce through piece #1 and your background at selected matching points. Slide the two fabrics together on the pin and secure with pins in the allowance. You can check the placement by lifting an edge of piece #1 to check that the fold line matches with the pattern design on the background piece (Fig. 2–1). Work on a flat surface, such as a tray or lap board, to ensure that the appliqué will lie flat.

Fig. 2–1. As the appliqué stacks up, it covers the design marked on your background fabric. The marks on your templates will aid in accurate placement by showing where the handle, leaves, stems, or petals intersect with your piece.

Before removing the template from a piece, use a marking pencil to extend the marks on the template into the turn-under allowance (Fig. 2-2). Snip the allowance to the fold line at any spot that is to remain flat (see *overlaps,* page 37) and at *twist* marks (page 31). Then carefully remove the template if desired, or you can leave the paper template attached while you stitch.

It is best to start sewing along the side of a piece, rather than at a point. When a leaf tucks into a basket, you can start at the base and sew up one side and back down the other. When you must sew completely around a piece, start at the straightest section. This will make it easier to finish the piece smoothly.

Needle-Turn Appliqué

To start appliquéing, hide your knot in the fold. With the tip of your needle, or with your thumb and index finger, fold under a short section of the allowance, only the length of a few stitches at a time. Hold the folded edge down with the thumb and index finger of your other hand as you sew.

Study Figure 2-2 for a few moments. Bring the needle and thread up through the appliqué piece at *A*, take a short stitch in the background fabric by inserting your needle tip at point *B* slightly beneath the fold to hide the stitch. Then angle your needle to come up at point *C* and catch just a few threads of the fold. Repeat for each stitch. After each stitch, pull the thread taut but not so tight that you cause puckering. Stitch around the piece, turning the allowance under with the tip of your needle as you go. Your stitches should be as short as possible; approximately 1/16" apart is ideal. If you are doing the appliqué stitch correctly, your stitches will be slightly slanted on the back of your work (Fig. 2-3). However, having your stitches nearly invisible on the front is more important than having them slant on the back.

Holding the work so that the allowance you are sewing is on top seems comfortable to many people. However, it may be more comfortable for you to sew along the bottom edge of the appliqué (Fig. 2-4). Either way is fine.

stitches from back

Fig. 2-3. Appliqué stitches should slant on the back.

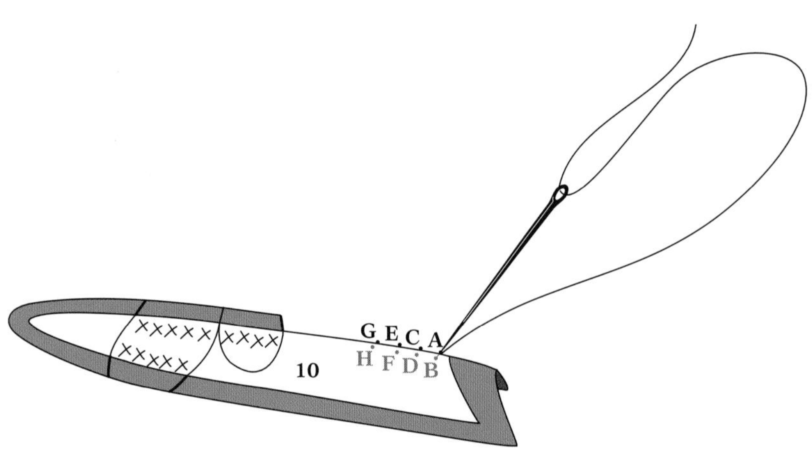

Fig. 2-2. Stitching along the top. Bring the needle up through the appliqué piece on the fold at *A* and go down through the background at *B* (*under* the fold), come up at *C*, down at *D*, up at *E*, etc.

Overlaps

There are many places where pieces overlap. It is better to leave the allowances flat where they lie under other pieces. If you turn an allowance under in those places, it will cause an unsightly ridge, not to mention the unnecessary sewing. To make a section of an allowance lie flat, snip the allowance to the fold line on both sides of the section (Fig. 2-5). If you have placed *X*'s on your templates to indicate the flat areas, they will be easy to identify. If necessary, refer to the pattern to determine which marks are to be snipped.

When you appliqué pieces with flat areas in the allowance, needle-turn up to the first snip and backstitch to secure the stitches (Fig. 2-6, page 38). Skip over to the next snip (the place where stitching will resume) by using a long running stitch in the allowance. On the other side of the flat area, fold the allowance under, take one stitch, backstitch as before, and continue sewing.

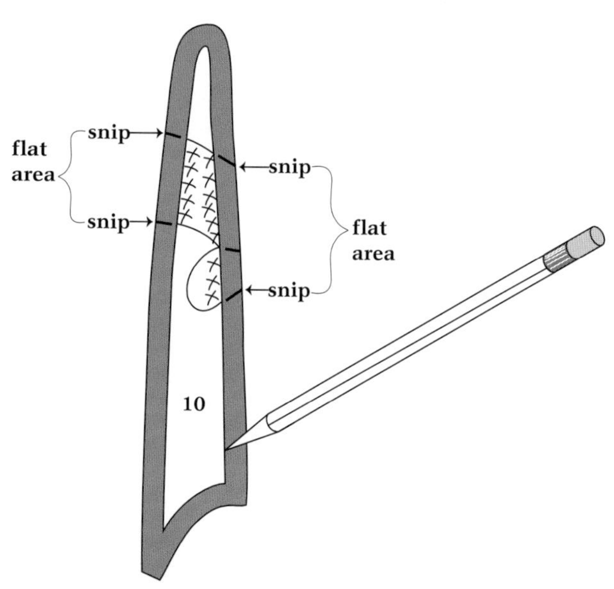

Fig. 2-5. Piece #10 from the Amaryllis Basket. Trace around each template to create a visible fold line for the turn-under allowance. Extend overlap marks into the allowance. Snip the allowance at the marks to leave a flat area to tuck under overlying pieces.

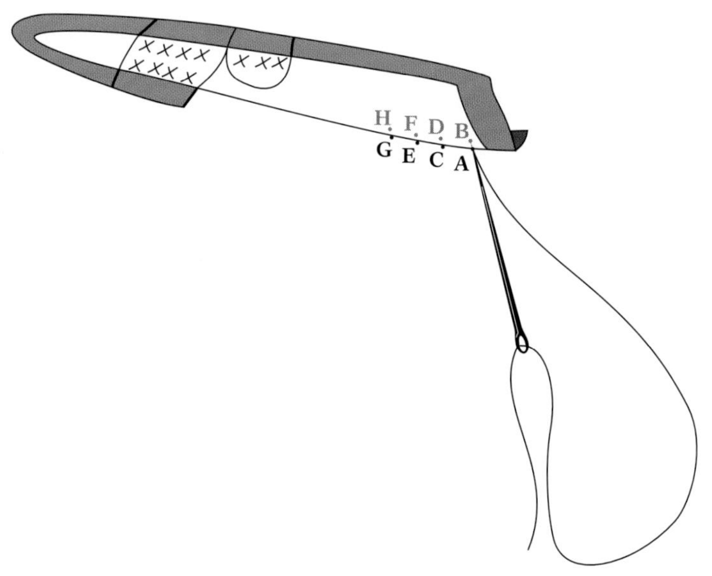

Fig. 2-4. You can stitch along the bottom, if you prefer.

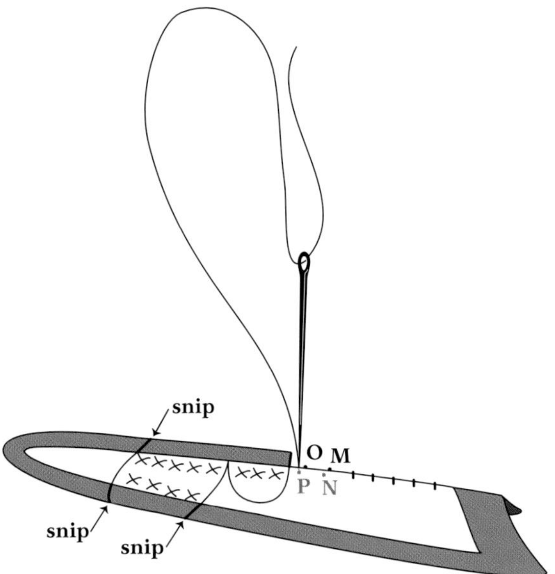

Fig. 2-6. Backstitch: Use this stitch to end a line of stitching or to secure an area. Stitch forward to *O*, go down through the background fabric at *P* (under the fold), up through the appliqué piece at *M*, then down at *N* (again, under the fold), and up at *O*.

Points

Sew up to the point and make a small anchor stitch to hold the point in place while you sew the turn. The anchor stitch is a stitch that goes nowhere. You simply catch a thread or two of the background fabric and bring the needle up through the appliqué exactly where it was before (Fig. 2-7). To remove excess bulk, carefully snip off the tip of the turn-under allowance at the angle as shown in Figure 2-8, slipping your scissor points between the leaf and background fabric to remove as much bulk as possible. With your needle, carefully fold under the allowance at the point (Fig. 2-9). Then, using your needle or your thumb and index finger, fold, pinch, or roll the allowance under until you are satisfied with the sharpness of the point. Continue sewing on the other side of the leaf (Fig. 2-10). Remember, turn under only enough allowance each time to take just a stitch or two.

Some leaves, like those in the Canna Basket, seem to require a more rounded point. To do this, simply use your needle to turn under the allowance gradually, folding under only enough to take one stitch before needle-turning a little more.

Dips

At a dip, clip the allowance to, but not through, the fold line. Sew to within a few stitches from the dip (Fig. 2-11). With your needle or fingers, fold under the allowance on the opposite side of the dip and pin it to hold in place. Slide your needle between the two fabrics and swipe across the dip to fold under the raw edge (Fig. 2-12). Continue stitching to the dip, take one anchor stitch in the dip, if necessary, and continue sewing.

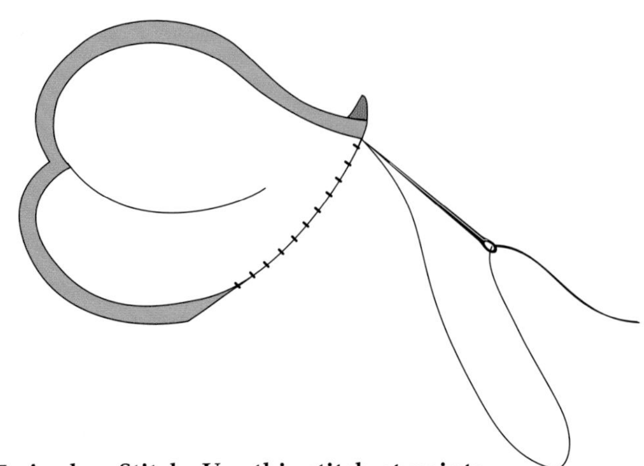

Fig. 2-7. Anchor Stitch: Use this stitch at points.

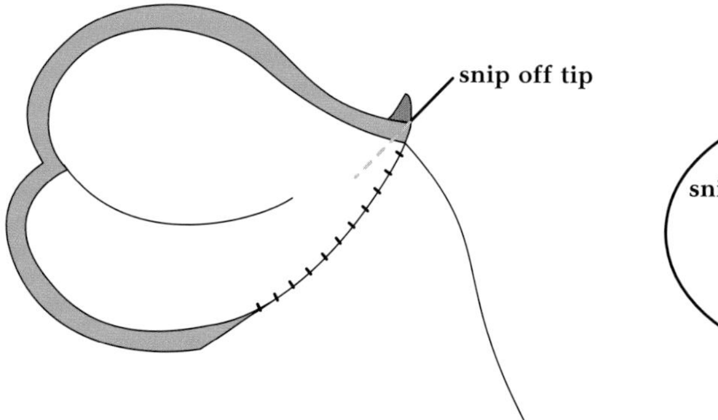

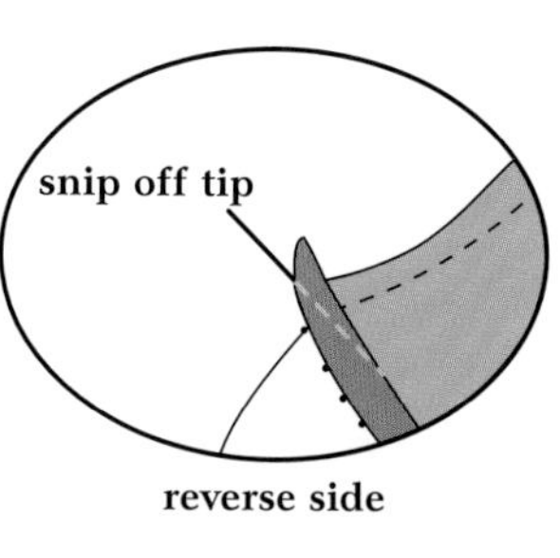

Fig. 2-8. Trim the tip of the allowance off at the angle shown to remove excess bulk.

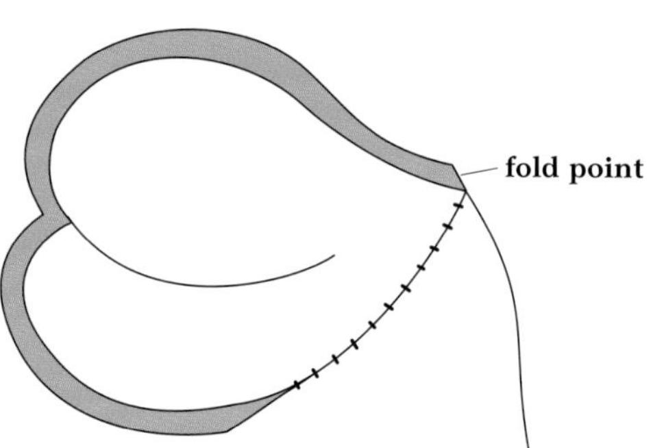

Fig. 2-9. Fold the point under.

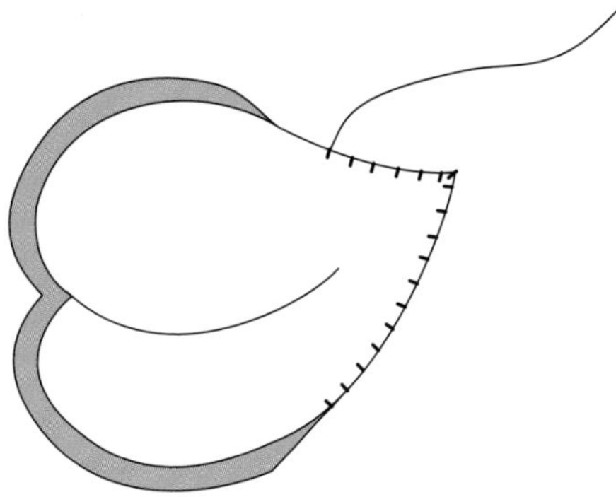

Fig. 2-10. Fold, pinch, or roll the allowance under, until the point is sharp, and continue stitching.

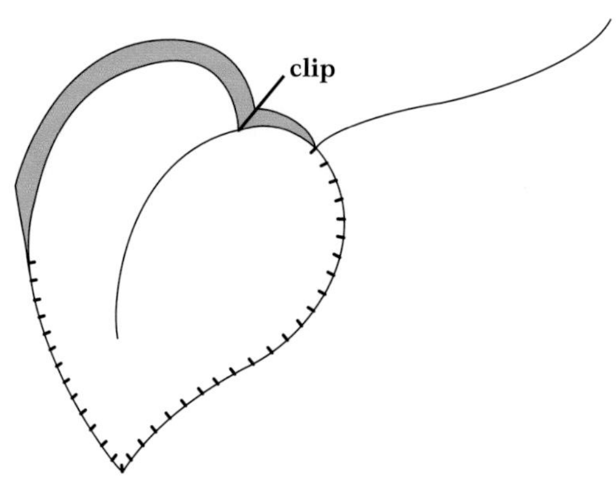

Fig. 2-11. Clip the allowance to, but not through, the fold line at the dip.

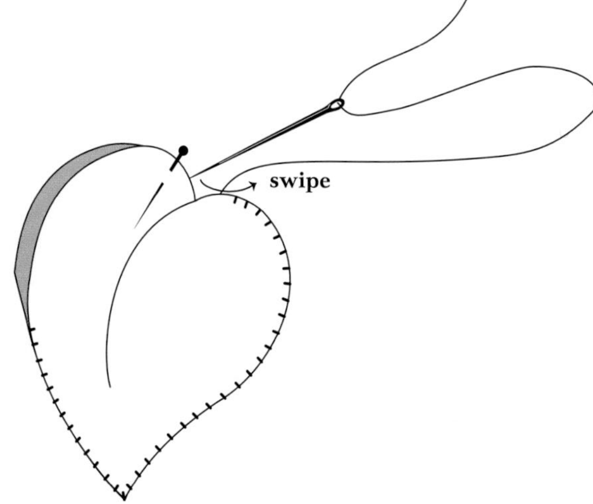

Fig. 2-12. Slide the needle between the fabrics and swipe across the dip, in the direction of arrow, with the side of the needle to fold under the raw edge.

For added insurance to prevent fraying, which is unlikely when the swipe has been done correctly, take a slightly bigger bite into the appliqué with your anchor stitch, catching a few more threads of the fold at the dip. When putting your needle down into the background fabric for the next stitch, place the needle point farther under the fold and pull the thread tight. This will cause a bit more fabric to fold under at the dip.

Stems and Handles

As mentioned in the section on template construction, page 29, templates will be used for all the stem and handle pieces. Therefore, you will need to treat the stems and handles like all the other appliqué pieces. This method is simpler than making bias strips in various widths, and the stems are easier to sew.

Special Techniques

Echo Appliqué

In key areas, your appliqué can be beautifully defined with a very narrow outline in a second fabric. Think of it as echo appliqué. This technique has many applications, both large and small. It was used to achieve the narrow red outline framing the Daffodil pillow, page 120. Although the outline baffles people who have never seen it, it is easier to do than it looks. Most people think that a bias strip has been inserted, like piping, but it is really much simpler than that.

Echo appliqué sample:

To make this sample, use piece #3 from the Primrose Basket, pages 134–137. You will need three fabrics: piece #2, the echo fabric; piece #3; and a background. The echo fabric should be in strong contrast to piece #3, or it will not create the definition you are trying to achieve.

1 Make a freezer paper template for piece #3, including the *X*'s for overlying pieces, and attach it to the right side of the fabric. (X's are shown in Figure 1–23, page 31.) Mark around the template.

2 Cut out the piece, leaving a ⅛" turn-under allowance all around, by eye. Snip the allowance on both sides of the flat areas, marked by *X*'s.

3 Pin piece #3 to the echo fabric (Fig. 2–13). Appliqué piece #3 along the top edge, remembering to leave the allowance flat (unstitched and unfolded) in areas that will later be covered by leaves or flowers. Don't forget to backstitch on either side of a flat area. Remove the template and cut away the echo fabric behind piece #3, leaving a ⅛" allowance, as shown.

4 The width of an echo outline can vary with its application and with your personal preference. In these patterns an out-

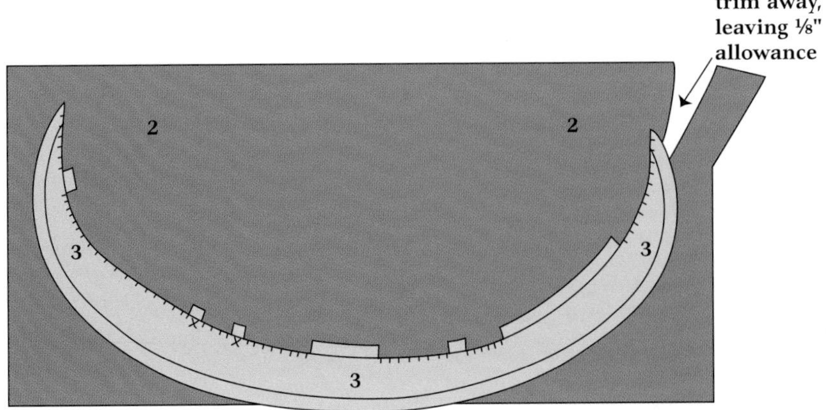

Fig. 2–13. Appliqué piece #3 to #2. Trim the allowance between #2 and #3 to ⅛".

line width of 1/16" is ideal. A good way to establish the fold line for the echo outline is to use your thumbnail to crease the fold as you "eyeball" the width of the outline. *Take care to keep a constant width throughout.*

An alternative to this method may help you achieve a uniform width for the echo appliqué (piece #2). You can use a soapstone marker to trace along the fold of piece #3. The marker is the right width (1/16" or less) to create an excellent echo line. If the fabric is too light for the soapstone to show, try a graphite pencil that comes in a holder like the soapstone.

5 Cut along the top edge of piece #2, adding a 1/8" allowance beyond the fold line by eye (Fig. 2-15).

6 Pin the combined piece #2/3 to your background fabric and appliqué the top edge in place, again leaving the areas flat that will be covered by the other pieces later (Fig. 2-16). Remember to backstitch on either side of the flat areas.

The beauty of this process is that you can achieve a fine, narrow outline of fabric without dealing with a very small piece. For it to enhance your baskets, the outline must be

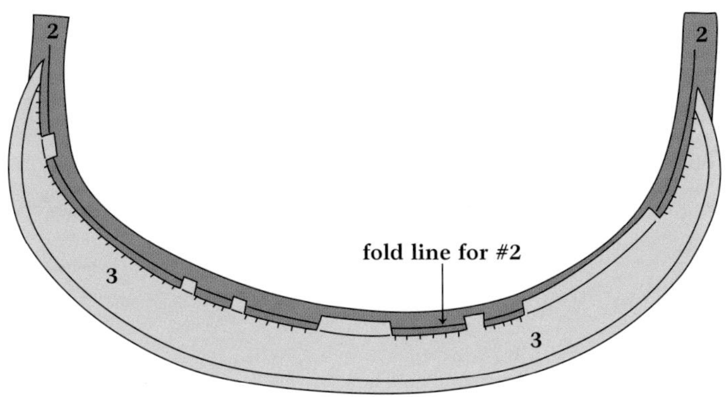

Fig. 2-15. Add a 1/8" allowance beyond the fold line by eye as you cut.

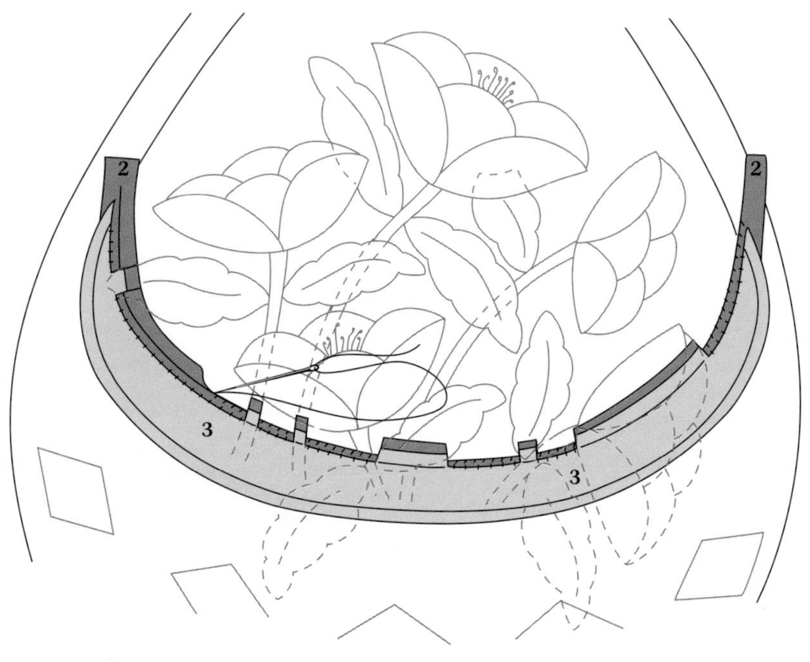

Fig. 2-16. Pin combined piece #2/3 to background fabric and appliqué the top edge. Remember to backstitch on both sides of a flat area.

uniformly narrow and smooth. Leave as little fabric showing as possible without it disappearing. The echo appliqué is not a numbered piece in every basket pattern because it is an optional feature. Echo appliqué can be omitted if you want to simplify the patterns.

The Twist

A method called the *twist* will be used numerous times in the construction of these basket patterns. The twist gives appliquéd flowers and leaves a more natural look and helps distribute excess bulk in the allowance.

Think of the twist as a twisted turn-under allowance. The allowance will be pressed to one side of a seam up to a snip in the allowance and to the other side beyond the snip. When a twist is indicated in your pattern, mark the slash and arrows on your templates. The arrows point to the portion of the allowance that will be on the bottom of, or tucked under, the overlying piece.

Using a different color of ink or lead to mark the slash on the templates may help you to spot it later. Attach the templates to your chosen fabrics. Trace around the templates to

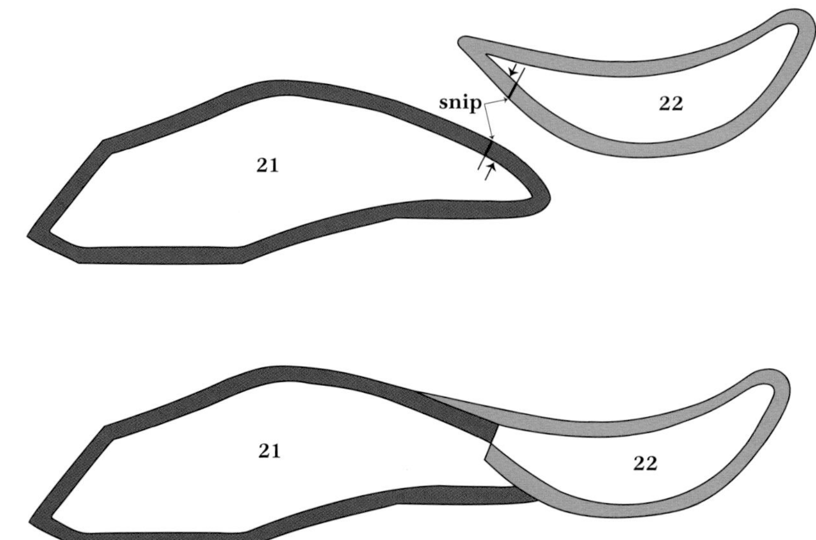

Fig. 2-17. Pieces #21 and #22 from the Tulip Basket. Snip the allowance at the slash mark and fit pieces together. If the pieces are fitted together correctly, the arrows on the templates will be covered by allowances.

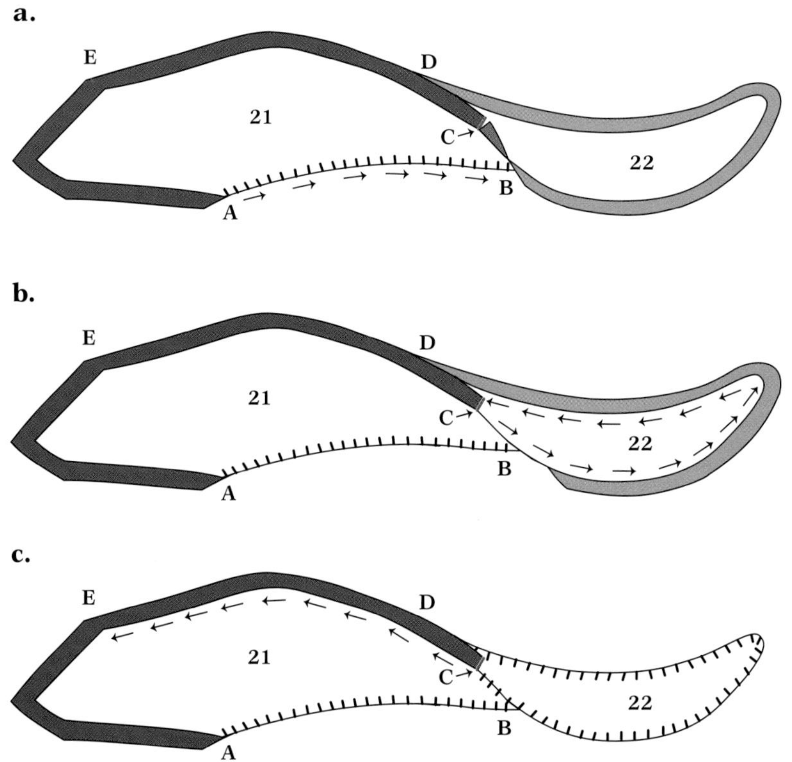

Fig. 2-18a-c. Sew from *A* to *B*, *C* to *D*, and *C* to *E* in the direction of the arrows.

mark the fold lines and snip the allowances at the slash marks.

Fit the two pieces together at the slashes (Fig. 2–17). Secure with pins in the allowance. The pieces are fitted together correctly if the twist-mark arrows are hidden from view by the turn-under allowances.

Pin the pieces to the background by carefully lining up the fold lines for the turn-under allowances and using the pin-piercing technique, described on page 35. Use a few pins in the allowances to hold the pieces together. Templates can be gently removed (freezer paper) or left in place (contact paper) while you sew.

To sew a twist, first look at Figure 2–18. The general idea is to sew between points *A* and *B* in the direction of the arrows. It will be necessary to lift piece #22 out of the way to sew to point *B* (Fig. 2–18a). Next, sew in the direction of the arrows from point *C* (which is at the slash mark) to point *D* (Fig. 2–18b), lifting piece #21 out of the way at point *D*.

When actually appliquéing, however, placing a knot in the allowance too close to the slash at point *C* can cause fraying. Therefore, after appliquéing to point *B*, it is best to start sewing approximately ¼" from the slash, in this case to the right of point *C*. Sew back to *C*, turn your work and sew around piece #22 to point *D*. To sew from *C* to *E*, again start ¼" from *C*, to the left this time. Sew back to *C* and turn your work to sew along piece #21 from *C* to *E* (Fig. 2–18c). (Left-handed people, and those who hold their work so that the allowance they are sewing is on the bottom, must sew in the reverse direction, sewing from *B* to *A*, *D* to *C*, and *E* to *C*.)

Appli-piecing

This technique involves appliquéing without a foundation. It's a method of constructing an appliquéd flower or other design before sewing it as a unit to a background. The unit is pieced together with appliqué stitches; hence, the term *appli-piece*. It is recommended, but not imperative, that the templates be left in place while sewing.

Appli-piecing has several advantages. In some cases, but not all, you can avoid working with very tiny pieces, and you get to see the finished flower before attaching it to the background. If the fabrics don't please you, you can change them or make an entirely new flower. This method works well for those of us who, as a rule, rarely remove pieces after they have been sewn down. Instead, we tend to "live with them" at that point.

Since you will stitch only the outer edges of the flower to your background fabric, cutting away excess layers from the wrong side of your work is less tedious and less confusing with appli-piecing. Without all those stitching lines to sort out, it is easier to spot the shapes to be cut away. Also, your stitches will remain tight if you haven't stitched through the layer that is removed.

Contact paper is recommended for appli-piecing templates because it will remain in place through the sewing process. Freezer-paper will release in handling. (You can leave freezer paper in place while sewing if you pin it to the fabric.) Regardless of which material you use, it is recommended that you mark around each template to make a back-up fold line in case the template comes loose. Be sure to extend the match-up marks into the allowance.

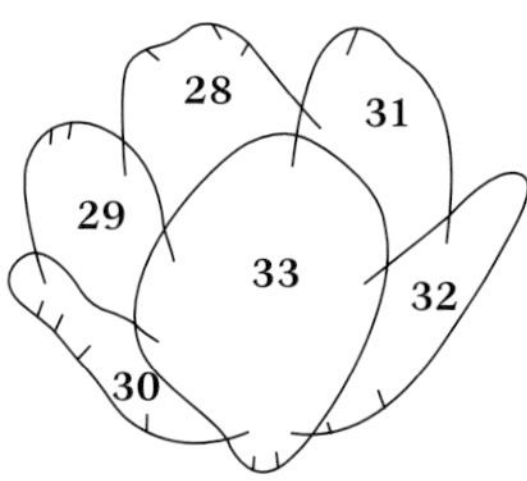

Fig. 2–19. Pieces #28–#33 from the Tulip Basket. Trace flower on contact paper.

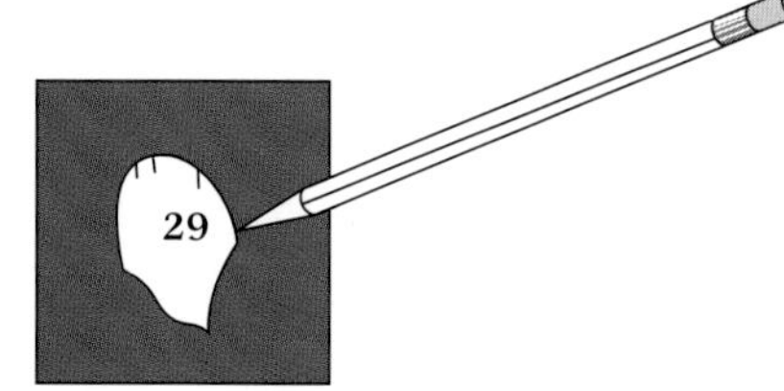

Fig. 2–20. Attach templates to right side of fabric and mark around each piece.

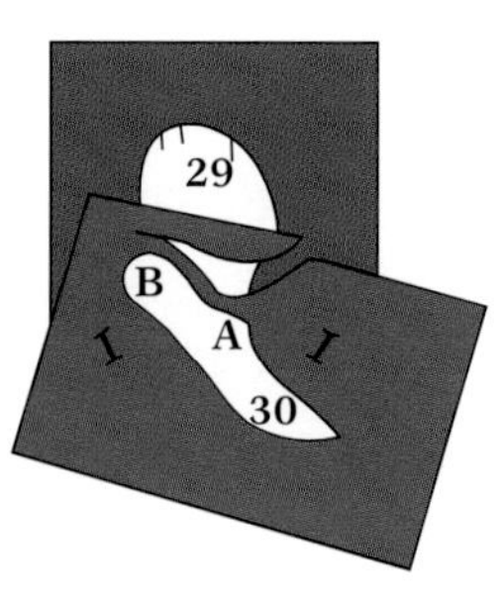

Fig. 2–21. Pin piece #30 to #29, matching fold lines. Trim allowance between *A* and *B* to ⅛".

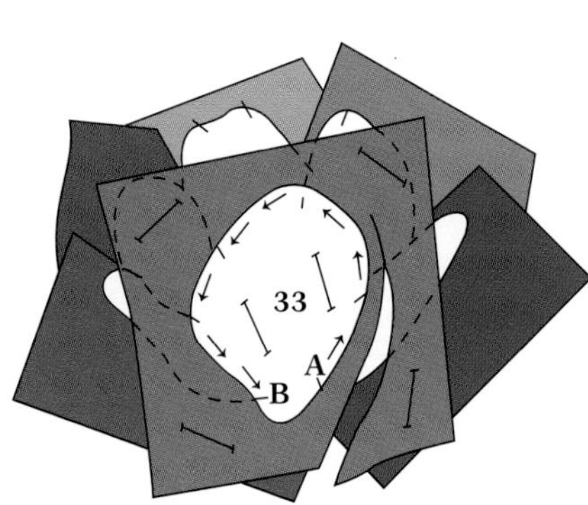

Fig. 2–22. Pin piece #33 to unit #29/32 and cut a ⅛" allowance around #33 as you sew from *A* to *B*.

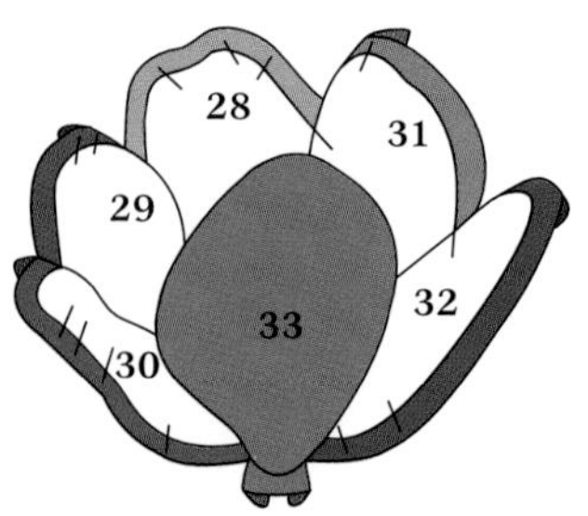

Fig. 2–23. If you left the templates in place while sewing, your flower will look like this after it has been sewn.

Fig. 2–24. Remove templates to reveal flower.

Appli-piecing sample:

To make this sample, use pieces #28–#33 from the Tulip Basket, page 54.

1 Mark the template as shown in Figure 2–19 and cut the template pieces apart. After the pieces have been cut apart, you can use the marks that extend into adjacent petals as reference points for matching the pieces as you sew them together.

2 Choose six petal fabrics and attach one template to each fabric. Rough-cut each appliqué piece, leaving extra fabric all around as shown in Figure 2–20. Mark around each template and extend the overlay marks to the edges of the turn-under allowances.

3 Starting with pieces #29 and #30, and without trimming any allowances yet, pin the two pieces so that the templates butt against each other (Fig. 2–21). Pinning from the wrong side will prevent the thread from catching on the pins as you sew.

4 Between *A* and *B*, trim the allowance of piece #30 to ⅛". Appliqué the two pieces together between *A* and *B*. When you complete this seam, turn your work over and trim the allowance for #29 to ⅛" between *A* and *B*.

5 In a like manner, attach #29 to #28, #31 to #28, and #32 to #31. Crease the seams with your thumbnail to keep them turned the way you have sewn them. Using the overlay marks as reference points, pin piece #33 to unit #29/32. Secure with pins when you are sure of the placement (Fig. 2–22).

6 Starting at the base of #33, cut a ⅛" allowance for a short distance and start appliquéing at point *A*. Continue cutting the allowance around #33 as you progress until you have sewn to point *B*. Trim the remaining allowances around the flower to ⅛". The flower will resemble the one shown in Figure 2–23.

7 Draw the overlay marks in the allowances so you can easily place the unit on the background square. Remove the templates to view the flower (Fig. 2–24).

To decide if you like your flower, place it on your background square and stand back a distance to look at it. It is important that you have sewn the flower accurately so that it will fit exactly in its space on your background square. To sew the flower to the square, pin it carefully and appliqué all the way around it. In learning to appli-piece, it will help if you leave extra-wide allowances, because the larger pieces are easier to work with, and the wider allowances are handy for pinning. As you become more experienced, you may want to try trimming the allowances to ⅛" from the start. Sometimes, you will find that it isn't necessary to use pins to hold the pieces together. Just use your thumbnail to crease the fold, line it up with the adjoining piece, and start sewing.

Although greater accuracy can be achieved by leaving the templates in place, if you find you don't like to sew that way, just remove the templates after marking the fabric pieces. Then you can use the marks in the allowances as your placement guides.

Appli-piece Twist

Twisted allowances are sometimes used in appli-pieced flowers. For these pieces, it is possible and even preferable to sew the seam as if the twist weren't there. Then, after the seam has been sewn, turn the piece over and snip the allowances at the slash mark. Press the allowances in opposite directions as indicated by the pattern arrows.

Reverse Appliqué

Reverse appliqué is used in the Primrose Basket, page 56. In regular appliqué, a piece of fabric is attached to a background by folding under the allowance and stitching around the outside edge of the piece. In reverse appliqué, a shape is cut out within the appliqué piece, and the edges of the shape are turned under and stitched, exposing the underlying fabric. The underlying fabric can be the background, or it can be a different fabric inserted between the appliqué and the background (Fig. 2–25, page 46).

Reverse appliqué sample:

Use the Primrose Basket on page 134–137.

1 Transfer the primrose basket design to the background square.

2 Make a template for the basket and cut the diamonds out of the template.

3 Attach the basket template onto the appropriate fabric (Fig. 2–26).

4 Trace around each diamond and the entire basket shape. You will be doing reverse

Fig. 2-25. The diamonds in the Primrose Basket are reverse appliquéd, revealing a fabric inserted between the appliqué piece and the background.

appliqué with the template attached.

5 Cut around the outside edge of the basket, leaving a ⅛" allowance by eye. To prevent possibly stretching the handle, you can leave the template attached to the basket while you to sew it to the background, if you like.

6 Slash each diamond, point to point, cutting to the fold line (Fig. 2-27). Choose the fabric you want to show through the holes, and cut a piece large enough to cover all of the holes. Pin the piece in place with its right side facing the wrong side of the basket.

7 Turn one edge of a diamond under at the fold line and start stitching half way between the points. Before you reach the first point, which is actually a dip, fold the next side under. (Refer to the instructions for appliquéing dips on page 38). Be sure that each fold has been turned under, opening the dip completely.

8 Slide the point of your needle between the fabrics and swipe around the dip to fold the raw edge under. Stitch past the dip and repeat this procedure for each point. Complete all the diamonds and, from the back, trim the allowances to ⅛" (Fig. 2-28).

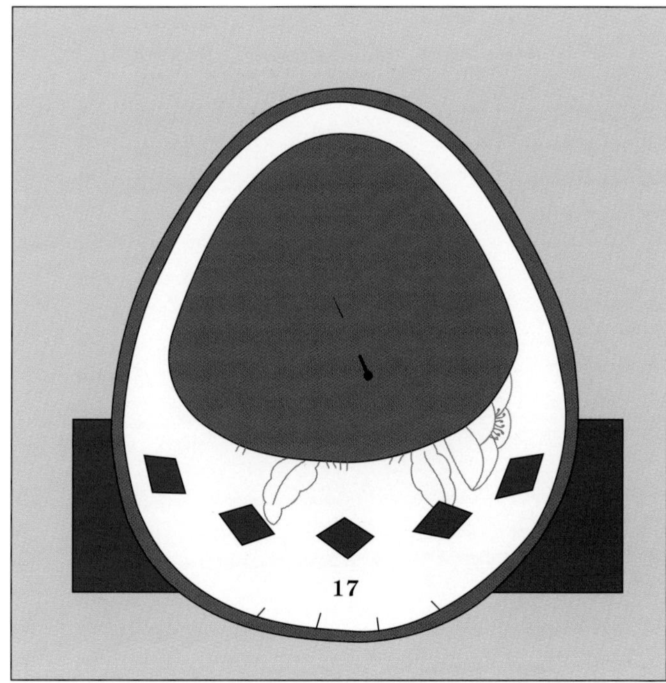

Fig. 2-26. Cut out the diamonds in template #17 before attaching the template to the fabric. Leave template attached to fabric as you sew the diamonds to prevent stretching the handle.

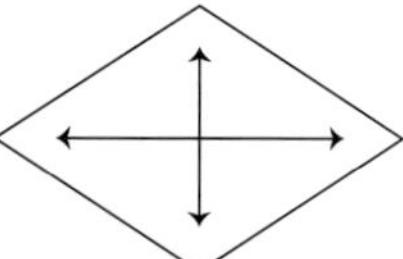

Fig. 2-27. Slash each diamond point to point.

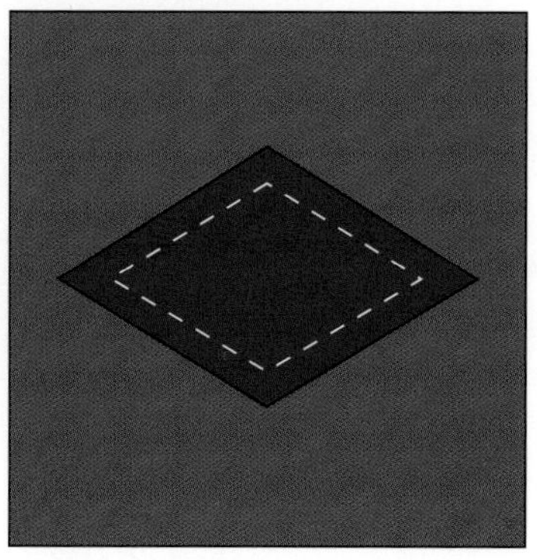

Fig. 2-28. From the back, trim the diamond allowances to ⅛".

Cut-Away Appliqué

This method is helpful for stems, like those of the lilies of the valley in the Rose Basket.

CUT-AWAY APPLIQUÉ SAMPLE:

Use a stem from the Rose Basket pattern, page 64.

1 Trace a lily-of-the-valley stem onto a background square and on to a piece of stem fabric. Do *not* cut the stem out for cut-away appliqué.

2 Place the stem fabric over the background square. Carefully match the stem fabric tracing to the background tracing by matching two or three points on their fold lines with pins. Secure the fabrics with pins in the allowances.

3 With small, sharp scissors, cut a ⅛" turn-under allowance around the stem for a short distance. Hide the knot in the fold and needle-turn the edge as you appliqué. Work your way around the stem, cutting just ahead of where you are working (Fig. 2–29). Do not fold the stem under at places that will be tucked under flowers.

4 Snip the allowance at inside curves and use the needle swipe, described on page 38 and illustrated in Fig. 2–12 on page 39, where necessary to get a smooth turn.

With this method, your stem will be one solid piece instead of numerous short sections. Of course, it is okay to appliqué the stems the more conventional way, if you prefer.

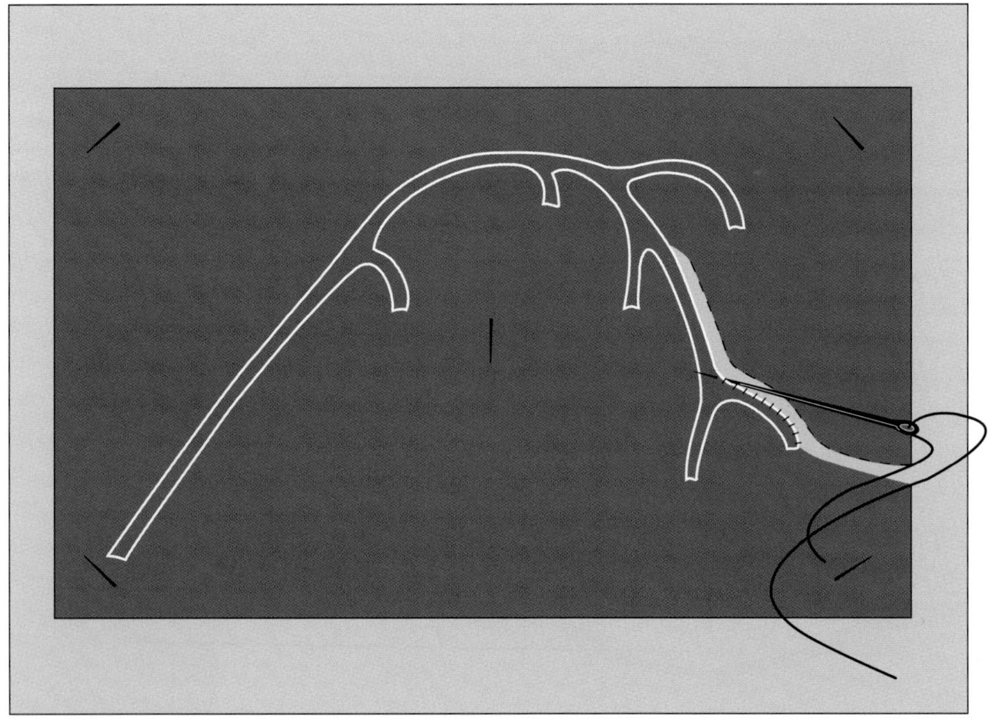

Fig. 2–29. Cut away small sections at a time as you stitch around the stem. Do not fold under the end of the stem where it tucks behind flowers.

Chapter 3

Gems of Summer

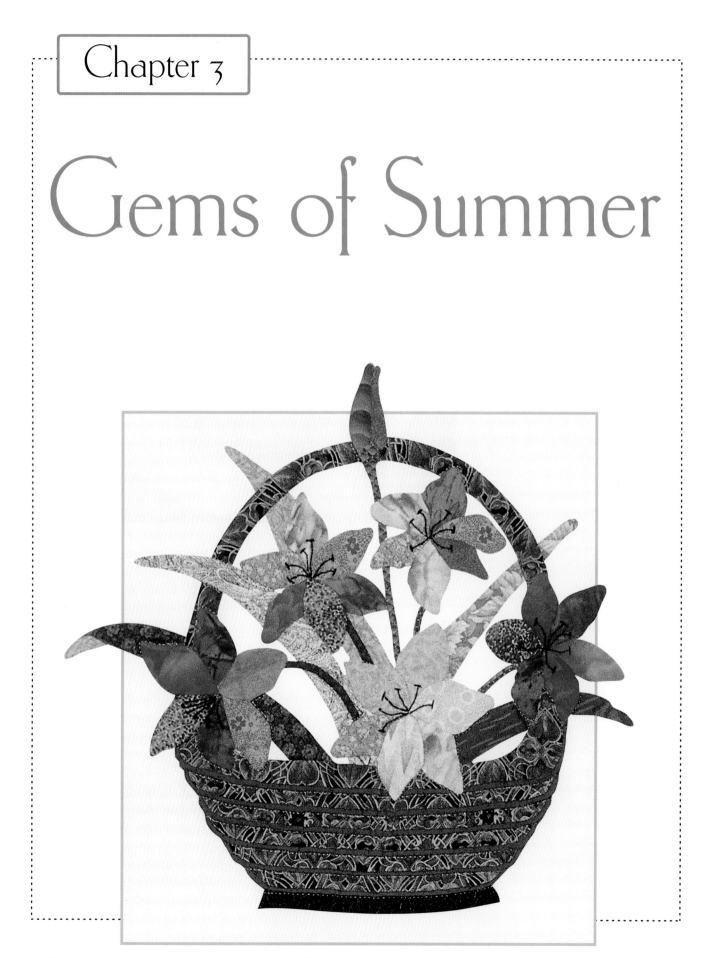

The flowers I have chosen for my designs are familiar favorites that conjure up memories of my mother's and grandmother's gardens. I was blessed with a strong gardening tradition in my family, and my love and appreciation of flowers and all living things are as deep as my love of quilts.

Before you begin, I recommend that you read the instructions carefully. Note that your basket designs will be oriented either on point or straight, depending on your choice of setting. Complete instructions for all techniques required to construct these patterns are included in Chapter 1. A Quick Find index to the various techniques is included with each pattern, for your convenience.

LILY BASKET

Lilies are breathtaking flowers found in abundance in Mother's garden. She has day lilies and spider lilies, but I think the tiger lilies are the most spectacular. I enjoy strolling with her in the garden while she points out and names each variety. The gardens have changed, but the flowers are each etched in my memory from those wonderful, leisurely, mother-daughter strolls.

1 Make a master pattern by tracing the four quadrants of the Lily Basket pattern, pages 122–125, on a large piece of paper. Include all instructional marks. Transfer the master pattern to a background square. (No instructional marks are needed on the background square.)

2 Make templates for all pattern pieces. Attach each template to a selected fabric.

3 Cut out either a 15" background square to be set on point or a 20" square to be straight-set, depending on the quilt setting you have chosen from Chapter 4. Fold the square in quarters diagonally, for placing on-point, or horizontally and vertically for straight-set. Crease the folds to use as guidelines for aligning the master pattern.

4 Appliqué the echo outline to basket piece #1 and appliqué the piece in place.

5 Appliqué pieces #2–#15. Notice that leaf pieces #2 and #3 are twisted.

6 Be sure to make the basket echo appliqué no wider than 1⁄16" or your basket will "grow" and not fit properly. Attach the echo appliqué to pieces *B–G*. Appli-piece *B* to *A* using the match-up marks for exact placement. Repeat, in turn, with *C* through *G*. When complete, the basket becomes piece #16 in the appliqué sequence. Appliqué the basket in place.

7 Appli-piece the lily units and appliqué them in place.

8 Cut away excess fabric layers from the back of the block and add embroidery details in the center of the lilies.

9 Size block to 13" (on-point) or 18½" (straight-set).

QUICK FIND

Lily Basket (updated version) – full-size pattern on pages 122–125. Photocopy this small pattern for your portable appliqué kit.

DAFFODIL BASKET

Some of my earliest memories involve daffodils. As a young girl, I remember the joy and anticipation I felt upon seeing the first daffodils in bloom each spring. We called them jonquils. In central Texas, spring came very early; the daffodils bloomed in late February. Our sidewalk was lined with these bright yellow beauties, and every morning, my sisters and I would pick bouquets to take to our teachers.

There are now many hybrid varieties of daffodils, and they can be white, orange, peach, or two-toned, as well as various shades of yellow. However, I will always be most fond of the original bright yellow harbinger of spring that I remember from my childhood.

1 Make a master pattern by tracing the four quadrants of the Daffodil Basket pattern, pages 126–129, on a large piece of paper. Include all instructional marks. Transfer the master pattern to a background square. (No instructional marks are needed on the background square.)

2 Make templates for all pattern pieces, including basket piece *A* (Fig. 3–1a). Attach each template to a selected fabric. Make a template *B* of the whole basket outline, but minus the handle (Fig. 3–1b).

a.

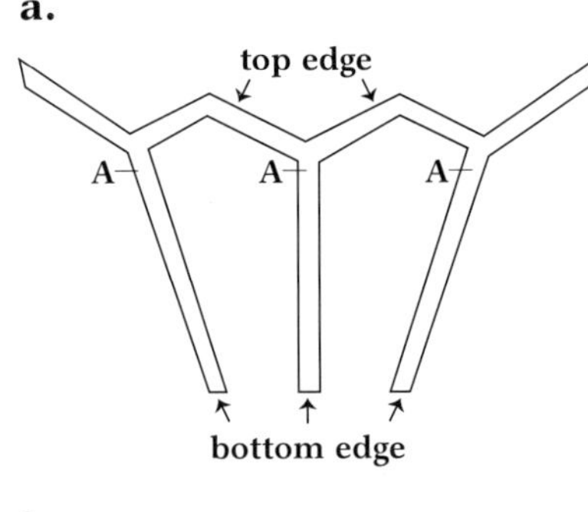

b.

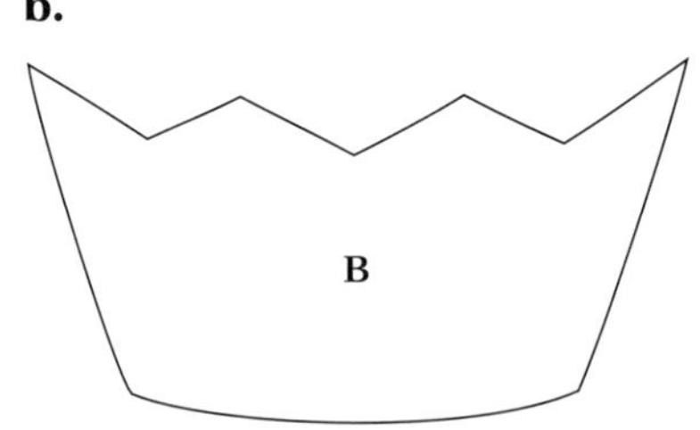

c.

Figs. 3–1a, b, and c.

3 Cut out either a 15" background square to be set on point, or a 20" square to be straight-set, depending on the quilt setting you have chosen from Chapter 4. Fold the square in quarters diagonally, for placing on-point, or horizontally and vertically for straight-set. Crease the folds to use as guidelines for aligning the master pattern.

4 Appliqué pieces #2–#24 to the background in numerical order.

5 For the basket (piece #25), cut one rectangle 5½" x 9" from your basket fabric and another from your coordinating basket fabric. Press template *A* to the coordinating fabric rectangle, being careful not to distort the shape. Mark around template *A*. Pin the wrong side of that rectangle to the right side of the basket fabric rectangle. Using the cut-away appliqué technique, sew piece *A* in place. Do not appliqué the top or bottom edges of *A*. The top of the basket will be turned under when the basket is attached to the background (Fig. 3–1c). The bottom edge will be covered by the base of the basket (piece *C*). Trim the top edge of the basket fabric that is behind piece *A* to ⅛".

6 Place template *B* over the basket section you have just appliquéd, aligning the top of *B* with the top of *A*. Mark all around template *B* and cut out the basket with a ⅛" turn-under allowance. Appli-piece the basket to piece *C*. Appliqué the basket unit to the background. Remember to leave turn-under allowances flat where covered by flowers.

7 Appli-piece flower units and appliqué them in place.

8 Cut away excess fabric layers from the back of the block and add embroidery details to the centers of the flowers.

9 Size block to 13" (on-point) or 18½" (straight-set).

QUICK FIND

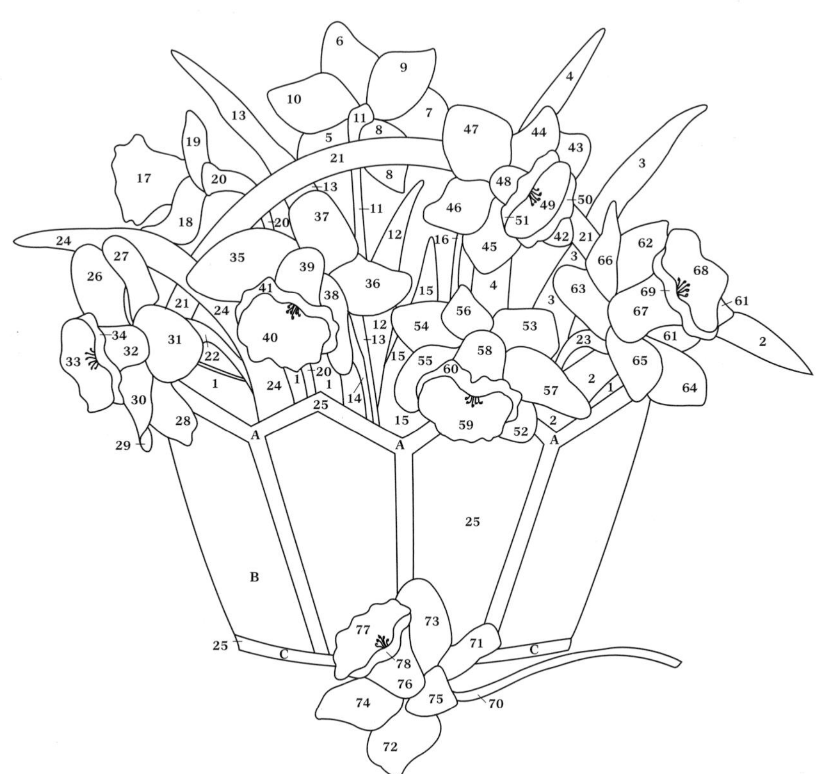

Daffodil Basket (updated version) – full-size pattern on pages 126–129. Photocopy this small pattern for your portable appliqué kit.

TULIP BASKET

I don't recall Mother having tulips when I was a child. Perhaps they were unavailable or we could not afford them. But, later, I remember Mom preparing the soil and planting tulip bulbs in the fall. They seemed very exotic to me, coming from Holland, and what a wonderful reward for her labor when they popped up each spring!

1 Make a master pattern by tracing the four quadrants of the Tulip Basket pattern, pages 130–133, on a large piece of paper. Include all instructional marks. Transfer the master pattern to a background square. (No instructional marks are needed on the background square.)

2 Make templates for all pattern pieces. Attach each template to a selected fabric. Make a template *A* for the basket, omitting pieces *I*, *J*, and the handle.

3 Cut out either a 15" background square to be set on point, or a 20" square to be straight-set, depending on the quilt setting you have chosen from Chapter 4. Fold the square in quarters diagonally, for placing on-point, or horizontally and vertically for straight-set. Crease the folds to use as guidelines for aligning the master pattern.

4 Appliqué the echo outline to basket piece #1 and appliqué the piece in place.

5 Appliqué leaves and stems #2–#24 in place.

6 For the basket, attach template *A* to the main basket fabric. Mark the placement of pieces *B–H* on *A* by extending the marks into the top and bottom allowance of *A*. Remove the template from piece *A* and appliqué pieces *B–H* to it. Piece *B* and piece *H* will be sewn only on their inner edges. Their outer edges will become the outside edge of the basket. Trim the edge of the basket under pieces *B* and *H* to 1/8". Appli-piece *I* to *A* and *J* to *A*. Remember to leave turn-under allowances flat where flowers overlap the basket. Appliqué basket to background square.

7 Appli-piece flower units and appliqué them in place.

8 Cut away excess fabric layers from the back of the block and add embroidery details to the flower centers.

9 Size block to 13" (on-point) or 18½" (straight-set).

QUICK FIND

Tulip Basket (updated version) – full-size pattern on pages 130–133. Photocopy this small pattern for your portable appliqué kit.

PRIMROSE BASKET

I remember, while playing along the creek of the farm in central Texas where I grew up, we chased frogs, waded in the stream, climbed trees, and filled our pockets with "precious" stones. I also remember picking wildflowers. One flower I particularly liked, we called a buttercup. Some were white, some pale pink, and some were a beautiful deep pink. When we sniffed their fragrance, the pollen would come off on our noses. I drew these flowers from memory and then tried to find a picture to verify the name, but no buttercup was listed in my books. The primrose was the closest to what I have drawn.

1 Make a master pattern by tracing the four quadrants of the Primrose Basket pattern, pages 134–137 on a large piece of paper. Include all instructional marks. Transfer the master pattern to a background square. (No instructional marks are needed on the background square.)

2 Make templates for all pattern pieces. Attach each template to a selected fabric.

3 Cut out either a 15" background square to be set on point, or a 20" square to be straight-set, depending on the quilt setting you have chosen from Chapter 4. Fold the square in quarters diagonally, for placing on-point, or horizontally and vertically for straight-set. Crease the folds to use as guidelines for aligning the master pattern.

4 Stitch the echo appliqué to basket piece #3, and reverse appliqué the diamonds (#16) in basket piece #17. To keep the handle from stretching, do not remove the basket template and do not cut out the section inside the handle until you are ready to sew the basket to the background.

5 Starting with the base of the basket (piece #1) appliqué all of the pieces in numerical order. To achieve a beautiful, smoothly folded edge on basket pieces #1 and #17, use your thumbnail to make a crease along the fold line before you remove the freezer paper. The bases of the leaves are tucked

under their stems. Notice the leave-open marks on stems #13 and #15, indicating that the area between the slash marks must be left unsewn until leaves #18 and #19 have been attached.

6 When it is time to appliqué the basket (#17), cut out the area inside the handle, pin the basket in place, and remove the basket template with great care to prevent stretching the handle out of shape. Appliqué the basket in place.

7 Appli-piece the flowers and appliqué them in place.

8 Cut away excess fabric layers from the back of the block and add embroidery detail to the centers of the flowers.

9 Size block to 13" (on-point) or 18½" (straight-set).

QUICK FIND

Primrose Basket – full-size pattern on pages 134–137. Photocopy this small pattern for your portable appliqué kit.

IRIS BASKET

In the late spring and early summer, my mother can usually be found tending or admiring her large collection of irises. These flowers have always been her passion and I believe they are her favorite. In the winter, she studies her catalogs and selects new and more exotic irises to add to an already vast assortment. The large, graceful flowers in their many colors are often found in an arrangement, adding untold color and beauty to her home. Have I mentioned that Mother is an award-winning floral arranger and a certified flower-show judge?

1 Make a master pattern by tracing the four quadrants of the Iris Basket pattern, pages 138–141, on a large piece of paper. Include all instructional marks. Transfer the master pattern to a background square. (No instructional marks are needed on the background square.)

2 Make templates for all pattern pieces. Attach each template to a selected fabric.

3 Cut out either a 15" background square to be set on-point, or a 20" square to be straight-set, depending on the quilt setting you have chosen from Chapter 4. Fold the square in quarters diagonally, for placing on point, or horizontally and vertically for straight-set. Crease the folds to use as guidelines for aligning the master pattern.

4 Appliqué the echo outlines to basket pieces #1 and #41. Appliqué piece #1 to the background square.

5 Appliqué pieces #2–#39 in place. Then appli-piece #41 to #40 and appliqué the basket in place. Leave the top of the basket open between the leave-open marks.

6 Appliqué leaves #42 and #43 in place, snipping the allowance of each at the basket's edge so the allowances will lie flat under the basket and the leaves will appear to drape out of the basket. Appliqué the top of the basket.

7 Appli-piece flower units and appliqué them in place.

8 Cut away excess fabric layers from the back of the block and add embroidery details to the irises.

9 Size block to 13" (on-point) or 18½" (straight-set).

QUICK FIND

Iris Basket – full-size pattern on pages 138–141. Photocopy this small pattern for your portable appliqué kit.

AFRICAN VIOLET BASKET

I was in my late twenties before I was introduced to the African violet. Again, my mother's influence comes to mind when I think about these delicate flowers. For a time, I simply admired hers. I was busy with my young son, so there was no time for house plants, I thought. But I lived in Dallas, Texas, and Volkmann Brothers Nurseries is there. So when Mom came to visit me, of course we had to go to the nursery. I had no idea there could be so many variations of one plant. Naturally, I came home with quite a selection. There was no way I could choose just one.

With my mother's guidance, I had great success and many years of enjoyment from those beautiful flowers. I still have African violets in my kitchen window, and they still take my breath away when they bloom. Thank you, Mom.

1 Make a master pattern by tracing the four quadrants of the African Violet Basket pattern, pages 142–145, on a large piece of paper. Include all instructional marks. Transfer the master pattern to a background square. (No instructional marks are needed on the background square.)

2 Make templates for all pattern pieces. Attach each template to a selected fabric.

3 Cut out either a 15" background square to be set on-point, or a 20" square to be straight-set, depending on the quilt setting you have chosen from Chapter 4. Fold the square in quarters diagonally, for placing on-point, or horizontally and vertically for straight-set. Crease the folds to use as guidelines for aligning the master pattern.

4 Appliqué the echo outline to piece #1 and appliqué the piece in place.

5 Appli-piece basket piece #3 to #2 and #4 to #3. Appliqué the basket in place. Notice the leave-open marks on the right side of piece #4 to allow handle piece #13 to be inserted later.

6 Appliqué pieces #5–#28 in place and finish the appliqué in the leave-open area on #4.

7 Appli-piece flowers and appliqué the units in place.

8 Cut away excess fabric layers from the back of the block. and add embroidery details to the violets.

9 Size block to 13" (on-point) or 18½" (straight-set).

QUICK FIND

African Violet Basket (updated version) – full-size pattern on pages 142–145. Photocopy this small pattern for your portable appliqué kit.

AMARYLLIS BASKET

My original design for this basket was an arrangement of fruit. But the one basket filled with fruit when all the others had flowers seemed out of place to me. So back to the design table I went and replaced the fruit with the amaryllis, another pretty flower found in Mom's garden. It's beautiful and showy and lends itself well to appliqué.

1 Make a master pattern by tracing the four quadrants of the Amaryllis Basket pattern, pages 146–149, on a large piece of paper. Include all instructional marks. Transfer the master pattern to a background square. (No instructional marks are needed on the background square.)

2 Make templates for all pattern pieces. Attach each template to a selected fabric.

3 Cut out either a 15" background square to be set on-point, or a 20" square to be

straight-set, depending on the quilt setting you have chosen from Chapter 4. Fold the square in quarters diagonally, for placing on-point, or horizontally and vertically for straight-set. Crease the folds to use as guidelines for aligning the master pattern.

4 Appliqué the echo outline to piece #1 and appliqué the piece in place.

5 Appliqué #2–#15 (stems, leaves, and handle) in place.

6 Appli-piece basket pieces *A–H* together (piece #16). (Or you can ignore the divisions and cut out a combined template *A–G* for the whole basket. Appli-piece the basket to *H*.) Appliqué the echo outline to top of the basket and appliqué the basket unit to the background square. Leave the top unstitched between the leave-open marks until leaf #18 has been appliquéd in place.

7 Appliqué remaining leaves. Then appli-piece flowers and appliqué the units in place.

8 Cut away excess fabric layers from the back of the block and add embroidery details.

9 Size block to 13" (on-point) or 18½" (straight-set).

QUICK FIND

Amaryllis Basket – full-size pattern on pages 146–149. Photocopy this small pattern for your portable appliqué kit.

ROSE BASKET

My grandfather's favorite flower was the yellow rose. I don't know if it was his favorite because Grandmother had a beautiful yellow rose bush or if she grew it because it was Granddaddy's favorite. Nonetheless, I remember enjoying their heady fragrance, while I often kept a wary eye on a nearby bee or wasp.

1 Make a master pattern by tracing the four quadrants of the Rose Basket pattern, pages 150–153, on a large piece of paper. Include all instructional marks. Transfer the master pattern to a background square. (No instructional marks are needed on the background square.)

2 Make templates for all pattern pieces. Attach each template to a selected fabric.

3 Cut out either a 15" background square to be set on-point, or a 20" square to be straight-set, depending on the quilt setting you have chosen from Chapter 4. Fold the square

Choosing Rose Fabrics

- *Examine the roses pictured in the quilts in the gallery, page 115–120, to get an idea of what fabrics make good roses. It may help to know that the rose centers, such as pieces #40, #48, and #61 in the Rose Basket pattern, should be the darkest fabrics. Choose lighter fabrics for pieces such as #41, #49, and #62.*

- *To audition your fabric choices before sewing them together, draw a paper foundation for each rose (Fig. 3–2).*

- *Cut the fabric for each petal, without turn-under allowances.*

- *Pin each petal to its corresponding place on the paper foundation.*

- *When you have pinned all the petals in place, hang the flower up and step back 8 to 10 feet. Ask yourself, does it look like a rose? Is there enough contrast in the fabrics or too little? If not, change it. You won't waste much fabric, and you will be happier with the end result.*

Fig. 3–2. Example of auditioning fabrics before appliquéing flower to background.

in quarters diagonally, for placing on-point, or horizontally and vertically for straight-set. Crease the folds to use as guidelines for aligning the master pattern.

4 Appliqué #1–#9 in place. Leaves #1, #2, #4, and #12 are large, and care should be taken in the fabric selection for them. Try using mid-range colors instead of your darkest ones that might overpower the space.

5 Appliqué the echo outline to basket piece #11 and appliqué the piece to the background square.

6 Appli-piece basket pieces *A* through *I* together, or if you prefer, make the body of the basket one piece and use these divisions as quilting lines. Appli-piece basket to *J* and appliqué the basket unit in place. Remember to leave flat and unstitched those areas that will be covered by other pieces. Also, do not sew between the leave-open marks on the basket rim until you have attached leaf #19.

7 Appliqué leaves #19–#21 and lily-of-the-valley blossoms #22–#35. Notice the slash mark on leaf #19. Snip the seam allowance of #19 at that point to allow it to drape out of the basket. Then appli-piece the roses and appliqué the units in place.

8 Cut away excess fabric layers from the back of the block and add embroidery details.

9 Size block to 13" (on-point) or 18½" (straight-set).

QUICK FIND

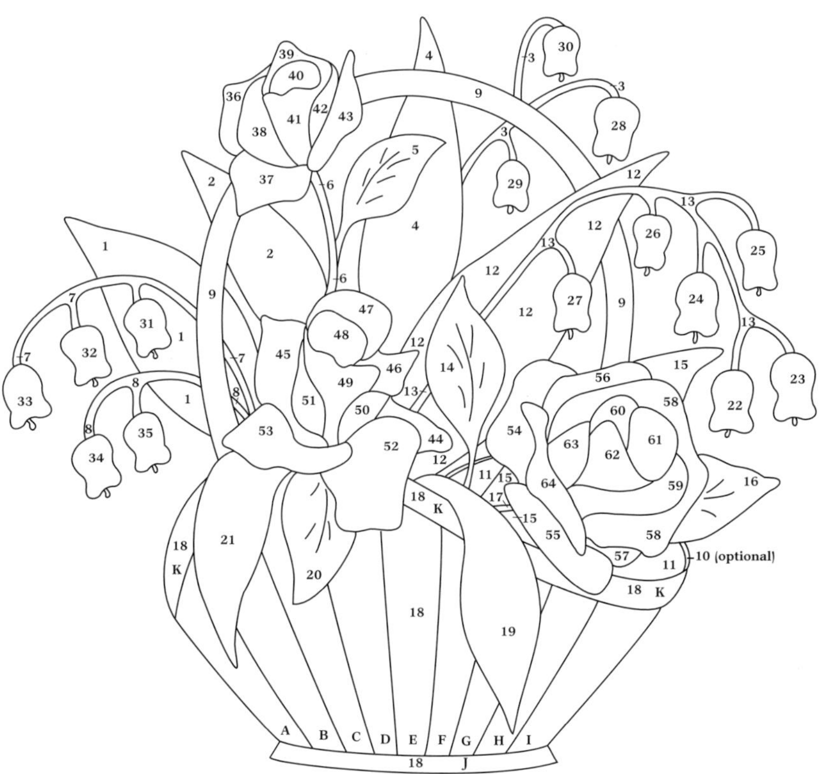

Rose Basket (updated version) – full-size pattern on pages 150–153. Photocopy this small pattern for your portable appliqué kit.

I had never seen a wild rose until I visited the Lake of the Ozarks in Missouri, where I spotted some in bloom. I picked one, only to have it wilt almost immediately. Of course, it saddened me that I had picked it. Oftentimes, nature is better left untouched. Its beauty can be appreciated more in its natural state. I find myself returning to the wild rose repeatedly in my designs, using it in quilting patterns, a medallion wreath, and in borders, clothing, etc. The viny plants and graceful flowers lend themselves to many creative applications.

WILD ROSE BASKET

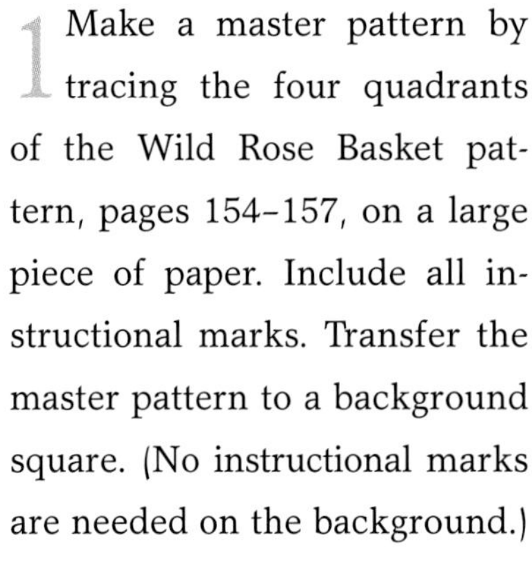

1 Make a master pattern by tracing the four quadrants of the Wild Rose Basket pattern, pages 154–157, on a large piece of paper. Include all instructional marks. Transfer the master pattern to a background square. (No instructional marks are needed on the background.)

2 Make templates for all pattern pieces. Attach each template to a selected fabric.

3 Cut out either a 15" background square to be set on-point, or a 20" square to be straight-set, depending on the quilt setting you have chosen from Chapter 4. Fold the square in quarters diagonally, for placing on-point, or horizontally and vertically for straight-set. Crease the folds to use as guidelines for aligning the master pattern.

4 Appliqué the echo outline to basket piece#1 and appliqué the piece in place.

5 Paying close attention to the numbering sequence, appliqué pieces #2–#23 in place. Notice the following marks:

a. The stem around the handle changes from #15 to #19 midway. You need to stop sewing at the slash and appliqué handle piece #16, stem portion #17, and leaf #18 in place before continuing with stem portion #19.

b. The leave-open marks on stem #15 will allow you to attach leaf #23 later. There are also leave-open marks on stem #19 for leaf #34 and on basket rim #24 for stems #27 and #29.

c. Stem #17 has a slash mark. Again, you need to stop sewing at this point and wait until you are ready for leaf #33 (attached to stem #17) in the numbering sequence.

d. Stem #15/19 is one continuous piece of fabric as is stem/leaf #17/33. Use a bias strip for #15/19 and a template for #17/33 because of the attached leaf at the end. Take care to keep the stems the same width throughout.

6 Appli-piece basket piece *A* to *B* and *C* to *A* and appliqué the basket in place.

7 Appliqué the rest of the leaves to the background. Appli-piece the flower units and appliqué them in place.

8 Cut away excess fabric layers from the back of the block and add embroidery details to the centers of the flowers.

9 Size block to 13" (on-point) or 18½" (straight-set).

Wild Rose Basket – full-size pattern on pages 154–157. Photocopy this small pattern for your portable appliqué kit.

QUICK FIND

DAISY BASKET

It is odd, with my special memories relating to all the other flowers in this series, that the Daisy Basket turned out to be my favorite. I am sure Mother had daisies, but I don't recall them. Perhaps, they were simply overshadowed by the more spectacular flowers in her garden.

1 Make a master pattern by tracing the four quadrants of the Daisy Basket pattern, pages 158–161, on a large piece of paper. Include all instructional marks. Transfer the master pattern to a background square. (No instructional marks are needed on the background square.)

2 Make templates for all pattern pieces. Attach each of them to a selected fabric.

3 Cut out either a 15" background square to be set on-point, or a 20" square to be straight-set, depending on the quilt setting you have chosen

from Chapter 4. Fold the square in quarters diagonally, for placing on-point, or horizontally and vertically for straight-set. Crease the folds to use as guidelines for aligning the master pattern.

4 Appliqué the echo outline to basket piece #1 and appliqué the piece in place.

5 Appliqué pieces #2–#20 in numerical order.

6 For the basket, appli-piece *B* to *A* and *A* to *C* and appliqué the basket unit in place. Leave the basket rim unstitched between leave-open marks until pieces #22 through #28 have been appliquéd. To allow #28 to drape out of the basket, snip the allowance to the fold line at the slash mark. Stitch basket between leave-open marks.

7 Appli-piece the flowers and appliqué the flower units in place.

8 Cut away excess fabric layers from the back of the block.

9 Size block to 13" (on-point) or 18½" (straight-set).

QUICK FIND

Daisy Basket – full-size pattern on pages 158–161. Photocopy this small pattern for your portable appliqué kit.

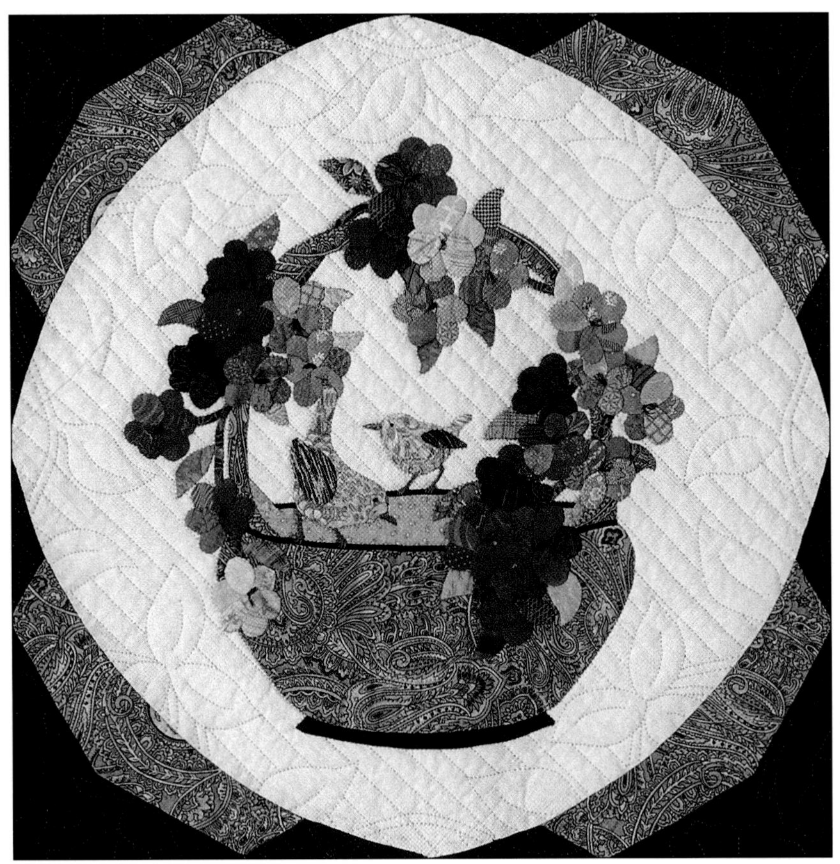

CLEMATIS BASKET

Years ago, I decided to feed wild birds. Soon, we had five feeders and a water station. We have been rewarded with hours and hours of enjoyment. Of course, the next step was to hang nesting boxes. We hung one birdhouse from a deck and were pleased when a wren quickly discovered it. We watched the nest-building activity for a few days and decided to hang another house in the hope of attracting another pair. Much to our amusement, our wren thoroughly checked out the new house and decided to move. The first house was abandoned, and a nest was built next door. What fun we had watching the activity as the family hatched, grew, and learned to fly. The first house remained empty all season. Apparently, it was too close for the territorial wrens. We later learned that the male wren builds the nest and often starts several, allowing the female to choose. It makes perfect sense to me.

1 Make a master pattern by tracing the four quadrants of the Clematis Basket pattern, pages 162–165, on a large piece of paper. Include all instructional marks. Transfer the master pattern to a background square. (No instructional marks are needed on the background square.)

2 Make templates for all pattern pieces. Attach each of them to a selected fabric.

3 Cut out either a 15" background square to be set on-point, or a 20" square to be straight-set, depending on the quilt setting you have chosen. Fold the square in quarters diagonally, for placing on-point, or horizontally and vertically for straight-set. Crease the folds to use as guidelines for aligning the master pattern.

4 Appli-piece basket piece #3 to pieces #1 and #2. Fold back the inner allowances of #1 and #2 and appliqué the echo outline to piece #3 (Figs. 2–13 to 2–16, pages 40–41). Appliqué this unit to the background square. Pieces #1 and #2 at handle base are minor details and may be omitted.

5 Appliqué an echo outline to the top of basket piece #7 and appli-piece #7 to #6. Appli-

qué the handle, basket, and stems #8 and #13 in place.

6 Appli-piece the flowers and appliqué the leaves, flower units, and birds in place. Legs, beaks, and eyes of the birds are embroidered.

7 Cut away excess fabric layers from the back of the block and add embroidery details to the flower centers and the birds.

8 Size block to 13" (on-point) or 18½" (straight-set).

Choosing Flower Fabrics

You will want to avoid a light-dark-light-dark petal arrangement in a flower. It is better to shade the petals from light to dark around the flower. Also, flowers that overlap or touch must have enough difference in value, intensity, or color to be perceived as individual flowers. The flowers that are lowest in the numbering sequence should appear to recede. Therefore, choose darker and duller fabrics for them. As you progress in the numbering sequence, choose lighter and brighter fabrics. It might be easier to make each flower distinct if you use multiple colors, making one flower purple, another yellow, one pink, etc. But if you prefer to use one color family for the flowers, expand your range by adding neighboring colors from the color wheel. For example, if using the red family, add oranges and purples. It is also possible to use just one fabric per flower.

Clematis Basket – full-size pattern on pages 162–165. Photocopy this small pattern for your portable appliqué kit.

QUICK FIND

CANNA BASKET

Mother used cannas as the backdrop in a well-planned flower bed to line a fence or as a striking addition to her vegetable garden. She has always loved red, so she plants mostly red cannas. Sometimes, she adds yellow ones for variety.

1 Make a master pattern by tracing the four quadrants of the Canna Basket pattern, pages 166–169, on a large piece of paper. Include all instructional marks. Transfer the master pattern to a background square. (No instructional marks are needed on the background square.)

2 Make templates for all pattern pieces. Attach each template to a selected fabric.

3 Cut out either a 15" background square to be set on-point, or a 20" square to be straight-set, depending on the quilt setting you have chosen from Chapter 4. Fold the square

in quarters diagonally, for placing on-point, or horizontally and vertically for straight-set. Crease the folds to use as guidelines for aligning the master pattern.

4 Appliqué pieces #1–#19 in place. Notice the leave-open marks on leaf #17. This piece will be completed after leaf parts #23 and #24 have been appliquéd in place.

5 Appliqué the echo outlines to basket pieces *A* and *B*, and appli-piece *B* to *A* and *B* to *C*. Appliqué basket unit to background fabric.

6 Appliqué pieces #21–#24 in place.

7 Appli-piece flowers and appliqué units in place.

8 Cut away excess fabric layers from the back of the block and add embroidery details to the flowers.

9 Size block to 13" (on-point) or 18½" (straight-set).

QUICK FIND

Canna Basket – full-size pattern on pages 166–169. Photocopy this small pattern for your portable appliqué kit.

EMBROIDERY DETAILS

Each of the baskets will benefit from a small amount of basic embroidery to define and finish such details as flowers, leaves, and birds. The stitches recommended are simple and add realism to the appliqué.

Choose a thread color that will stand out. It makes no sense to do the embroidery and not be able to see it.

In almost all cases, you will be using a single strand of thread. Exceptions will be noted.

You can use an embroidery needle if you want, but an appliqué or quilting needle will also work since you will be using only one, or sometimes two, strands of thread or embroidery floss. A #26 tapestry needle will work best for the Iris and Clematis.

A small embroidery hoop is recommended to stabilize your fabric and prevent puckering.

Stem Stitch

From the back of the work, bring your needle up at *A*, then down at *B*, and up again at *C* (Fig. 3-3). Pull the needle and thread all the way through, while holding the thread to the left of the needle.

Go down at *D* and come up at *B*, still keeping the thread to the left of your needle. Pull thread through, then go down at *E* and come up at *D*. Continue to the end of the line.

Make stitches equal in length. Pull thread to the back and either tie a knot or weave the thread through the stitches on back. Fig. 3-4 shows how the stitches should look from the back of your piece.

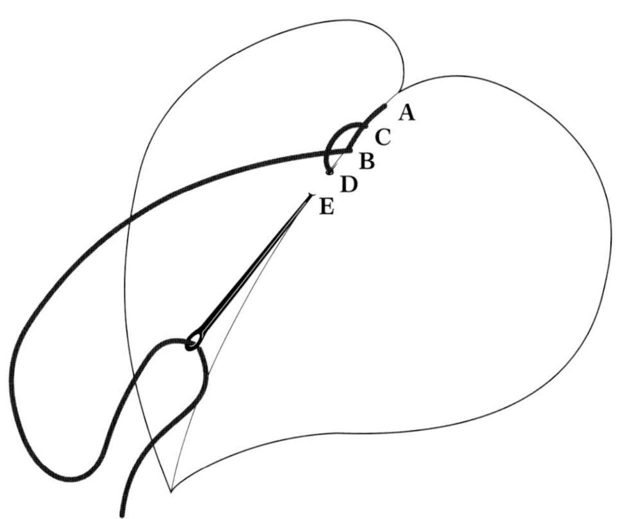

Fig. 3-3.

Veins of leaves may also be quilted.

Fig. 3-4.

French Knot

Bring the needle up at *A* and loop the thread twice around needle as shown (Fig. 3–5). For a smaller French knot, wrap the thread around the needle only once, and for a larger knot, wrap three times. You can also vary the size of the knot by using more strands of floss.

Put the needle point in the flower just beside *A* (Fig. 3–6), pull the thread taut around the needle, slide the loops down close to fabric, and pull the needle and thread to back, while holding the loops in place with your other hand.

When French knots are short distances apart as in the Clematis Basket, you can travel from knot to knot without tying off until the last knot.

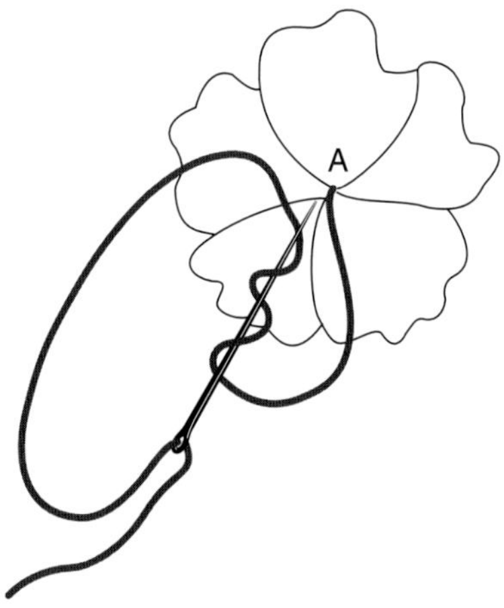

Fig. 3–5.

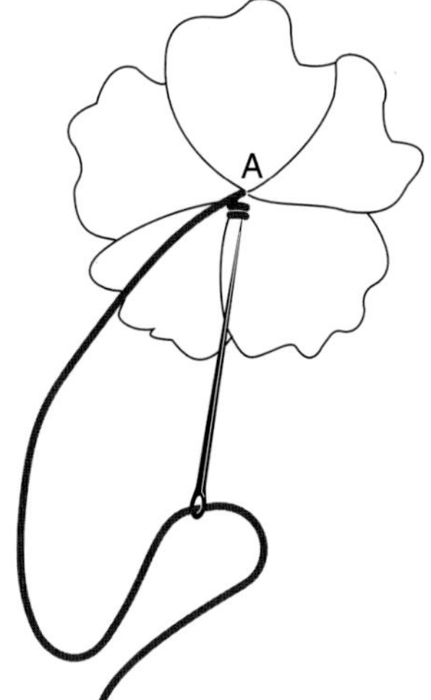

Fig. 3–6.

Candlewicking Knot

You may want to try this knot in place of the French knot. It is slightly more involved, but it is a little more distinctive. Vary the size of your knots by changing the number of strands of floss.

Bring the needle up at *A*, loop the thread around the needle (Fig. 3–7). The needle tip should point toward the fabric.

Hold the thread taut to keep the loop on the needle and pivot the needle point up (Fig. 3–8). Loop the thread around the needle.

Still holding the looped thread taut, pivot the needle down again and loop the thread around the needle a third time. The thread will form a figure-8 on the needle (Fig. 3–9).

Insert the needle again at *A*, taking care to avoid going through the same hole (Fig. 3–10). Pull the looped threads close to the needle and next to the fabric as shown. Pull the needle and thread to the back and tie a knot. You may travel to another candlewicking knot.

Fig. 3–7.

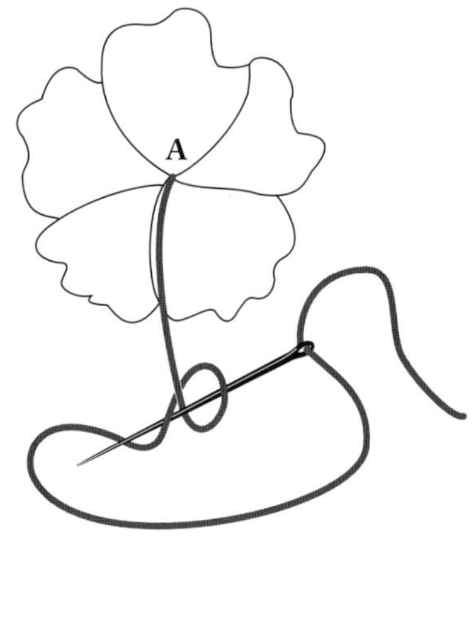

Fig. 3–8.

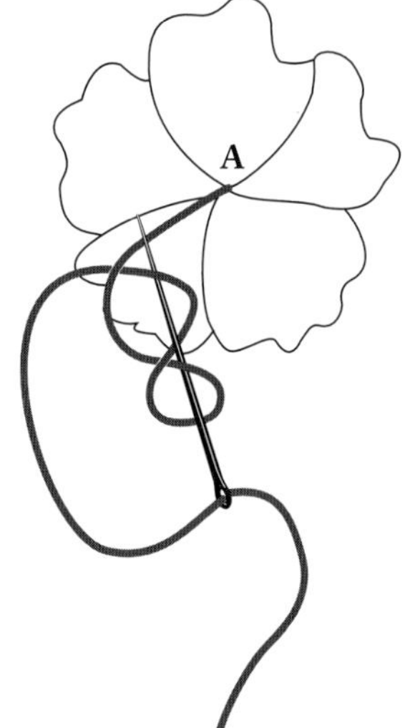

Fig. 3–9.

Fig. 3–10.

Couching

With a single thread, bring the needle up through the fabric at *A* and go down at *B*. Then come up at *C* and go back down at *C* on the opposite side of the thread as shown (Fig. 3-11). By offsetting the anchor stitch at C, you can make a stamen slightly crooked or create a bend in a bird's leg.

By laying down more than one thread between *A* and *B*, you can create the top portion of each lily stamen (Fig. 3-12).

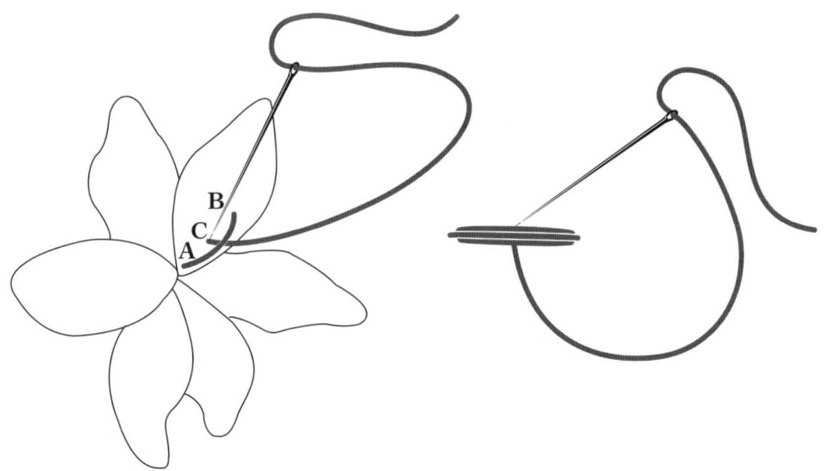

Fig. 3-11. **Fig. 3-12.**

Satin Stitch

This stitch is useful for filling in an area, such as the beaks of the birds in the Clematis Basket pattern. Outline stitch the beak first with a single strand of thread. Then fill in with parallel stitches (Fig. 3-13). The stitches should lie evenly side by side, not crowded, but leaving no fabric showing between them.

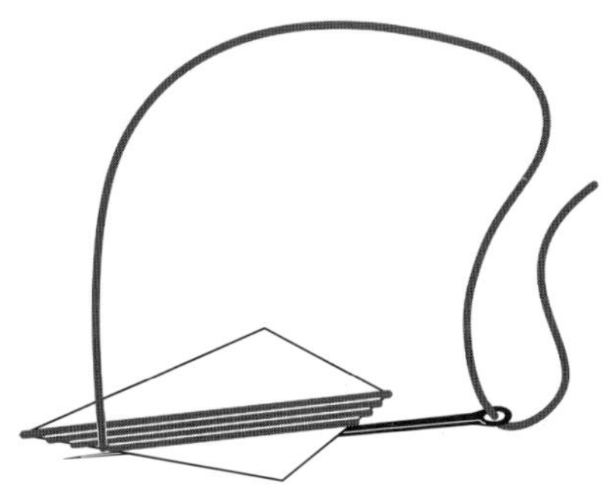

Fig. 3-13.

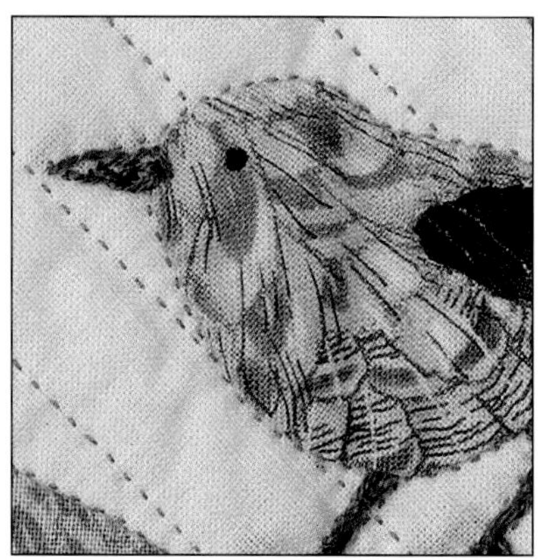

Outline Stitch

Outline stitches are used to define shapes and areas (Figs. 3-14 and 3-15). When an outline stitch must span excessive lengths, it may be couched at intervals to keep it in place.

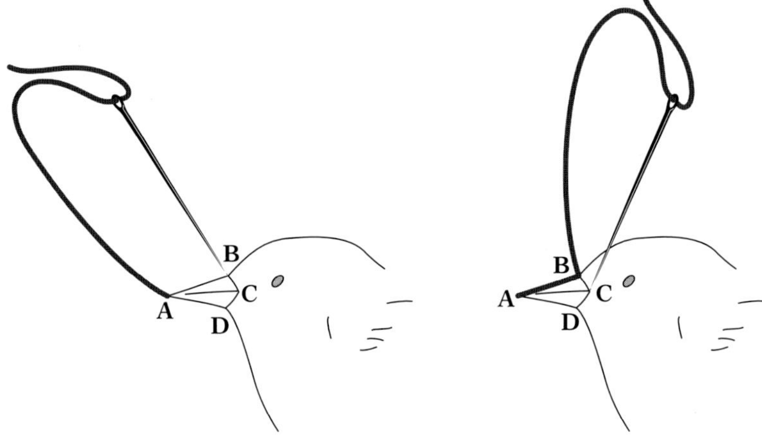

Fig. 3-14. **Fig. 3-15.**

Chain Stitch

This stitch can be used to make the stamens for the lily-of-the-valley blossoms in the Rose Basket pattern. Bring the needle up through the background fabric at *A*. Make a loop with the thread as shown (Fig. 3-16) and hold the loop down with your finger as you take the needle back down at *A*. Come up at *B* and go back down at *B* on the other side of the thread, as shown, to secure loop (Fig. 3-17).

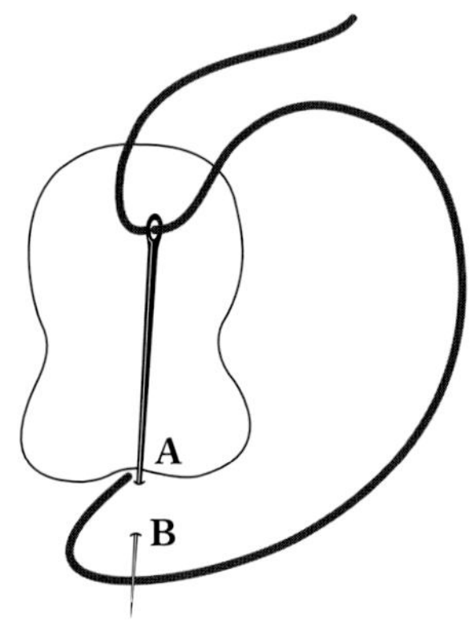

Fig. 3-16.

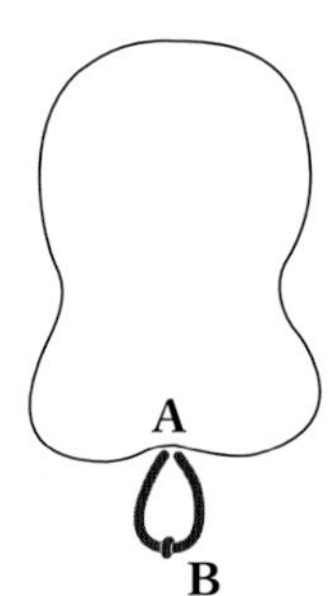

Fig. 3-17.

Beards and Stamens

I don't know the name for this one or even if there is a name. It was my solution to the problem. It works quite well, and it is easy. A tapestry needle is best.

With the thread knotted as shown in Fig. 3-18, slide your needle between the flower and the background, coming up at the flower center. Pull the thread through until the knot catches in center of the flower. You may have to tug a bit to get the knot past your appliqué stitches at the edge of the flower. Snip the thread approximately ¼" from the fabric. Trim shorter for irises to get a more velvety appearance. Repeat as needed to add more threads to the center (Figs. 3-19 and 3-20). For the iris, form enough knots to fill the beard area.

It is possible to do this stitch by bringing the needle and knot up from the back. But because the threads are just snipped off and not secured, you should wait to add this detail until it is time to baste the quilt sandwich.

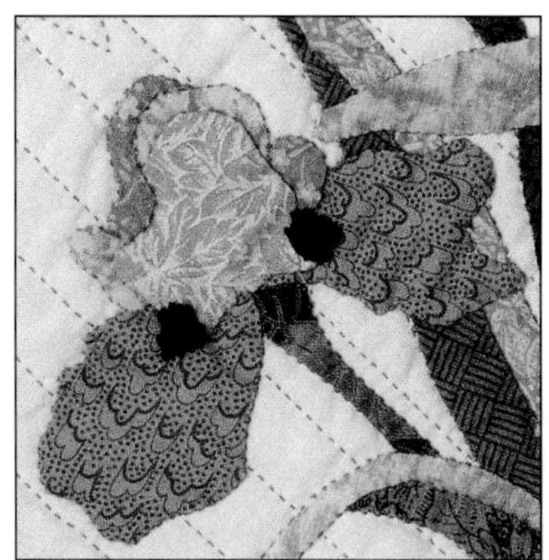

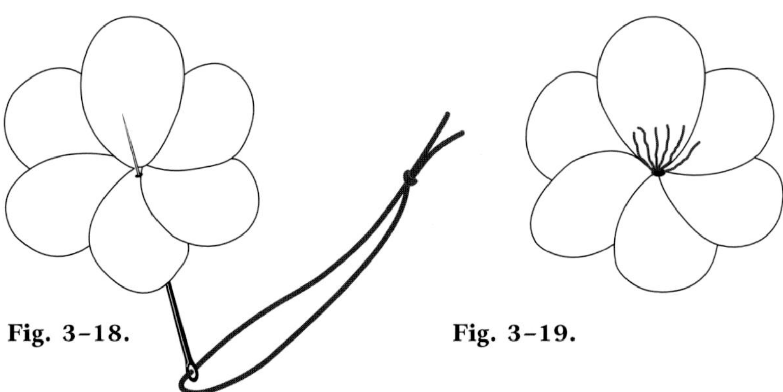

Fig. 3-18.

Fig. 3-19.

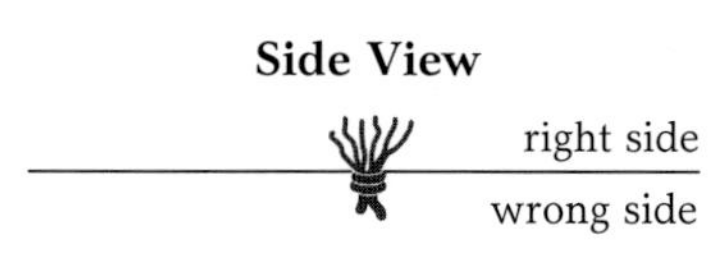

Fig. 3-20.

FINISHING APPLIQUÉ BLOCKS

Removing Markings

Upon completing your appliqué blocks, it will be necessary to remove any visible pattern marks. The method you use will depend on the type of marker. Hopefully, you tested each one, and you know they will come out easily. Try the least abusive removal methods first: dry brushing; plain water; a paste of baking soda and water applied with a soft brush; and finally, soap. If necessary, gently hand wash in a mild soap like Orvus, Dreft, or Clear Ivory Liquid. When no marks remain, completely rinse the block and gently blot it dry in a towel. Remove as much excess water as you can without wringing. Place the block where the air can circulate, on a sweater rack perhaps, and place a fan in the room to speed the drying process. Or, if you prefer, place the block on an ironing board, face down on a thick terry towel, and gently press with a medium to hot iron to dry it. Take care not to distort the shape of the block.

Fig. 3–33. On-point: crease 15" block as shown. Make sure crease lines form a right angle in the center. Measure 6½" and mark on each side of both crease lines to find the cutting lines.

Sizing Blocks

Originally, you cut your blocks larger to allow for the shrinkage that naturally occurs during appliqué and to give you an opportunity to remove edges that may have been stretched and frayed from handling.

Depending on the setting you have chosen, your blocks will be cut to 13" (on-point) or 18½" (straight-set). To size a block to the required measurement, locate the center by folding the block as shown in either Fig. 3-21 or 3-22, depending on the type of block. Check that your creases form a 90° angle. If they do not, correct them now, or you will not have a square when you cut off the excess.

Lay the block on your cutting mat and line up the center creases with the mat's crosswise and lengthwise grid lines. For the 13" block, measure out 6½" from the center creases in all four directions. Make certain the 13" block has a full ¼" seam allowance from the basket foot on the two sides at the bottom (Fig. 3–21). If not, adjust the position of the square so that it does. For the 18½" block, measure out 9¼". Lightly mark the cutting line on all four sides with a wash-out marker and check the measurement again. Make sure each block is square before you cut.

Removing Excess Layers

The very nature of appliqué produces numerous layers of fabrics. If these layers are added to the backing, batting, and background, in some areas you would be quilting through four, five, or more layers of fabric. Removing excess layers has advantages besides facilitating quilting. The areas where excess layers have been removed will puff up more when you quilt around them. There will also be a noticeable reduction in the overall weight of the quilt.

When removing excess layers, you will be working on the wrong side of your appliqué. A pair of sharp embroidery scissors is the tool of choice. Gently separate the background fabric and the appliquéd fabric by pinching each one while pulling them apart. Then carefully snip the background fabric to be trimmed away. This is a small cut, just enough to allow the blade of your scissors to slide between the fabrics.

Trim inside the area you are removing, leaving a ⅛" seam allowance all around. If you are trimming away the background fabric behind a basket, for example, trim inside the stitches around the entire basket area. Where a leaf or flower has been appliquéd over the basket and the stitches prevent the background fabric from falling away, carefully cut very close to the stitching line. Then, gently tug the background fabric on the opposite side of the stitching line. It will fray and release, revealing the wrong side of the basket. In the same manner, cut away the basket fabric from behind a flower or leaf that is appliquéd to the basket.

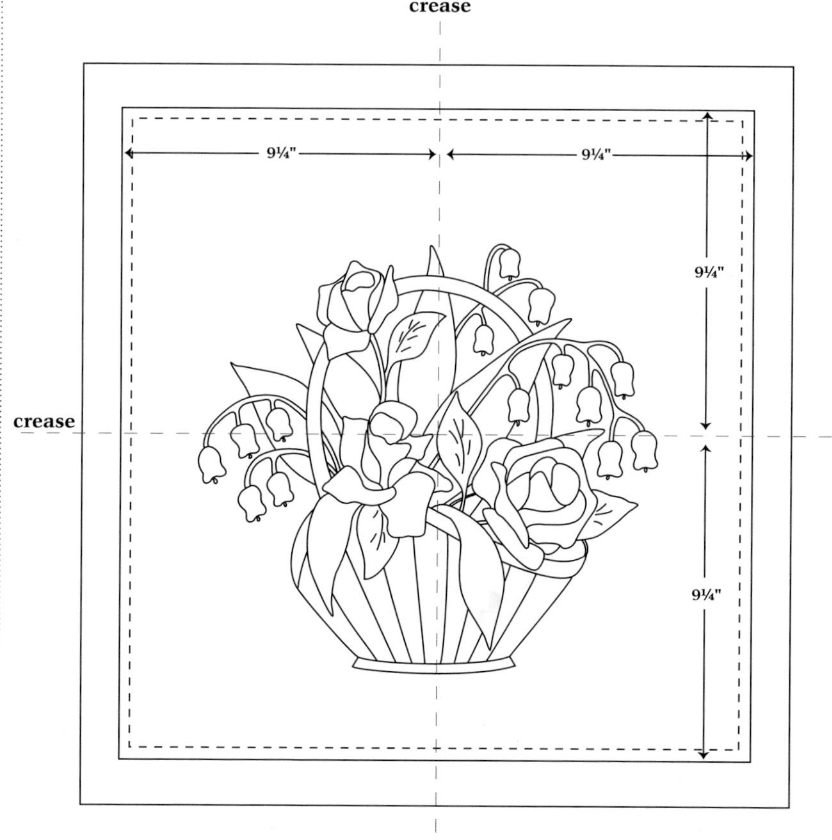

Fig. 3–22. Crease 20½" block as shown. Make sure crease lines form a right angle. Measure 9¼" and mark on each side of both crease lines. This is the 18½" cutting line.

Fig. 3-23a. Front of work that has had excess layers removed.

Fig. 3-23b. Back of work that has had excess layers removed.

Only fairly large areas will be removed. It is not necessary to trim behind the handles, stems, or many of the leaves. You will have to decide what is too small. Keep one hand under the block so you can feel that there is a layer of fabric between your hand and the scissors. Turn your work to the front frequently to be sure you are not cutting through the appliqué.

It is best to attempt this procedure only when you are fresh, have no distractions, and have adequate lighting. If you are tired, in a hurry, in a bad mood, or don't feel well, you are much more likely to make a mistake. This process is more time-consuming than you might think, so plan accordingly. The thing you must not do is cut the final layer of fabric, especially not the background fabric in a spot that has nothing appliquéd over it. A mistake such as this would be difficult to fix, but not impossible. It is even possible to change an entire flower after the fabric behind it has been removed.

You will find it necessary in most instances to wait to cut away excess layers until your work is finished for reasons that will become obvious as you proceed. The background, after all, is your stabilizer, and until all the appliqué has been attached, the background is the only thing holding everything together.

Trimming excess fabric is considered by some to be a rather radical procedure. Some quilters feel that it weakens the piece and makes it less repairable. However, if good-quality, tightly woven fabrics are used, if the appliquéd stitches are small and tight, and if a backstitch has been made at every intersection that will be trimmed away, appliqué in which the excess layers have been removed is no weaker or less repairable than pieced work. In essence, it has become an appli-pieced work (Figs. 3-23a and 3-23b).

Chapter 4

Quilt Settings

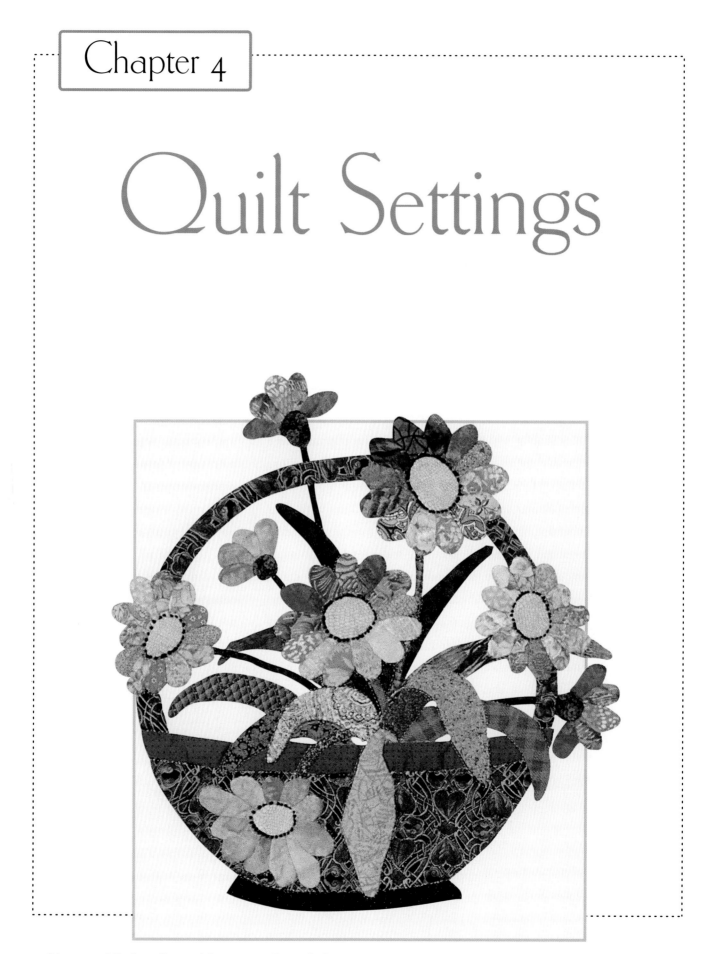

General Instructions

The possibilities for setting these patterns are endless. Complete instructions for four settings are given on pages 89–100. More possibilities are pictured in the gallery section. Medallion settings have been popular with my students because of the intriguing arrangement options. A wreath pattern, found in the pull-out pages, can be appliquéd to a center medallion square, or you can create your own design with flowers from the basket patterns. You could also use fancy quilting in the center instead of the appliqué. The following general instructions apply to all the quilt settings presented.

Yardage

Caution: Before cutting, it is a good idea to establish a cutting plan to make the best use of your fabric. If you purchase the yardage recommended, you will have ample fabric, but without excess. However, a poorly thought-out plan might result in not having enough length left for borders.

Measurements

The measurements given for all the pieces of the quilt top include ¼" seam allowances. The basket blocks and the center square of the three medallion settings will be cut 1½"–2" larger to allow for the shrinkage that often occurs with appliqué as well as the wear and tear of the edges that occurs with handling. Borders, corner triangles, and side triangles are also oversized to allow room for error. Oversized pieces will be trimmed during quilt assembly, as directed in the instructions for each quilt setting. Even though some pieces are cut large, it is suggested that you wait to cut the pieces for each section as needed, giving you a chance to check the measurements of the actual quilt as it progresses.

Grain Line

Remember to mark the grain line on all your setting pieces as you cut them out so that no wayward patterns or mismatched shading occurs in your quilt. Attention to the grain line will also make a difference in how your quilt lies or hangs.

Seam Allowances

Before starting to sew a top together, test the width of your ¼" seam allowance as follows: Sew a section together, such as a row of sashing strips and cornerstones. Press the allowances to one side. Check the finished measurement of each piece in the section, in this case, the length of each sashing strip and cornerstone. If the measurements are incorrect, adjust the width of your seam allowance and test again. An inaccurate allowance width is the most common cause of quilt pieces not fitting together properly.

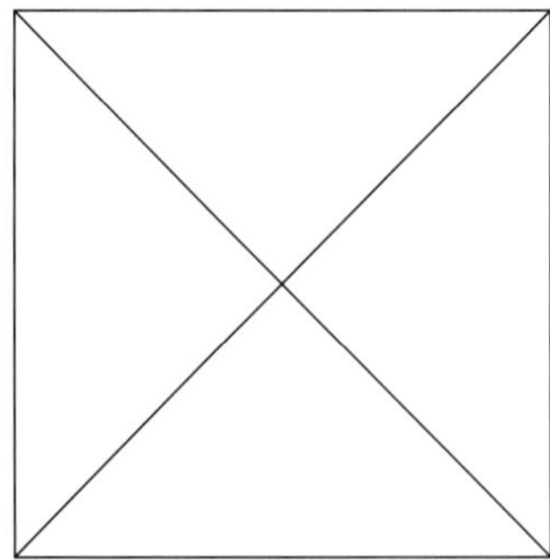

Fig. 4-1. Making side triangle: Cut a square diagonally in both directions to yield four triangles.

Pressing

Press each section before attaching it to the next, and press seam allowances to one side, preferably toward the darker fabric whenever possible. Grade seam allowances where necessary to prevent shadowing.

Accent Strips

The actual width needed for the accent strips and cornerstones in Settings 2 and 3 is not a convenient measurement, so they are about 1⁄16" too wide. This is a minute difference, and you may find that you do not need to trim any off, but if you find it is necessary, trim the excess width all around, leaving a ¼" seam allowance beyond the medallion points.

Side Triangles

Cut a square of the size listed for your chosen pattern, in fourths diagonally as shown in Figure 4–1. Handle triangles carefully so as not to stretch bias edges.

Corner Triangles

To prevent stretching, stay-stitch the squares as shown in Figure 4–2. Number the triangles as shown, then cut the squares in half to yield the four corner triangles. By using this method, all four triangles can be placed with the lengthwise grain running the length of the quilt.

Borders with Cornerstones

To determine the exact length to cut for a border, measure the length of the quilt top at both sides and in the center. Subtract the ½" seam allowances from each. Add the three measurements together and divide by three to find the average border length. Then add ½" back in for seam allowances. Repeat this procedure to determine the border length across the top and bottom of the quilt.

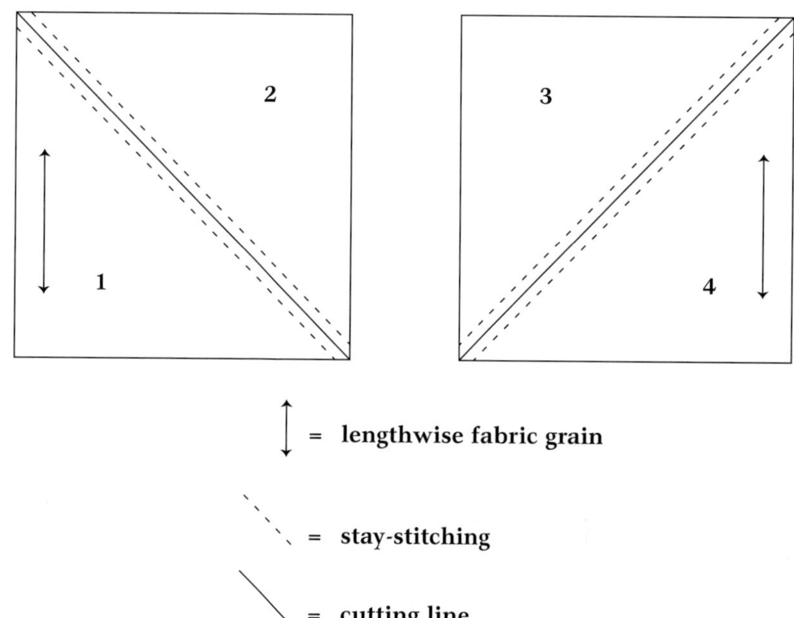

Fig. 4–2. Making corner triangles: Before cutting corner triangles apart, stay-stitch the long sides of the triangles to prevent stretching the bias edges. Cut and number as shown so that the triangles, when set in quilt top, will all be on the lengthwise grain.

Borders with Mitered Corners

Method I:

At one corner, fold the quilt top right sides together, as shown in Figure 4-3, forming a 45° angle at the corner. Spread the folded top on a flat surface and carefully align the raw edges of the borders and the seam lines where the borders are sewn to the quilt top. Place the 45° line of a quilting ruler along the raw edges of the borders and align the edge of the ruler with Point *A*, at the intersection of the seams. [Note: The ruler does not need to line up perfectly with the diagonal fold. It does need to align with the borders' raw edges and Point *A*.] Draw a line from Point *A* to the raw edge of the border. Pin and sew by machine or hand along the marked line from point *A* to the border edges (Fig. 4-4). Open the miter and check to make sure that it lies flat. If not, you can adjust the seam or redo the miter. Trim the miter's allowances to ¼" and press them to one side.

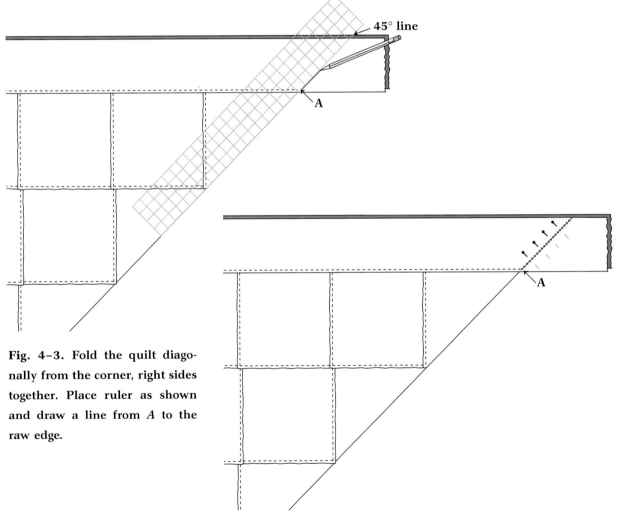

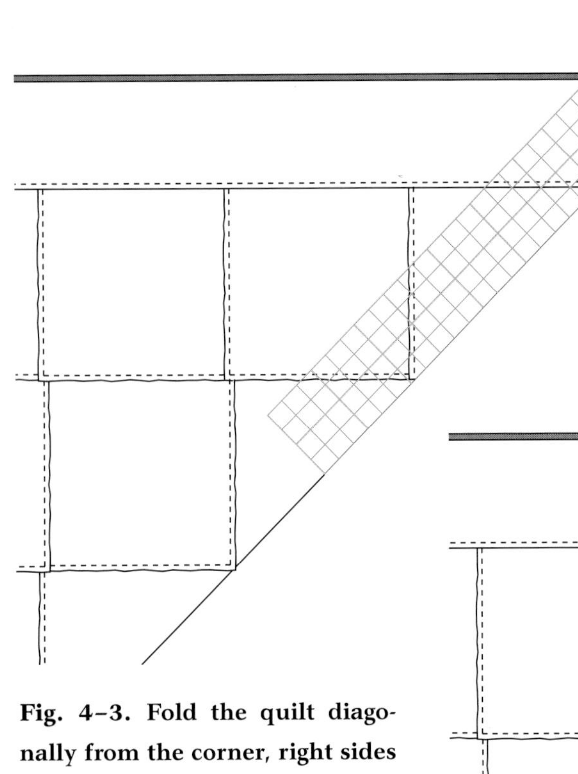

Fig. 4-3. Fold the quilt diagonally from the corner, right sides together. Place ruler as shown and draw a line from *A* to the raw edge.

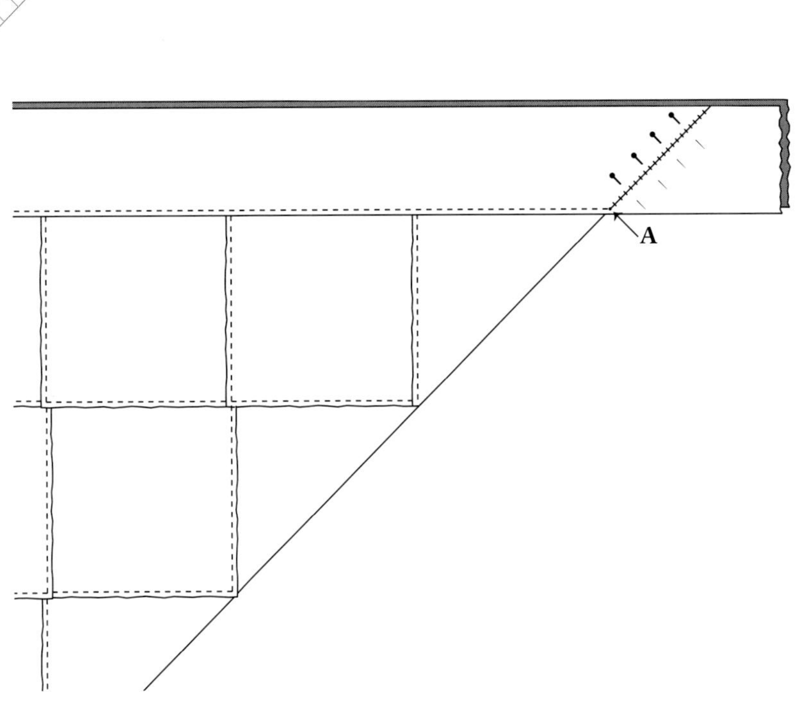

Fig. 4-4. Pin the borders together along the drawn line and sew from *A* to the edge.

Method II:

Spread the quilt top out on a flat surface. Allow the borders to extend straight out with one overlapping the other at each corner, as shown in Figure 4-5. At one corner, angle a straight edge from point *A* to point *B* and mark a line. Fold the overlying border under along the line and crease (Fig. 4-6). Pin the borders together at the miter and hand sew them with an appliqué stitch. To sew them by machine, unfold the top border. Align the borders carefully, as in Fig. 4-4, and pin them. Sew along the crease between Point A and the raw edge of the border.

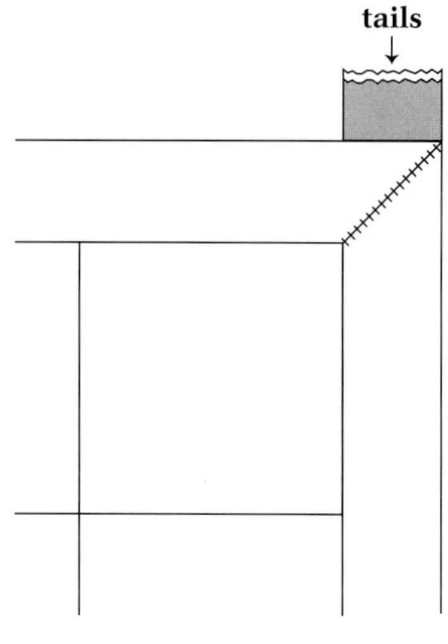

Fig. 4-6. Fold top border under along the line and crease the fold. Appliqué the fold.

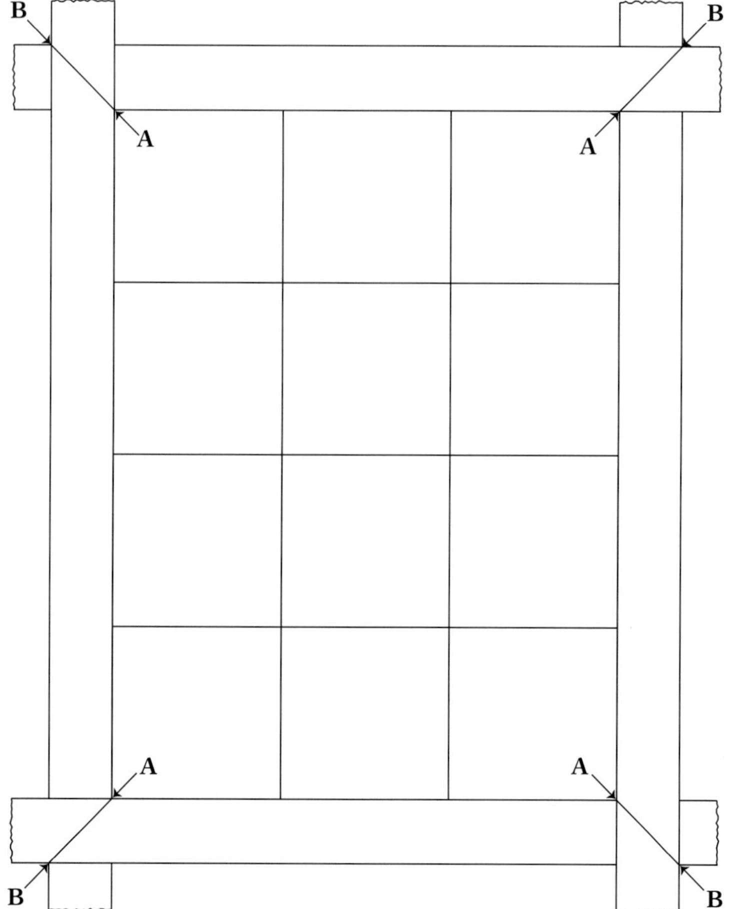

Fig. 4-5. Draw a line from *A* to *B* at each corner.

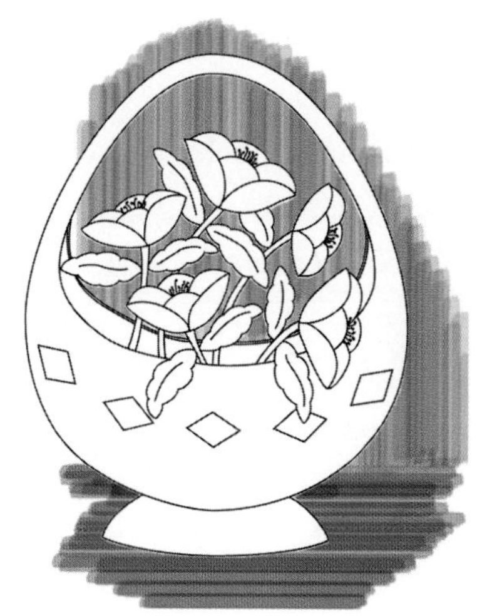

Quilt Setting 1
Medallion I

86" x 86"

Fabric Requirements

Pieces	Cut	Yds.
Medallion square	1 square, 38½" x 38½"	1¼
Background blocks	12 squares, 20½" x 20½"	3¾
Accent borders	4 strips, 2½" x 78"	2⅜
Outside borders	4 strips, 5½" x 88"	2¾
Backing	3 panels, 30½" x 90"	7⅞
Binding	2½" x 10 yards	⅞
Main basket fabric		1
Coordinating basket fabric		½
Accent basket fabric		½

Floral appliqué - you will need assorted, small amounts.

Quilt Top Assembly

1 After all appliqué has been completed, trim and size basket blocks to 18½".

2 Lay basket blocks around the center square as shown in the Setting 1 assembly diagram, Fig. 4-7, page 89. Sew the top row together as shown. Before continuing, press seam allowances to one side and measure the length of this unit to check for accuracy. The total length should be 72½". If not, adjust the width of your seam allowances and test again. Sew another unit like this for the bottom row.

3 Trim and size the medallion square to 36½". Sew two sets of two basket blocks together and then to each side of the center square. Attach the top and bottom rows to center section.

QUICK FIND

Accent strips . . . . .p. 85
Borders . . . . .p. 85
Corner triangles . . . . .p. 85
Miters . . . . .p. 86
Side triangles . . . . .p. 85
Sizing blocks . . . . .p. 80
Sizing corner triangles . . . . . . .p. 90
Stay stitching . . . . .p. 85

4 Matching centers, pin each accent border strip to a side of the quilt top. Sew each strip, starting and stopping your sewing ¼" from the raw edge of the quilt top to allow for mitering. Miter the corners by folding the quilt so that adjacent borders are aligned with each other, right sides together. Sew the corner seam at a 45° angle to complete the miter. To prevent gaping or puckering at the corner, be sure that all three corner seams meet precisely. Trim off any excess border length, leaving a ¼" seam allowance along the miter.

5 Cut the four outside border strips, as listed under Fabric Requirements. Sew on the borders and miter the corners as described for the accent borders in Step 4.

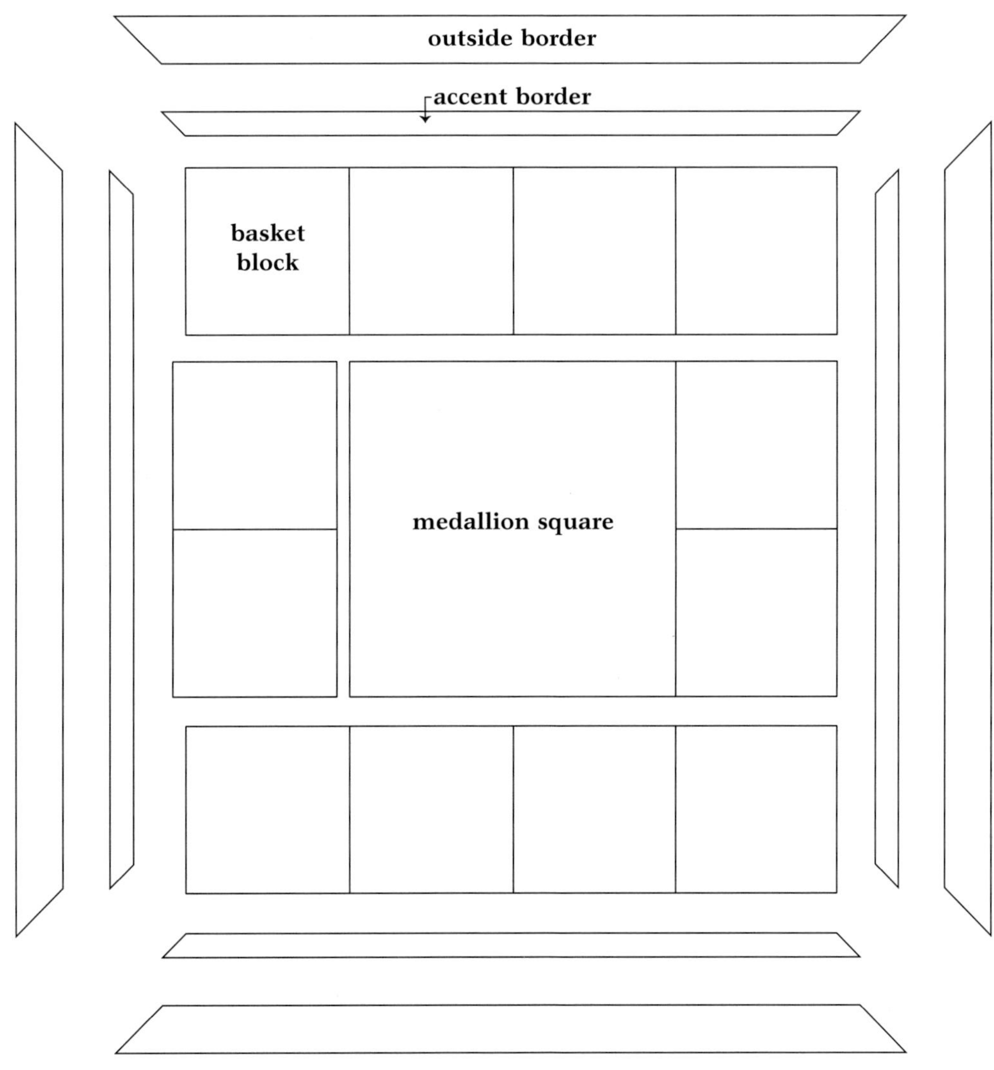

Fig. 4-7. Setting 1 assembly.

Sizing Corner Triangles

If your medallion section does not measure the size given in your pattern, it will be necessary to adjust the size of the corner triangles to fit. Here's a way to figure the size in four simple steps:

1 Measure the center section between points *A* and *B* (Figs. a and b). This is the measurement of the finished long side of a corner triangle. Measure all four sides.

2 Add the four measurements together and divide by 4 to find their average length.

3 Divide the answer by 1.414. Round the result to the nearest ⅛". This is the finished length of the short sides of the corner triangles.

4 Add ⅞" (.875") for seam allowances. Use this measurement to cut the two squares for the corner triangles.

For example:

1. Side one, 55.5" + side two, 55.25" + side three, 55.625 + side four, 55.375 = 221.75.

2. Divide by 4 = 55.44.

3. Divide by 1.414 = 39.21. Round to nearest ⅛" = 39.25"

4. Add .875 = 40⅛".

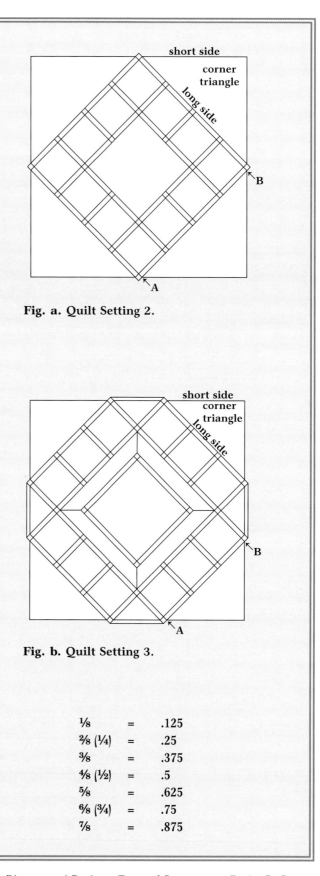

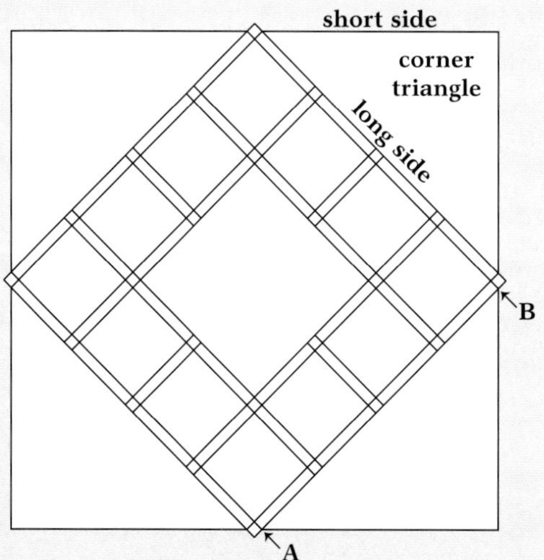

Fig. a. Quilt Setting 2.

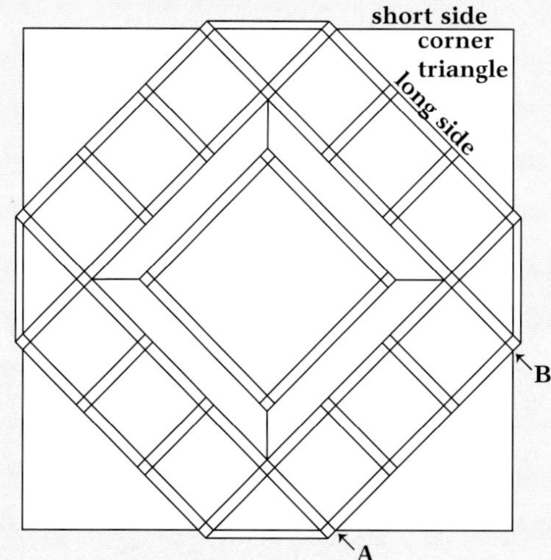

Fig. b. Quilt Setting 3.

⅛	=	.125
2/8 (¼)	=	.25
⅜	=	.375
4/8 (½)	=	.5
⅝	=	.625
6/8 (¾)	=	.75
⅞	=	.875

Fabric Requirements

Pieces	Cut (42"-wide fabric)	Yds.
Medallion square	1 square, 29½" x 29½"	1
Background blocks	12 squares, 15" x 15"	2¾
Corner triangles	2 squares, 42" x 42"	2½
Sashing	36 strips, 2½" x 13"	1
Sashing cornerstones	24 squares, 2½" x 2½"	¼
Accent borders	8 strips, 2" x 44"	⅝
Accent cornerstones	4 squares, 2" x 2"	⅛
*Outside borders	4 strips, 5½" x 87¼"	2⅝
*Outside cornerstones	4 squares, 5½" x 5½"	¼
Backing	3 panels, 33½" x 99"	8¾
Binding	2½" x 11 yards	1
Main basket fabric		1
Coordinating basket fabric		½
Accent basket fabric		½

Floral appliqué: You will need assorted, small amounts.

**If you prefer to miter the outer border corners, substitute 4 strips 5½" x 97" (3 yds.) for the outside borders and cornerstones.*

Quilt Setting 2 Medallion II

95" x 95"

Quilt Top Assembly

1 After all appliqué has been completed, trim and size basket blocks to 13".

2 Size the medallion square to 27½" and cut the sashing strips and cornerstones.

3 In an arrangement that is pleasing to you, position your basket blocks with the center square and sashings as shown in the Setting 2 assembly diagram, Fig. 4-8, page 92. Using a ¼" seam allowance, sew blocks, medallion square, and sashing strips into rows; then sew the rows together to complete the medallion section.

4 To fit the corner triangles, the center medallion section should measure 56" between points *A* and *B* on the assembly diagram. If it does, you can cut

QUICK FIND

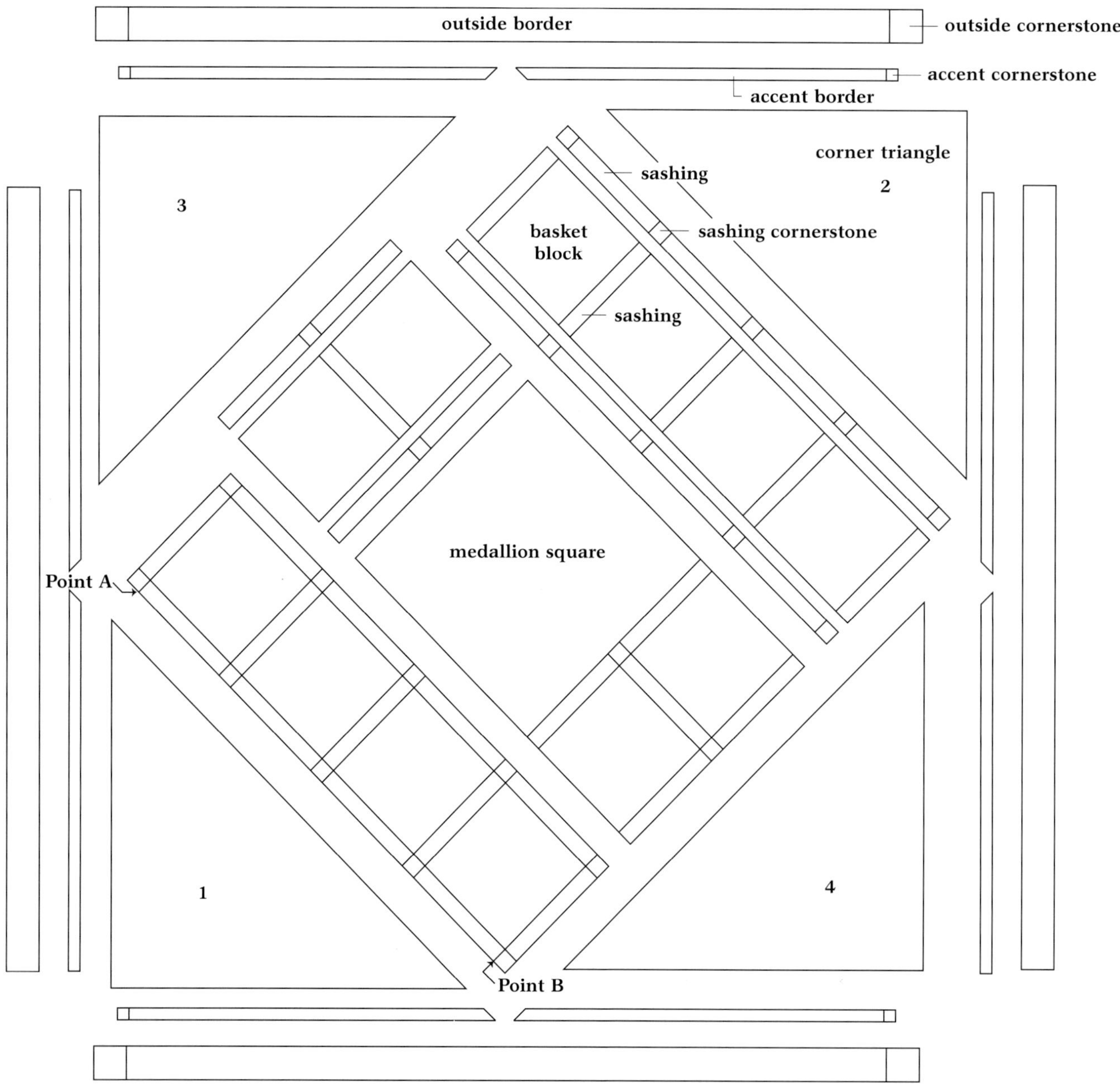

Fig. 4–8. Setting 2 assembly.

the squares for the corner triangles, using the sizes listed in Fabric Requirements. If it does not, see Sizing Corner Triangles. Stay-stitch the bias edges of the corner triangles before cutting the squares in half to prevent stretching. Cut the squares in half diagonally to yield four corner triangles.

5 Attach an accent border to a corner triangle as shown in Figure 4-9. Trim the strip even with the long edge of the triangle. Sew a cornerstone to one end of another strip and sew the strip to the other side of the triangle. Trim as before. Repeat for the other three corners.

6 Lay the corner triangles around the medallion section as shown in the assembly diagram. With right sides together, pin a corner triangle to the medallion section, matching the centers of the two pieces. Also match the cornerstone seams to the accent border seams. Sew the triangle to the section. Repeat with the remaining three corner triangles.

7 Determine the exact length of your outside borders. Trim the four border strips to this length. Pin two of the borders to opposite sides of your quilt top, matching centers and ends, and sew. Sew a cornerstone to each end of the two remaining borders and sew the borders to the quilt.

cut off

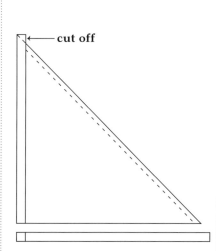

Fig. 4-9. Attach accent borders to corner triangles. Press seams to one side. Use the long edge of the triangle as a guide and cut off the extra length of the accent border as shown.

SUMMER'S SYMPHONY (95" x 95"), by Anna Kephart, Prairie Village, Kansas, and quilted by Toni Fisher, Springfield, Missouri. Anna used Medallion Setting 2 to make this quilt. It received an honorable mention at Silver Dollar City in 1997. Toni quilted an unusual spider-web pattern behind the corner swags.

Fabric Requirements

Pieces	Cut (42"-wide fabric)	Yds.
Medallion square	1 square, 30" x 30"	1
Background blocks	12 squares, 15" x 15"	2¾
Medallion sashing	4 strips, 2½" x 28"	⅜
Medallion border	4 strips, 5½" x 44"	1⅜
Sashing	40 strips, 2½" x 13"	1¼
Sashing cornerstones	32 squares, 2½" x 2½"	¼
Corner triangles	2 squares, 32" x 32"	2
Side triangles	1 square, 21" x 21"	⅝
Accent borders		¾
Corners	8 strips, 2" x 34"	
Sides	4 strips, 2" x 24"	
Accent cornerstones	4 squares, 2" x 2"	⅛
*Outside borders	4 strips, 5½" x 87½"	2⅝
*Outside cornerstones	4 squares, 5½" x 5½"	¼
Backing	3 panels, 32½" x 99"	8¾
Binding	2½" x 11 yards	1
Main basket fabric		1
Coordinating basket fabric		½
Accent basket fabric		½

Floral appliqué: You will need assorted, small amounts.

**If you prefer to miter the outside border corners, substitute 4 strips 5½" x 97" (3 yds.) for the outside borders and cornerstones.*

Quilt Setting 3 Medallion III

95" x 95"

Quilt Top Assembly

1 After all appliqué has been completed, trim and size basket blocks to 13".

2 Size the medallion square to 28" and cut the sashing strips, sashing cornerstones, and the medallion sashing and border strips.

3 Take a moment to study the Setting 3 assembly diagram, Fig. 4-10. To make the center section, sew two medallion sashing strips to opposite sides of the medallion square. Sew cornerstones to both ends of the remaining two medallion sashing strips and sew the strips to the other two sides of the square. Add the medallion border strips, mitering the corners.

4 Construct two units of three basket blocks, each with their sashings and cornerstones,

QUICK FIND

Accent strips . . . . .p. 85
Borders . . . . .p. 85
Corner triangles . . . . .p. 85
Miters . . . . .p. 86
Side triangles . . . . .p. 85
Sizing blocks . . . . .p. 80
Sizing corner triangles . . . . . .p. 90
Stay stitching . . . . .p. 85

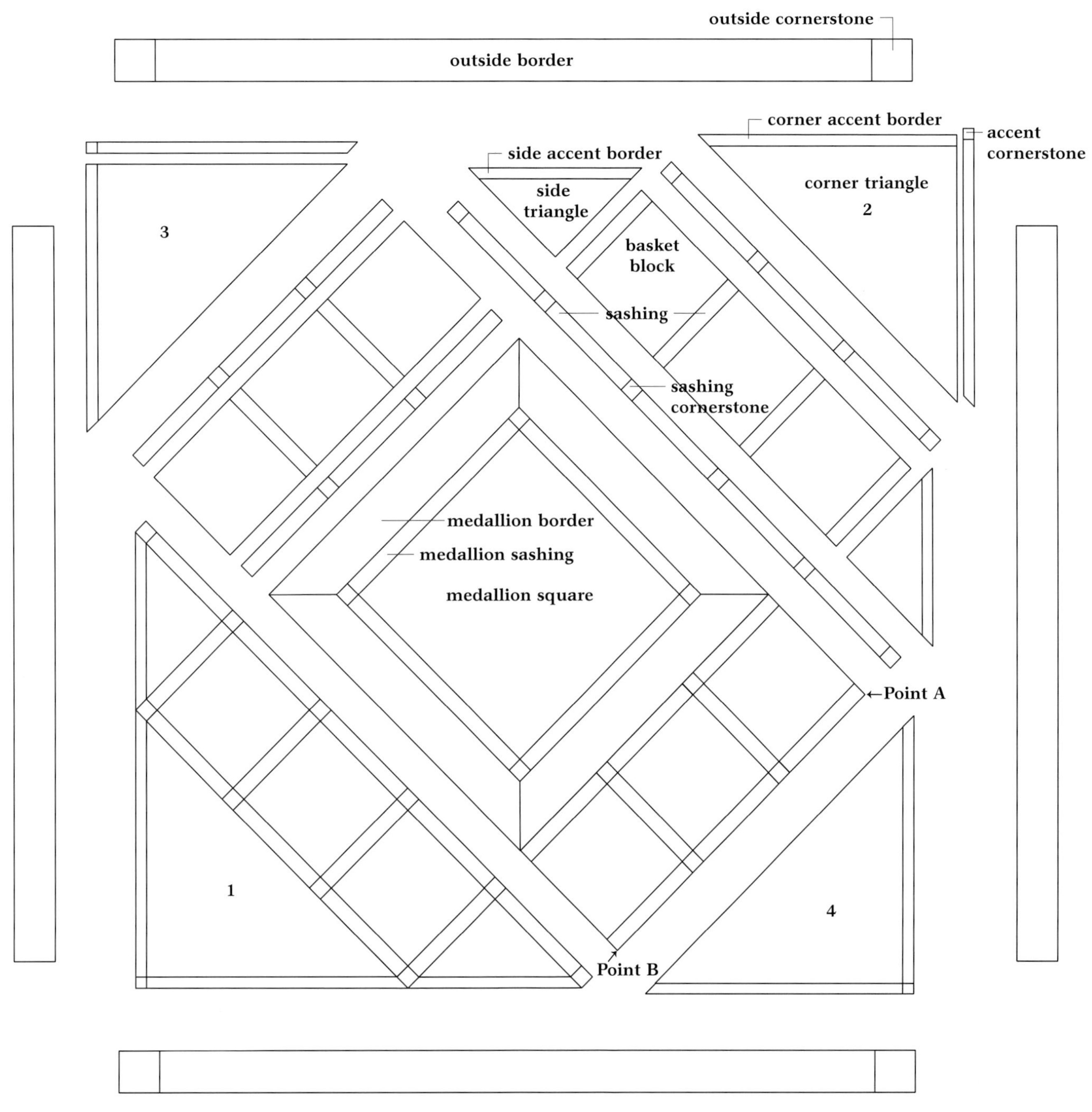
outside cornerstone
outside border
corner accent border
accent cornerstone
side accent border
side triangle
corner triangle
2
3
basket block
sashing
sashing
sashing cornerstone
medallion border
medallion sashing
medallion square
Point A
1
4
Point B

Fig. 4–10. Setting 3 assembly.

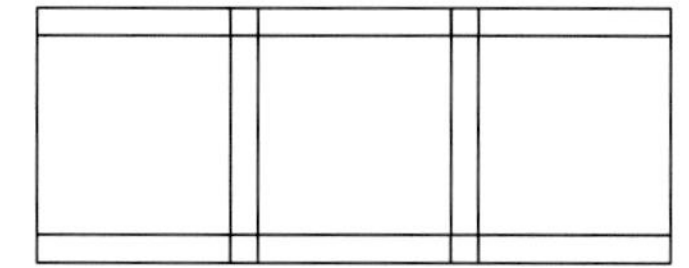

Fig. 4–11. Three-block unit.

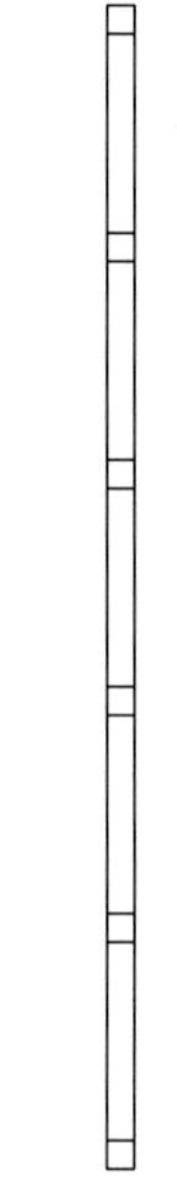

Fig. 4–12. Sashing and cornerstone unit.

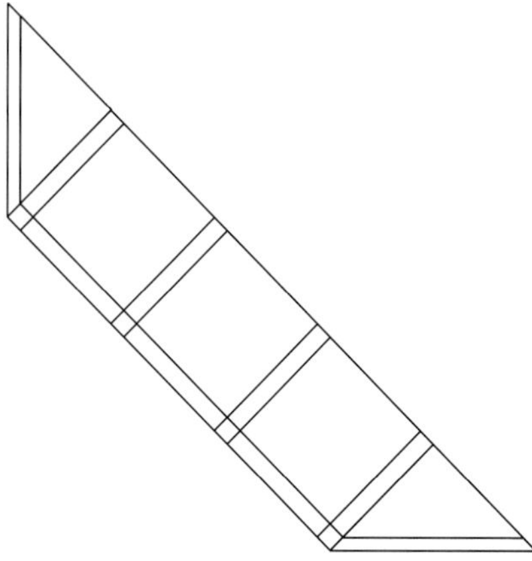

Fig. 4–13. Block and side triangle unit.

as shown in Figure 4–11. Attach these units to opposite sides of the medallion center. Construct two long units of five sashings and six cornerstones (Fig. 4–12), and attach them to the long sides of the medallion section.

5 Cut the side triangles, and sew the accent borders to their long sides. Trim borders even with the short sides of the triangles. Construct the two remaining basket units and add a side triangle to each end, as shown in Figure 4–13. Sew these units to the medallion section.

6 The quilt top should measure 41½" between points *A* and *B*. If it does, cut the squares for the corner triangles and cut the accent border strips as listed in Fabric Requirements. If it does not, see Sizing Corner Triangles, page 88. Stay-stitch the bias edges of the corner triangles before cutting the squares in half to prevent stretching. Cut the squares in half diagonally to yield four corner triangles.

7 Attach one accent border to each of the four corner triangles, matching one end of the border strips to the right-angle end of the triangles (Fig. 4–9, page 93). Trim the strips even with the long edges of the triangles. Sew a cornerstone to one end of each of the four remaining accent border strips and sew the strips to the four triangles and trim as before.

8 Lay the corner triangles around the medallion section as shown in the assembly diagram. With right sides together, pin a corner triangle to the medallion section, matching the centers of the two pieces. Also match the cornerstone seams to the accent border seams. Sew the triangle to the section. Repeat with the remaining three corner triangles.

9 Determine the exact length of your outside borders. Trim the four borders strips to this length. Pin two of the borders to opposite sides of your quilt top, matching centers and ends, and sew. Sew a cornerstone to each end of the two remaining borders and sew the borders to the quilt.

Quilt Setting 4 Alternate Blocks

63" x 80¾"

Fabric Requirements

Pieces	Cut (42"-wide fabric)	Yds.
Background blocks	12 squares, 15" x 15"	2¾
*Alternate plain blocks		2
Squares	6 squares, 13" x 13"	
Side triangles	3 squares, 21" x 21"	
Corner triangles	2 squares, 9¾" x 9¾"	
*Or alternate pieced blocks		
Piece 1	48	1¾
Piece 2	48	1
Piece 3		⅞
Whole	34	
Half	28	
Piece 4		1¼
Whole	6	
Half	10	
Quarter	4	
Borders		2½
Short sides	2 strips, 5½" x 65½"	
Long sides	2 strips, 5½" x 83¼"	
Backing	2 panels, 34" x 84¾"	5
Binding	2½" x 8⅜ yards	⅞
Main basket fabric		1
Coordinating basket fabric		½
Accent basket fabric		½

Floral appliqué - you will need assorted, small amounts.

You can keep this setting simple with plain alternate blocks or you can dress it up with pieced blocks. Full-sized patterns for the pieced blocks are provided on pages 99–100.

Quilt Top Assembly

1 After all appliqué has been completed, trim and size basket blocks to 13".

2 Cut 6 alternate plain blocks or construct 6 pieced blocks as shown in the block diagram, Fig. 4-15, page 99.

3 Lay out basket blocks with alternate blocks (either plain or pieced) and the side and corner triangles as shown in the Setting 4 assembly diagram, Fig. 4-14, page 98. Rearrange basket blocks if necessary until the arrangement pleases you. Sew the basket pieces and alternate blocks together in diagonal rows and sew the rows together.

4 Cut the four border strips, as listed under Fabric Requirements. Matching centers, pin each border strip to a side

QUICK FIND

of the quilt top. Sew the strips, to the quilt and miter the corners. To prevent gaping or puckering at the corners, be sure that all three corner seams meet precisely. Trim off any excess border, leaving a ¼" seam allowance along each miter.

Piecing Alternate Blocks

Directions given are for hand piecing, so the templates do not include seam allowances. (Machine piecers need to add ¼" seam allowances to the templates before cutting them.)

1 Make templates for pieces #1–#4. For piece #3, you will also need to make a half template, and for piece #4, you will need a half template and a quarter template (shown on pieces.)

2 Paying close attention to grain lines, mark the number of pieces needed from each template on your fabrics, as listed under Fabric Requirements, page 97.

3 Cut out the pieces, adding ¼" seam allowances by eye as you cut.

4 Hand piece 6 full blocks, 10 half blocks, and 4 quarter blocks. Press seam allowances and grade them, if necessary, to prevent shadowing.

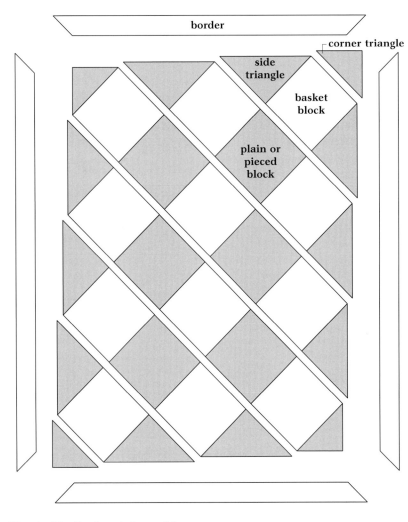

Fig. 4–14. Setting 4 Assembly.

EVERLASTING GEMS OF SUMMER, detail, by the author. This close-up is an example of the alternate block. Full quilt shown in the front of the book.

PIECED ALTERNATE-BLOCK

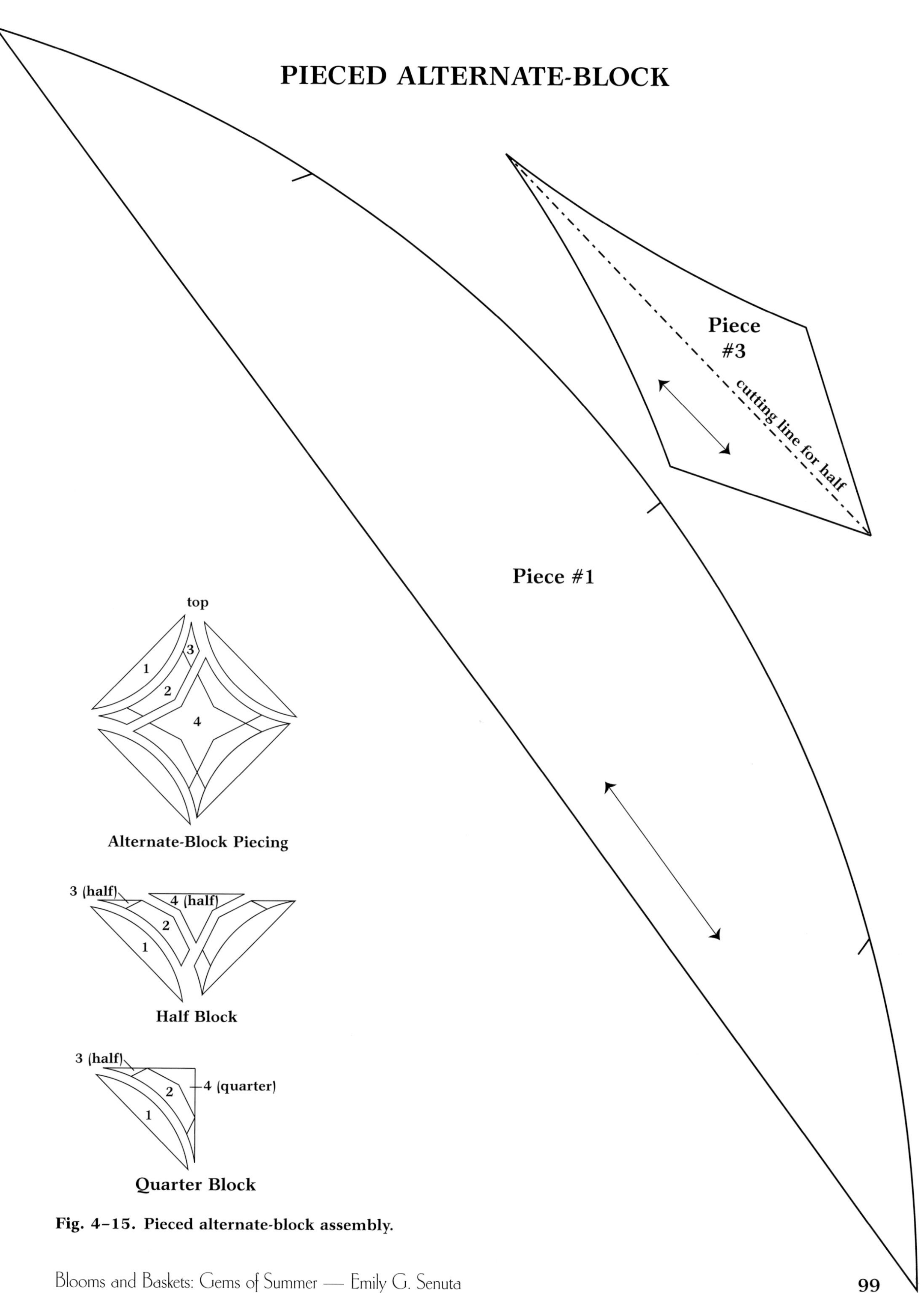

Fig. 4–15. Pieced alternate-block assembly.

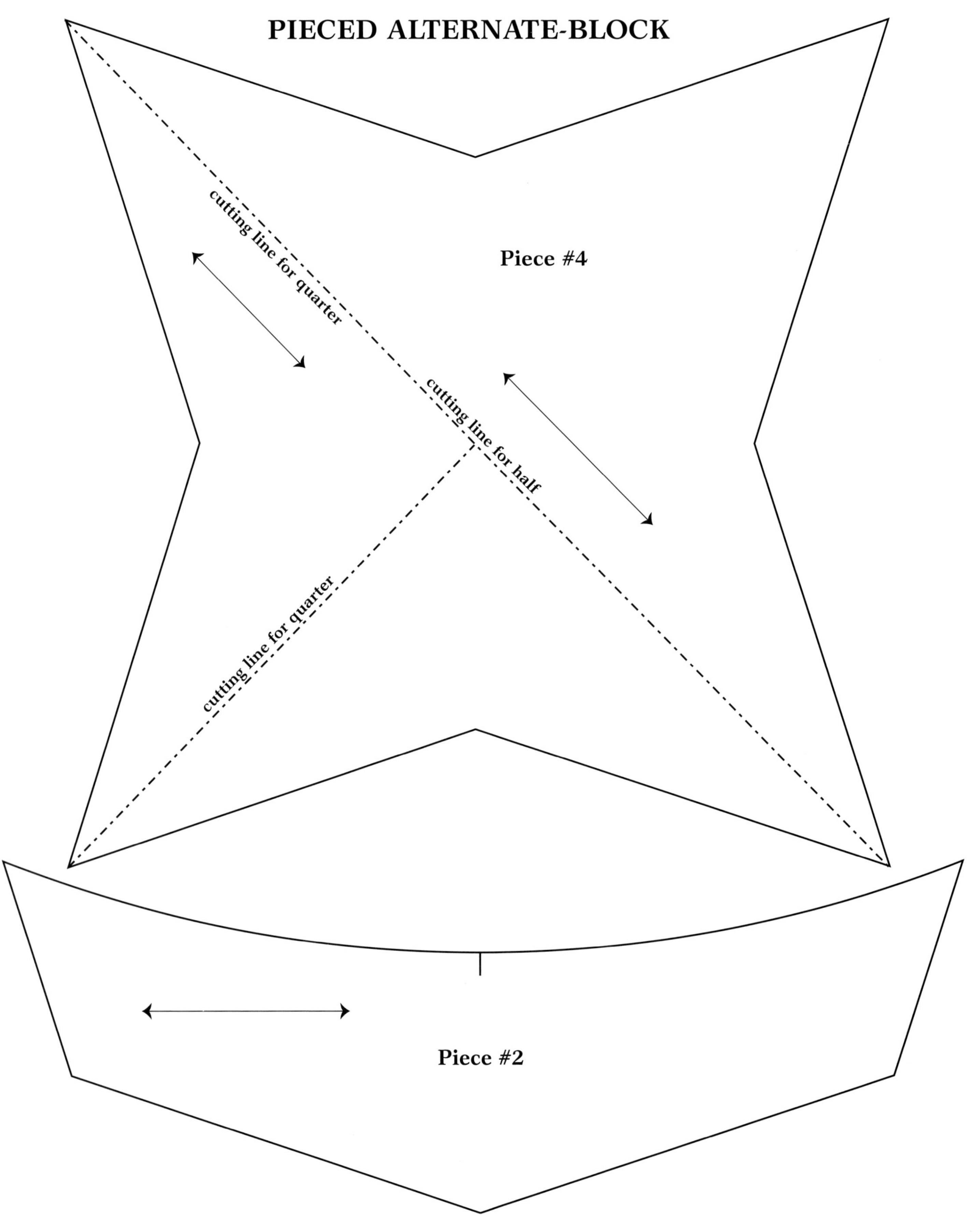
PIECED ALTERNATE-BLOCK
cutting line for quarter
Piece #4
cutting line for half
cutting line for quarter
Piece #2

Chapter 5

Quilting and Finishing

Quilting Designs

Once your top has been completed, you have reached a major milestone, one of relief and satisfaction, and possibly disbelief that you ever made it this far. It is at this point that many tops are placed in a box or trunk to languish because the maker didn't know how to continue or have time to quilt. Many tops are hurried onto the quilt frame with the only thought being to get them quilted as quickly as possible. Essentially, they are quilted by rote, with the same quilting pattern (in the ditch around the appliqué, with a grid or crosshatching to fill the rest of the space) used over and over.

Please don't misunderstand, this quilting strategy is very effective. You are encouraged, however, to take the time at this point to plan your quilting carefully. You may have already put a lot of thought into possible quilting ideas while you were sewing the top together.

We have all heard repeatedly, "It's not a quilt 'til it's quilted" and "The quilting makes the quilt." Both statements are true. The suggestions and patterns offered here and the beautiful quilts included in the Gallery, pages 115–120, should help you create a quilting plan for your quilt. Two additional and invaluable sources of information for exceptional quilting ideas are the books *Surface Textures*, by Anita Shackelford (AQS, 1997) and *The Encyclopedia of Quilt Designs*, by Phyllis Miller (AQS, 1996).

Your fabric colors will dictate the type of utensils necessary for marking the quilting designs on your quilt top. Choose markers that you can see but that you have tested to make certain they will wash out when you finish. Soapstone, graphite, and wash-out pencils are excellent choices. Mark as lightly as possible, just enough so you can comfortably see the lines to quilt.

Wild Rose Border

This is a quilting pattern, but it would also be pretty appliquéd. The Wild Rose was designed for the medallion border of Quilt Setting 3, but you can adjust the length of the repeat so that the design can be used in other places. If the design is to be quilted, the borders can be sewn to the top before you mark the design. If the design is to be appliquéd, mark and appliqué the design on the borders before sewing them to the top. The corners must be appliquéd after the borders are attached and the miters have been sewn.

The pieces are numbered in case you decide to appliqué the design. Notice that every other flower has been reversed, top to bottom. If you need help with the appliqué, read the basic instructions, beginning on page 36, especially the instructions describing how to sew a twist, page 42.

This Wild Rose pattern can be enhanced with trapunto. A good method for adding trapunto can be done as follows: After marking the quilting design on your border, place a piece of batting under the border. To hold the batting securely to the top, outline each leaf and flower that will be padded with a basting stitch, about ⅛" inside

WILD ROSE BORDER

repeat section 5" x 10½"

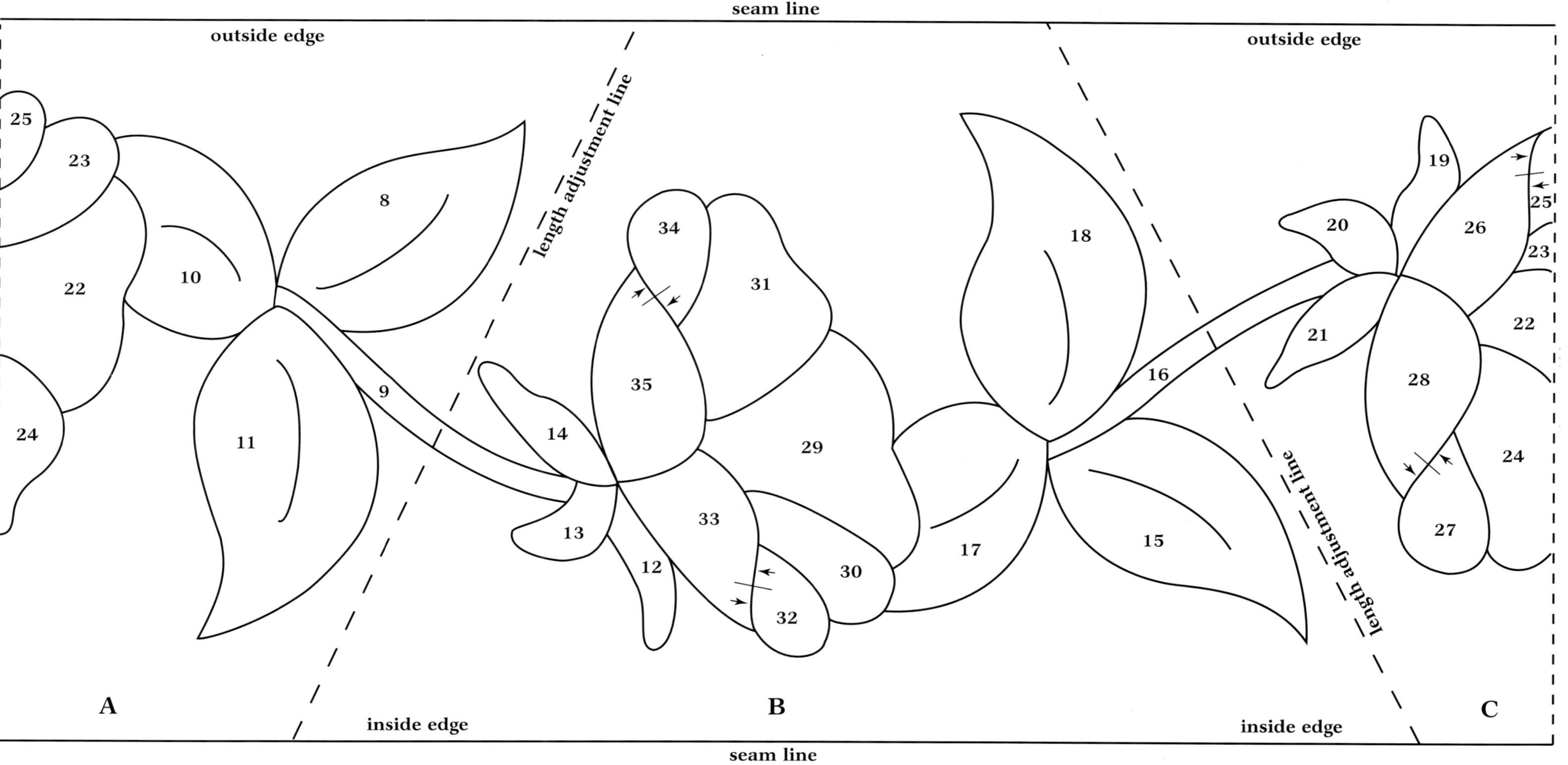

the lines. Pick a color for your basting thread that you can easily see. Turn the fabric over with the batting on top and carefully cut the batting away along the basting stitches, leaving batting within the leaves and flowers only. Now, when you make your quilt sandwich, the extra batting is already in place. Remember, raised quilting shows up best on solid-color fabrics.

To use the Wild Rose Border, trace or photocopy the repeat and corner sections. It is helpful to have at least two copies of the repeat pattern. Cut the photocopies out on the seam lines. If your border fabric is light enough to see through, pin the corner pattern under the fabric, both right side up. Be sure the outside edge of

WILD ROSE BORDER

corner section 5" x 5"

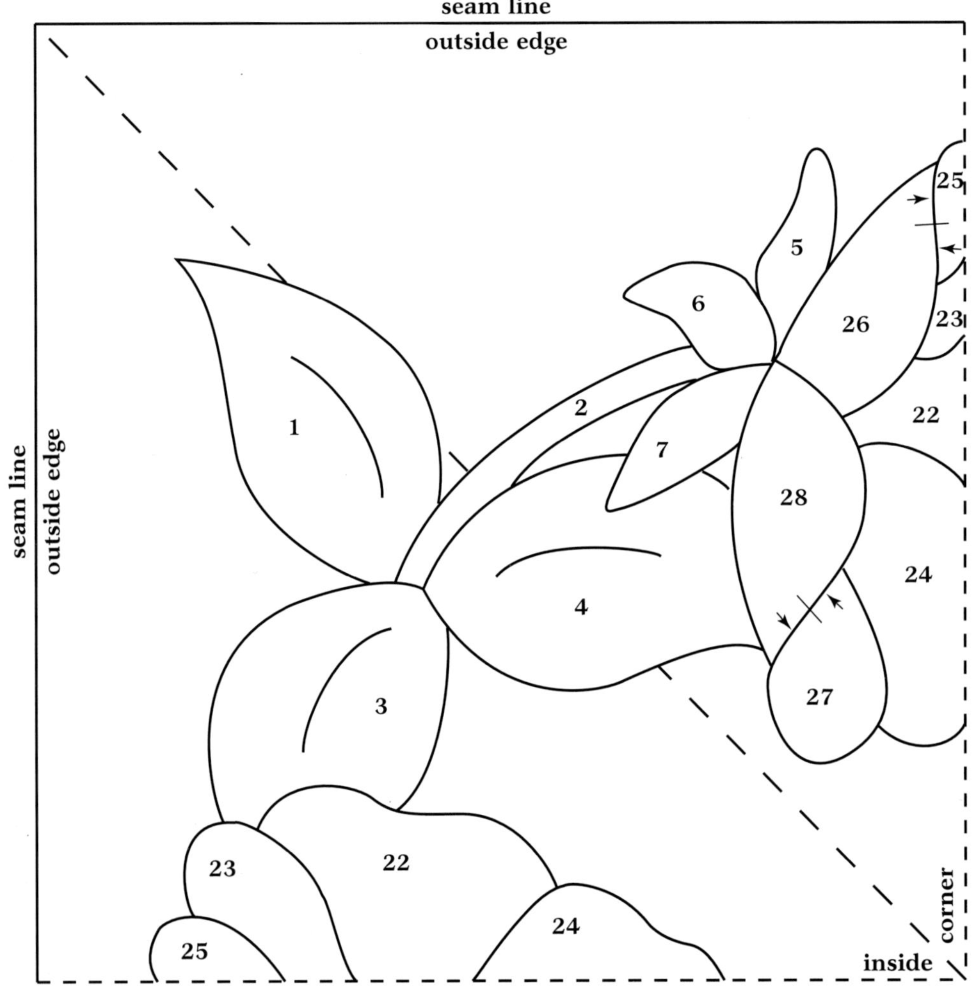

the pattern is on the outside edge of the border. Trace the pattern on the fabric with a wash-out marker.

If your border fabric is too dark, pin the corner pattern right side up on top of the border fabric. Slide a piece of wash-out dressmaker's carbon, carbon side down, between the two and carefully trace with a medium-tip, ball-point pen. Next, butt the repeat pattern to the corner pattern, again taking care that the outside edge of the pattern is on the outside edge of the border, and trace. Move the repeat pattern again and butt it to the end you just marked. Trace the pattern. Repeat, tracing the pattern one more time. Now, move the corner pattern and butt it to the last repeat pattern you just traced. Always keep the inside edges of the pattern and the border seam lined up. Continue in this manner to mark around the entire border.

Two corner and three repeat patterns per side should fit exactly if your border is 41½" long (finished length). If your border is not this measurement, cut the repeat pattern apart on the dashed lines to make your adjustments.

The Wild Rose Border can also be used on the outside border in Quilt Setting 3. Between points 1 and 2, as shown in Fig. 5–1, divide the outside border of your quilt into eight equal sections. An easy way to do this is to fold the border in half and crease the fold with your fingers to mark the center. Then fold each half in half again (one at a time for greater accuracy) and crease to mark the fourths. Finally, fold each fourth in half and crease to complete the eight equal sections.

Measure the sections to make certain they are equal in length and make a paper pattern 5" wide by the length of one section. Trace or photocopy the repeat and corner patterns of the Wild Rose Border and cut them out on the seam lines. Cut the copy of the repeat pattern apart on the slanted dashed lines. Trace or tape section *A* to the paper pattern you just made of the ⅛ section of your border, lining the left ends up exactly. Do the same with section *C*, only line up the right ends. Now center section *B* between sections *A* and *C*, and trace or tape. Re-draw the stems to make them meet with a natural and pleasing arc. By following these directions, this design can be adjusted longer or shorter to lengths between 9½" to 12". You could use it almost anywhere. Transfer the new pattern to the border in the same manner as described previously.

Grid Designs

If you have decided that outlining the appliqué is the most attractive option for your quilt, you are left with large spaces that need to be quilted. All the beautiful appliqué that you have done will be greatly enhanced if these spaces are

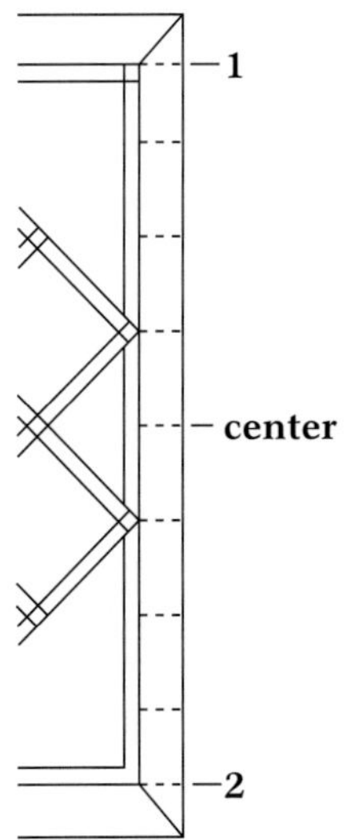

Fig. 5–1. Divide the outside border into eight equal sections between points 1 and 2.

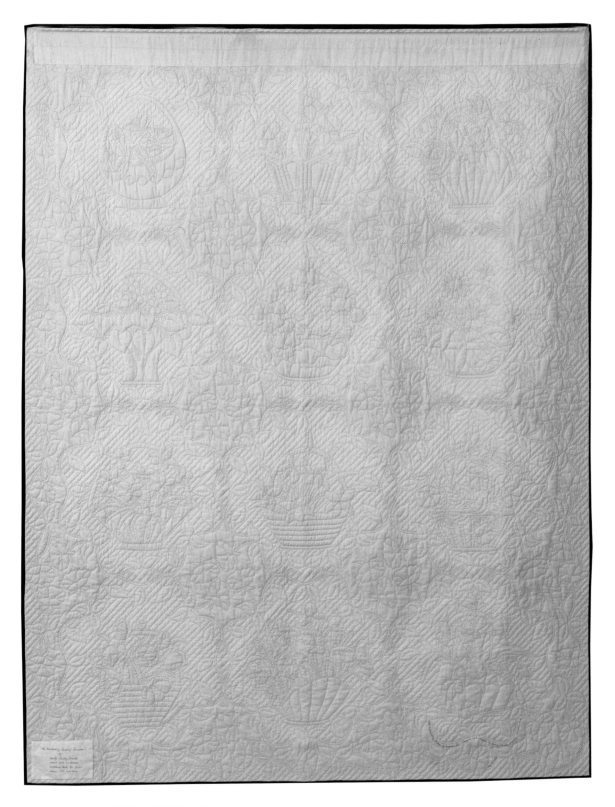

EVERLASTING GEMS OF SUMMER (back), 60" x 70", by the author, shows the quilting patterns for the baskets and the use of grid quilting.

quilted effectively and attractively. Grids are the most common choice. Parallel lines or a variety of crosshatch options can be used. Your goal when marking a grid is to achieve straight, evenly spaced lines. Good tools are necessary for good results. Either a 6" x 24" or a 3½" x 24" see-through ruler with accurate markings will be needed. If you will be using a particular grid pattern more than once, make a full-size paper pattern of the grid and transfer it to your quilt top rather than marking the grid directly on the fabric.

It is more pleasing to the eye to have a variety of grids or other fillers in a quilt as opposed to the monotony of the same grid all over. In addition, it can be difficult to keep the same grid straight and even throughout. When choosing a grid or filler, first consider the design to be emphasized or enhanced, then decide on a scale that will be most effective.

The basket appliqué patterns are busy with a lot of curves, so it is reasonable to assume that straight lines will make a good contrast. On the quilt Everlasting Gems of Summer, opposite page, parallel diagonal lines, spaced ½" apart, were used. However, straight lines were combined with a floral design in the alternating blocks and in the borders to break the monotony and add some excitement. A variety of grids has been used in the quilts shown in this book. It is hoped that the pictures will give you some ideas for your quilt.

It is easy to mark even or uneven parallel-line grids or crosshatches. Here is a tip to get you started. Wherever possible, use the seam lines within the quilt as a guide to start the grid and as a gauge to keep the lines straight, which makes one more good argument for straight and accurate piecing. If it is necessary to fudge a bit to keep a line even or straight, make the adjustment behind the appliqué or sashing. Instructions for marking two unusual grids (radiating lines and spirals) follow.

Doreen's Radiating Lines

This quilting pattern is effective for large right triangles, such as the side or corner triangles in Quilt Settings 2 and 3, pages 91 and 94 (Fig. 5-2, page 108).

To establish a pivot point for the radiating lines, mark the center of the long side of the triangle. On the two short sides, place dots every ½", ¾", or 1", depending on how dense you want your quilting to be. Because all the lines cannot converge at the pivot point (too many stitches in one place), a design similar to the Crown Design (Pattern 5-3, page 109), should be chosen to cover the pivot. Mark the design in the triangle before marking the radiating lines. Mark any other pattern in the triangle, such as the Wild Rose on page 104.

To mark the radiating lines, use a straight edge that is long enough to reach from the pivot point to the farthest distance on the short sides. Place one end of your straight edge on the pivot point and the other on the 90° angle and draw a line, skipping over the design at the pivot point and all parts of the Wild Rose pattern. For the next line, keep the end of the straight edge on the pivot point, swing the other end of the ruler to the first dot on one of the short sides and draw a line, skipping over the center design and the Wild Rose as before. Continue in this way until you have drawn a line from the pivot point to each dot on both short sides of the triangle.

It will become apparent that, even with the Crown Design in the center, the lines will be very close together near the pivot point. Quilting so densely may cause puckering or distortion in your quilt. To alleviate this problem, you can stop stitching every other line before reaching the center design. If you like, lightly draw a half circle with a compass to give yourself a constant stopping point for the shorter lines.

Doreen's Spiral

The spiral grid can be used to enhance your appliqué blocks. To mark this grid, you will need a compass, template plastic, and a permanent pen or pencil for marking the plastic.

To draw the spiral on your block patterns, you will need to make two templates, one for scribing the arcs in the spiral and one for measuring the distance between the arcs. Follow these simple directions to cut the two templates from one piece of plastic.

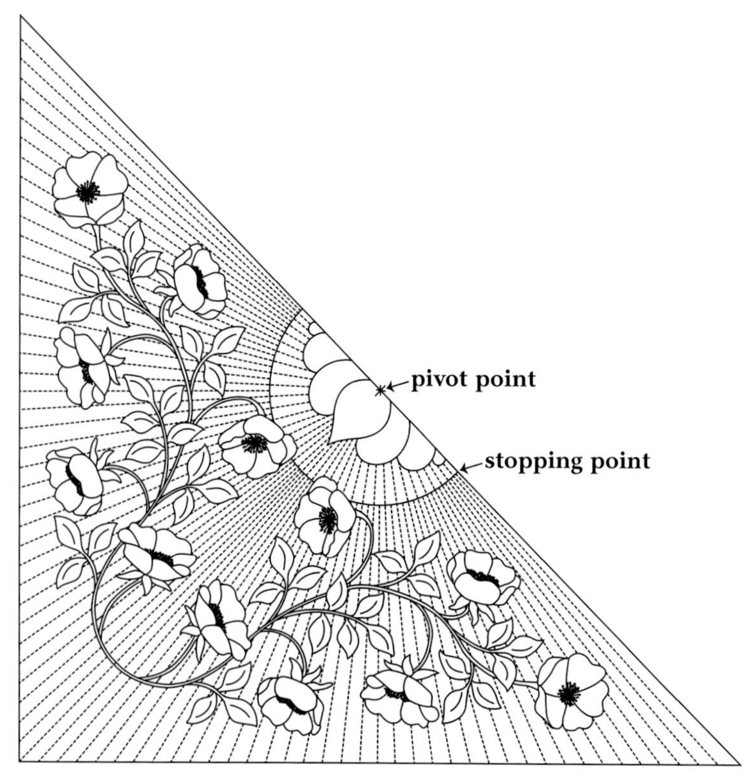

Fig. 5–2. Radiating quilting lines in corner triangle.

1 Find the center of an appliquéd block by placing a straight edge across opposite corners and another straight edge across the other two corners, forming an *X* with the rulers. Place a pin or mark a dot at the center. Measure the distance from the center to any corner and set your compass at this distance to make an arc.

2 Use this measurement to draw a quarter-circle arc on the template plastic. (You need only the arc, so it is okay if the compass point is off the template plastic.) Label the inside of the arc *A* and the outside *B*. (The *A* section will be used for scribing, and the *B* section will be marked for measuring.)

3 Before cutting the arc apart, mark a 12½" distance (the finished block measurement) on the arc. To do this, simply place a ruler with the zero on the arc at one end and the 12½" mark on the arc at the other end and mark both ends on the arc (Fig. 5–3, page 110). Next, on the *B* section, place marks on the arc ½", ¾", or 1" apart, depending on how dense you want your quilting to be. Cut the *A* and *B* section apart along the arc to make the template.

CROWN DESIGN

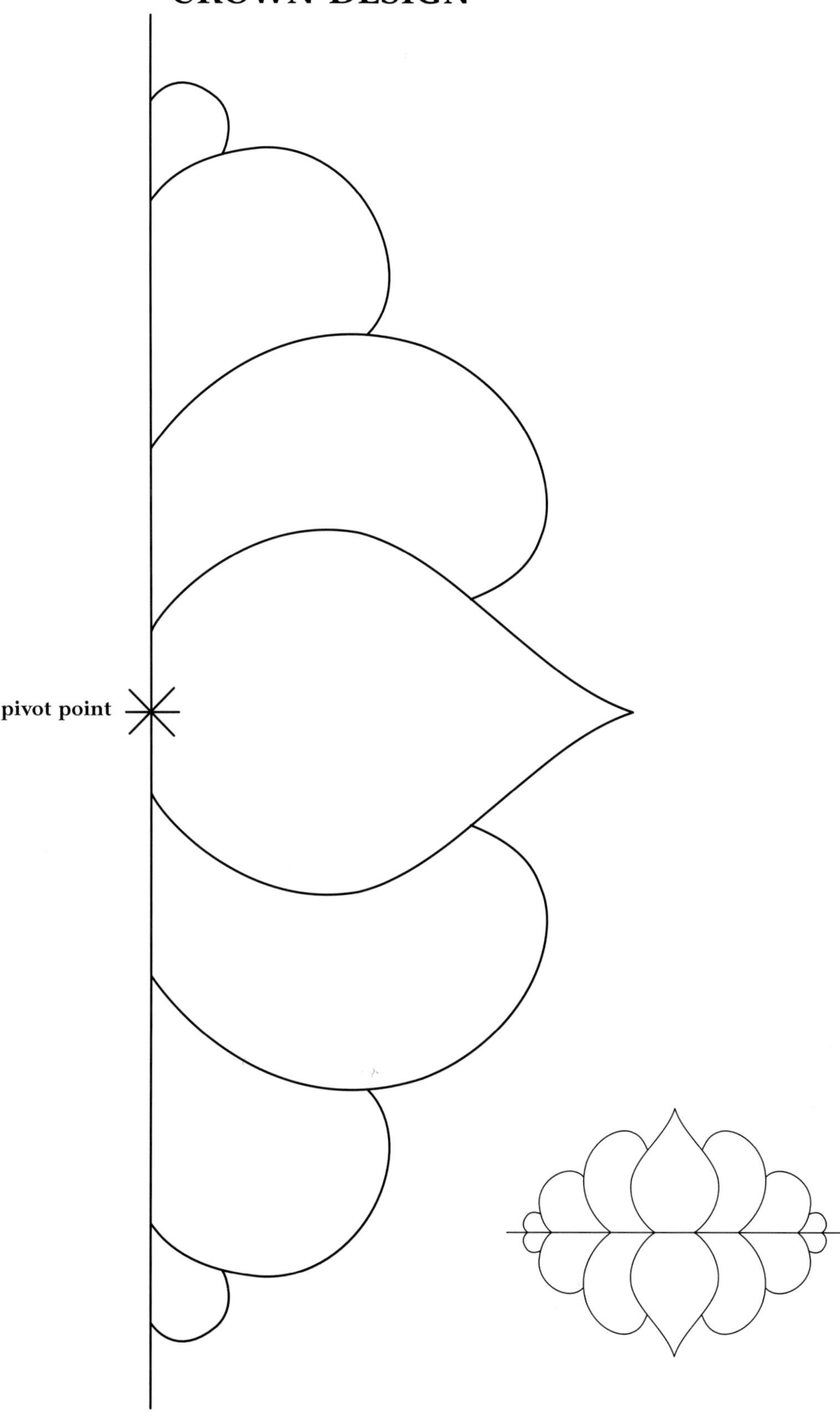

Crown Design. This is a simple feather, designed to be used with Doreen's Radiating Lines, page 107. By combining it with its mirror image, it becomes a nice design to fill an oval or rectangular space.

4 Find the center of the block to be marked, as described in Step 1. Place template *B* on one side of this block as shown in Figure 5-4, lining up the zero at one corner and the 12½" mark at the other corner. Template *B* may be taped to your fabric to stabilize it while you mark the quilting line.

5 Using template *A*, place one end of the arc on the center pivot point and the other end of the arc on the corner of the block and draw a line, skipping over any appliquéd areas. Pivot template *A* to the first mark on template *B*, making sure to keep the other end of template *A* on the pivot point. Draw another line, again skipping over any appliquéd areas. Continue in this way around the entire block, moving template *B* to each of the four sides in turn.

If all these lines converge in the center, they will create a mess because the quilting will be too dense and could cause distortion. The appliqué on many of the blocks covers most of the center, providing a natural place to stop the lines before reaching the center. For those that don't have covered centers, take only every third or fourth line to the center. Stop the rest at varying distances away from the center to provide pleasant and uniform background quilting for your appliqué.

When marking more than one block with this pattern, keep the spiral traveling in a uniform direction, either clockwise or counter-clockwise, on all blocks.

Finishing

Final Clean-up

Now that the quilt top has been marked, it is tempting to leave out a very important aspect of the process of making a quilt. It is a good idea to take time to do some final clean-up before layering your quilt or mounting it on your frame.

If it has been necessary to press an allowance toward a light fabric, that seam should be graded, that is, the darker fabric should be cut 1⁄16" shorter than the light fabric to prevent the dark fabric from shadowing through the top after it has been quilted.

Pick all the loose threads off the wrong side of the quilt top for the same reason that

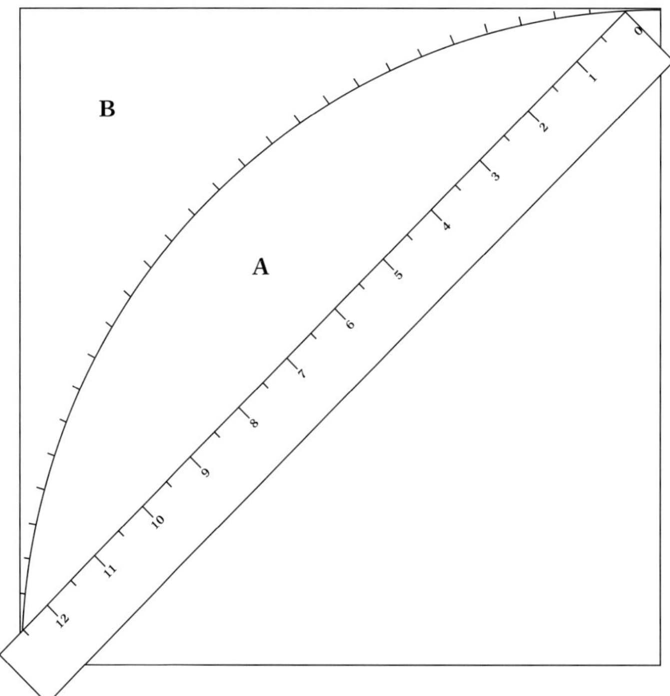

Fig. 5-3. Mark a 12½" distance across the arc on plastic to make templates for Doreen's Spiral.

you graded the seams. It is very difficult to remove a thread that is inside the quilt sandwich once the quilt has been basted.

Spread out the top. Measure it. Is it square? Does it lie flat? Now is the time to correct any problems.

When you prepare to baste your quilt, take care not to stretch the top out of shape.

You have devoted too much time to this project to let these important details slide because you are anxious to start quilting.

Layering the Quilt

The backing fabric and batting must each be wider and longer than your quilt top by 4" to 6".

Most of us do not have a large quilting frame, either because we don't have room or because we prefer to quilt with a smaller frame or hoop. Some quilters get very good results without using any frame or hoop at all when quilting.

Without a large frame, it is necessary to baste the three layers before quilting can begin. This is not difficult to do, but if it seems like a daunting task to layer a large quilt by yourself, try enlisting the help of four to six friends. It's a good way to get the job done more quickly and have a good time doing it.

With a large quilt, you will need a large area to spread it out. The floor (which can "break" your back), a Ping-Pong table, or two to three rectangular banquet size tables pushed together are all areas that will suffice. Assuming that you don't like the floor idea, let's concentrate on the large table method (not your formal dining table because the needle will mar the surface). First, spread out the backing fabric, wrong side up, and center it with equal amounts hanging from the ends and sides of the table. If possible, tape each edge of the backing fabric to the underside of the table, stretching the backing fabric slightly. Then carefully spread the batting on top of the backing, centering it as you did the backing. *Place the lengthwise grain of the batting going the same direction as that of your backing.* (You can determine the batting grain by gently pulling a small portion of a

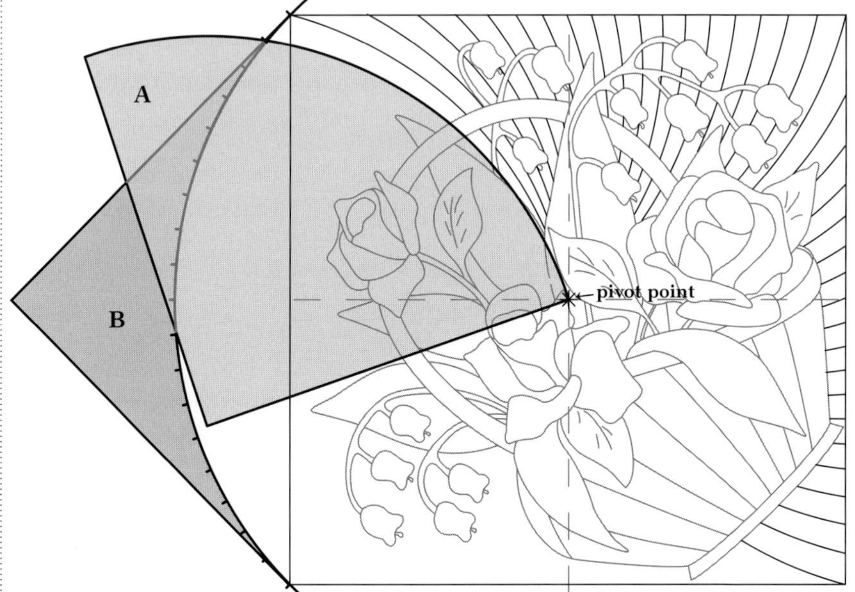

Fig. 5-4. Doreen's Spiral: Line up template *B*, on one side of block and tape it to prevent it from moving. Using the arc of template *A*, connect each dot on template *B* to the pivot point.

corner in both directions. The lengthwise grain will not stretch or give as much as the crosswise grain.) Smooth out the batting, but try not to stretch it. Finally, center your quilt top over the batting with the right side up. Smooth it out and make certain that the batting and backing extend beyond the edge of the quilt top on all sides.

Thread numerous basting needles (either darning needles or milliner's needles) with an arm's length of thread. Start basting in the middle and work toward the outside, making grid lines 4" to 6" apart. Use long stitches. They don't have to be pretty as long as they hold the three layers together securely. The amount of basting is up to you, but if the sandwich will be handled a lot during quilting, you will do well to baste heavily. After you have basted the area of the quilt that rests on the table, gently slide the sandwich to one side, exposing another area to be basted. Smooth out all three layers again and baste. Repeat this process until all areas of the quilt sandwich have been basted. Finally, fold the excess backing fabric up and over the batting and edge of the quilt top and baste. This fold protects the edge of the top and prevents the batting from shredding apart. Now you are ready to quilt.

Documenting the Quilt

A label with the following information should be attached to your quilt to provide future generations with vital statistics and to satisfy historians: quilt name, date started and date completed, pattern name and source, name of maker(s) and owner (if different), methods and techniques used (if desired), and geographic location where quilt was made. An address and phone number may also be included; however, you may prefer to make a separate, smaller label with this information, which can easily be changed, if necessary.

Methods of making labels and attaching them vary. To make the label, you can write with indelible ink directly on the quilt backing if you are bold. This is the most permanent way to mark your quilt to declare ownership. If anyone obtains possession of your quilt illegally, they cannot remove the label without damaging the quilt. Another way to make a label is to write the information on a separate, small piece of muslin, and stitch it to the back of the quilt. It is suggested that this be done before you start quilting so that it will be quilted into the quilt, making it more difficult to remove. Some quilters keep a journal and take photographs while making a quilt and slip them into a special pocket hidden in the quilt. Whatever information you choose to include, this is an important part of the completion of your quilt.

Binding

A French-style double binding is recommended. You can use bias or straight-grain strips. If you plan to use your sewing machine to attach the binding to your top, as opposed to sewing it on by hand, it is helpful to use a walking foot to prevent stretching and distorting the binding. Bias bindings are said to wear better, but a straight binding is fine and in some instances preferred, such as when the binding fabric has a directional pattern. When you trim the excess batting and backing off your quilt, leave enough to completely fill the binding. Binding wears better if the batting extends all the way to the edge.

1 To make the binding, cut enough 2" strips so that, when they are sewn together end-to-end at a 45° angle, the continuous strip will encircle the quilt plus 20". The extra length is for turning corners and connecting the ends (Figs. 5-5 and 5-6). The angled seams between the strips will distribute the bulk of the seam allowances when the binding is folded over the edge of the quilt. Press binding in half lengthwise.

2 On the starting end of the binding, press under a ¼" seam allowance. With your quilt face up, and beginning on the top side of the quilt rather than a corner, align the raw edges of the binding strip with the raw edge of the quilt top. Leave a few inches of the binding free at the starting point to allow you to finish the ends. Begin with a backstitch to anchor the seam.

3 To miter a corner, simply stitch to ¼" from the edge and backstitch (Fig. 5-7). Raise the needle and presser foot and

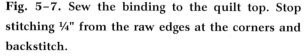

Fig. 5-5. Cut 2½" strips for binding, which can be bias or straight grain. Cut ends at a 45° angle.

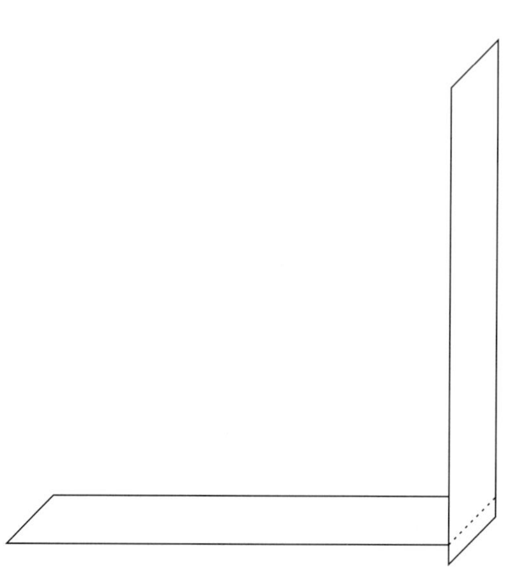

Fig. 5-6. Sew strips together on the diagonal. Press seams to one side. Trim off the "dog ears."

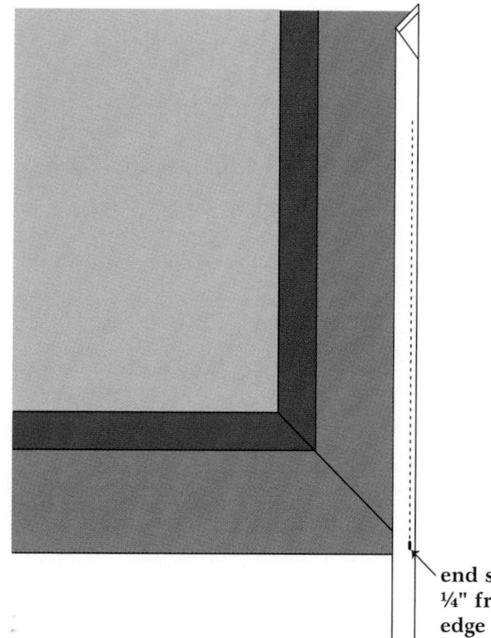

Fig. 5-7. Sew the binding to the quilt top. Stop stitching ¼" from the raw edges at the corners and backstitch.

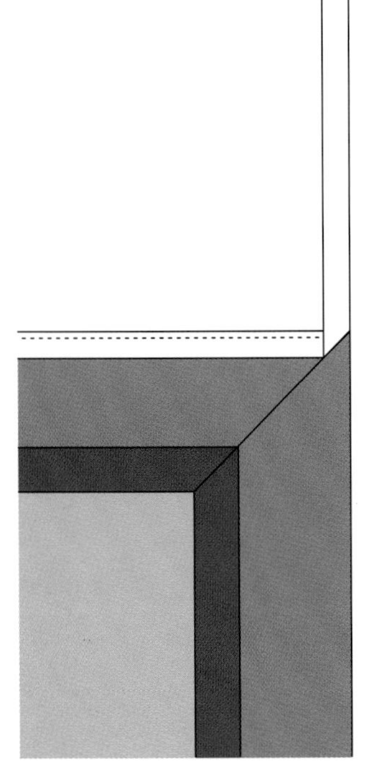

Fig. 5-8. Cut the threads and fold the binding up to form a 90° angle.

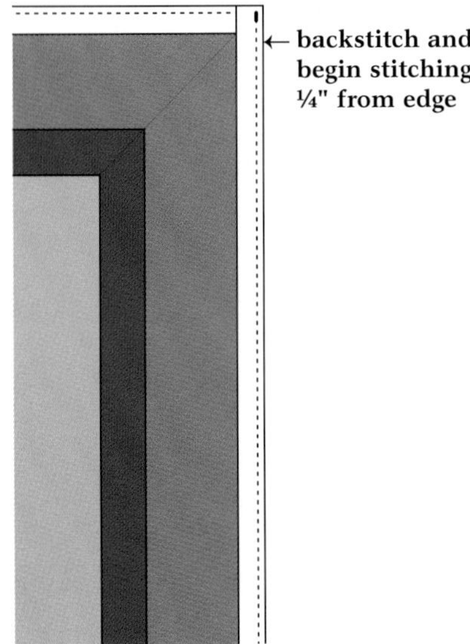

Fig. 5-9. Fold the binding down along the raw edge.

cut the threads. Turn the quilt to begin sewing the next side. Fold the binding up and away from you, as shown in Figure 5-8, to form a 90° angle. Then fold the binding down (Fig. 5-9). Starting ¼" from the top edge, take one stitch forward and one back. (To avoid gaps or puckers, the stitching lines need to meet in the corner.) Then sew to the next corner and miter as before. Continue sewing all the way around the quilt.

4 When you are approximately 6" from the place you started, stop sewing, backstitch, and cut the threads. Cut off any extra length of the binding, leaving enough to tuck into the starting tail. Open the fold of the starting tail and tuck the ending tail inside it (Fig. 5-10). Refold the tail and stitch the rest of the seam, backstitching to anchor it.

5 To finish, fold the binding to the back of the quilt making sure the binding covers the machine stitches. Hand stitch the binding to the backing with the appliqué stitch. Your stitches should go into the batting but should not go through to the front of your quilt. When you come to a corner, simply fold in one side of the binding and then the other to create a miter, and pin. (It is best to tuck the back fullness at the miter to the opposite side from the front fullness so the corner will lie flatter.) Stitch the fold of the miter closed on the front and on the back and then continue sewing around the quilt. Where the binding starts and ends, appliqué the binding closure together.

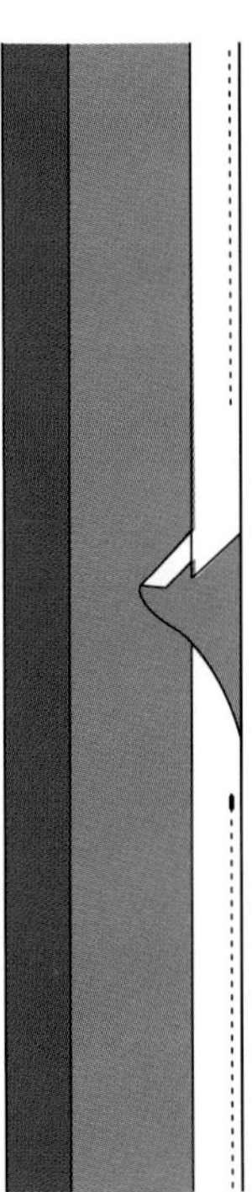

Fig. 5-10. To finish, tuck tail of binding inside the fold of starting tail. Refold the starting tail and stitch to the starting point.

Chapter 6

Gallery

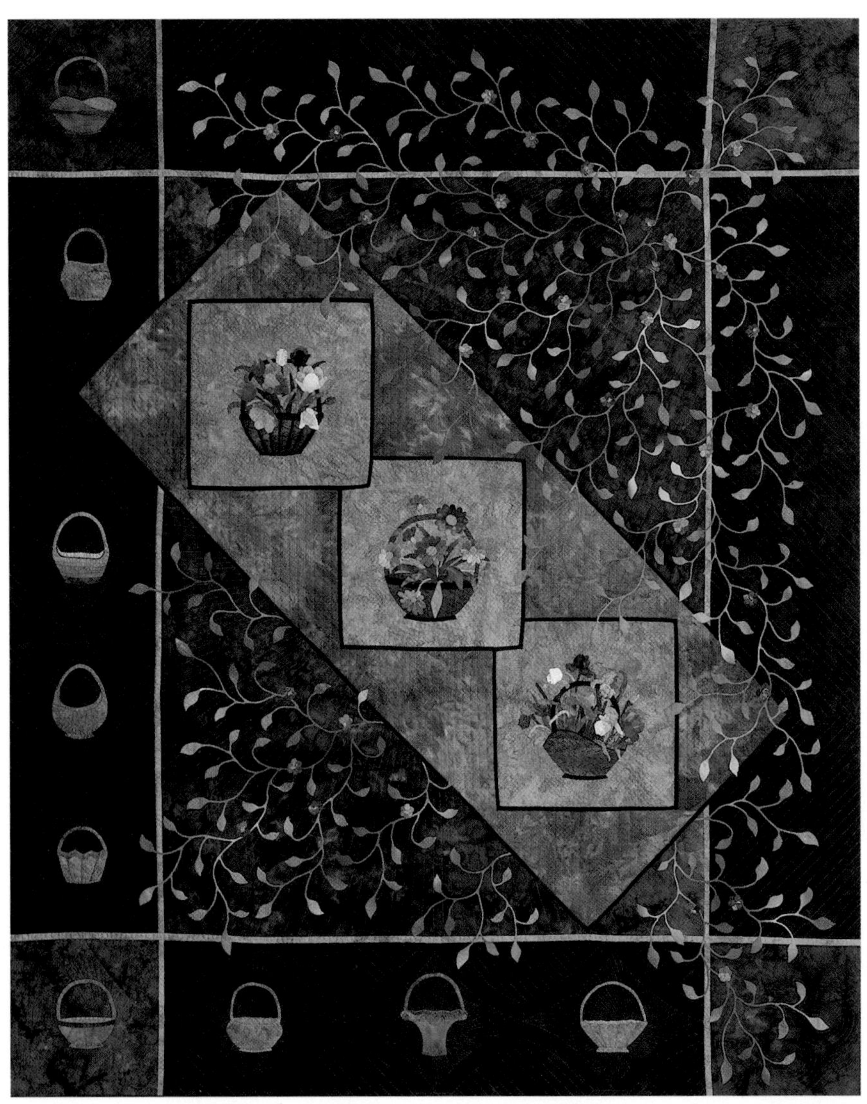

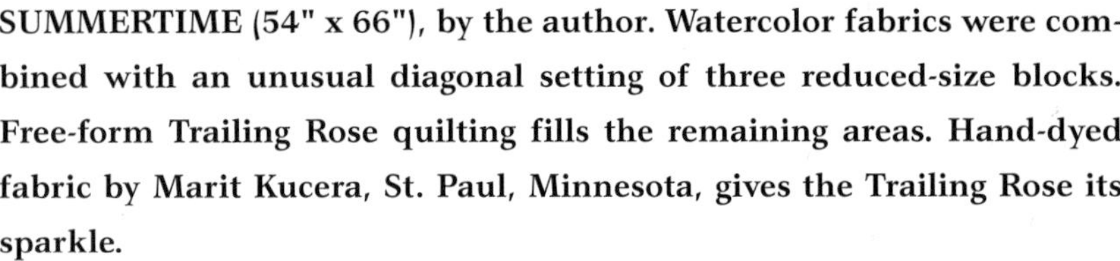

SUMMERTIME (54" x 66"), by the author. Watercolor fabrics were combined with an unusual diagonal setting of three reduced-size blocks. Free-form Trailing Rose quilting fills the remaining areas. Hand-dyed fabric by Marit Kucera, St. Paul, Minnesota, gives the Trailing Rose its sparkle.

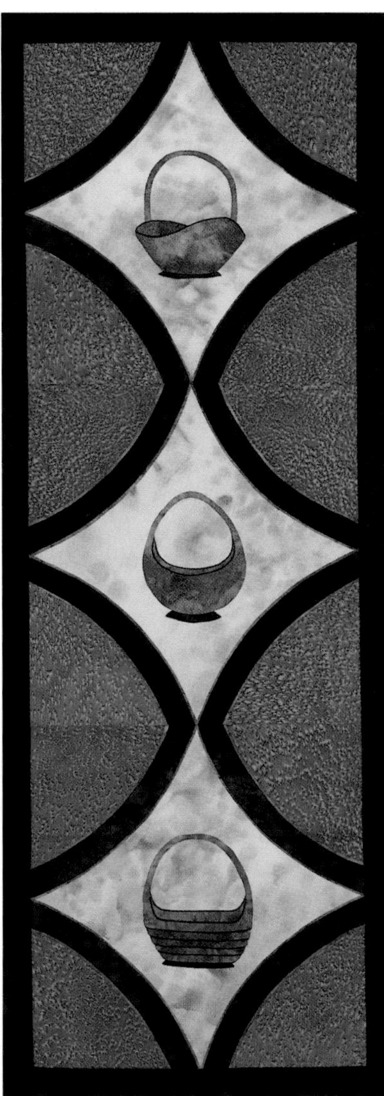

DEFINITIONS (12" x 36"), by the author. The Primrose, Lily, and Iris Baskets were reduced to approximately 5", placed in a 12" setting block, and appliquéd without the floral arrangements.

THE SECRET GARDEN (35" x 35"), by the author, is an octagonal contemporary-style piece. The irises from the Iris Basket were rearranged slightly for this guild challenge, requiring that all fabrics used be in the blue family.

SNAILS TRAILS (38" x 45"), by Doreen Perkins, Kansas City, Missouri. A member of the first Gems of Summer class, Doreen designed an asymmetrical setting for her two blocks, used brilliant colors, and framed them with an unusual pieced sashing she calls Snails Trails.

SUMMER FRAGRANCE (97" x 97"), by Ora Lee Eastland, Stanley, Kansas. Ora Lee shows a remarkable sense of color in her first-ever quilt. The 12½" blocks were alternated with plain blocks. To make a king-size quilt, she used all the Gems of Summer patterns, including the four that were retired or redesigned.

GEMS OF SUMMER (51" x 51"), by Reiko Watanabe, Tokyo, Japan. A member of the first Gems of Summer class, Reiko revived an abandoned project to make this sample. She updated and improved her blocks by changing many fabrics. Flowers and feathers are stuffed.

IMPERIAL GARDEN (80" x 80"), by Kathy Delaney, Overland Park, Kansas; center wreath appliquéd by Leanne Baraban, Overland Park; quilted by Toni Fisher, Springfield, Missouri. This quilt is a dramatic example of the use of a black background.

SUMMER'S SYMPHONY (95" x 95"), by Anna Kephart, Prairie Village, Kansas; quilted by Toni Fisher, Springfield, Missouri. Anna used Medallion Setting 1 to make this quilt. It received an honorable mention at Silver Dollar City in 1997.

BASKETS, BLOOMS, BUTTERFLIES, AND BOWS (92" x 92"), by Joan Streck, Overland Park, Kansas. The central medallion is from a Sarah Ann Nelson Edwards quilt, circa 1850 found in *Red and Green* by Jeana Kimball. Joan's quilt was awarded second place at the 1995 American Quilter's Society Show.

TRAILING ROSE (39" x 39"), by the author; quilted by Toni Fisher, Springfield, Missouri. The Rose basket was reduced to fit the 12" center block and placed in a diamond-in-a-square setting. The Trailing Rose pattern was created to fill the corner areas.

FLIRTING WITH FLOWERS (68" x 84"), by Kathy Scott, Louisburg, Kansas. Kathy has added pieced corners to her squares to make 18" blocks that, when sewn together, create a window pane effect.

GRACE (22" x 36"), by the author; quilted by Anita Shackelford, Bucyrus, Ohio. The African Violet Basket is combined with Trailing Rose appliqué. The leaf fabric is hand-dyed fabric by Marit Kucera, St. Paul, Minnesota.

TICKLED PINK (22" x 22"), by Anita Shackelford, Bucyrus, Ohio. Anita added dimensional appliqué to her daffodils to show how flat appliqué can be changed to three dimensions. A narrow palette (just six fabrics) creates a charming mood.

SUMMER GARDEN (95" x 95"), by Margaret Berglund, Stanley, Kansas; quilted by Janice Walden, Scottsville, Kentucky. Using Medallion Setting 2, Margaret spot-lighted her baskets with a light background fabric that contrasts with the rest of the quilt.

Vest by Katherine Stubbs Ward, Riviera Beach, Florida. Kathy sprinkled the front of a denim vest with reduced-size Wild Roses to dress it up.

Vest, by Doreen Perkins, Kansas City, Missouri. Sueded cotton provides a beautiful background for the Wild Roses that grace Doreen's vest.

Canna Pillow, by Anna Kephart, Margaret Berglund, and the author.

Daffodil Pillow, by LaDonna Marks and the author.

African Violet Pillow, by Margaret Berglund and the author.

Chapter 7

Patterns

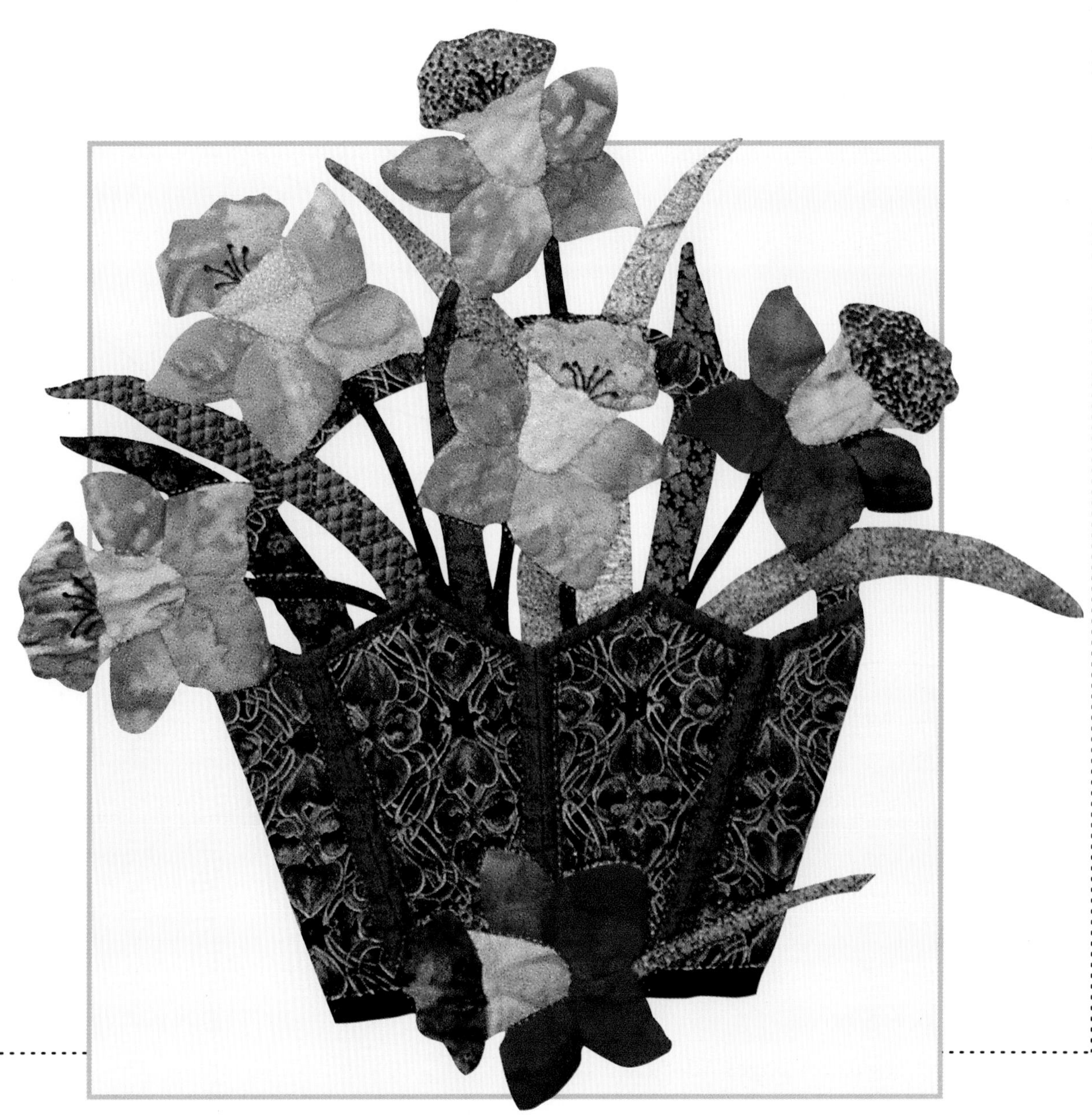

LILY BASKET

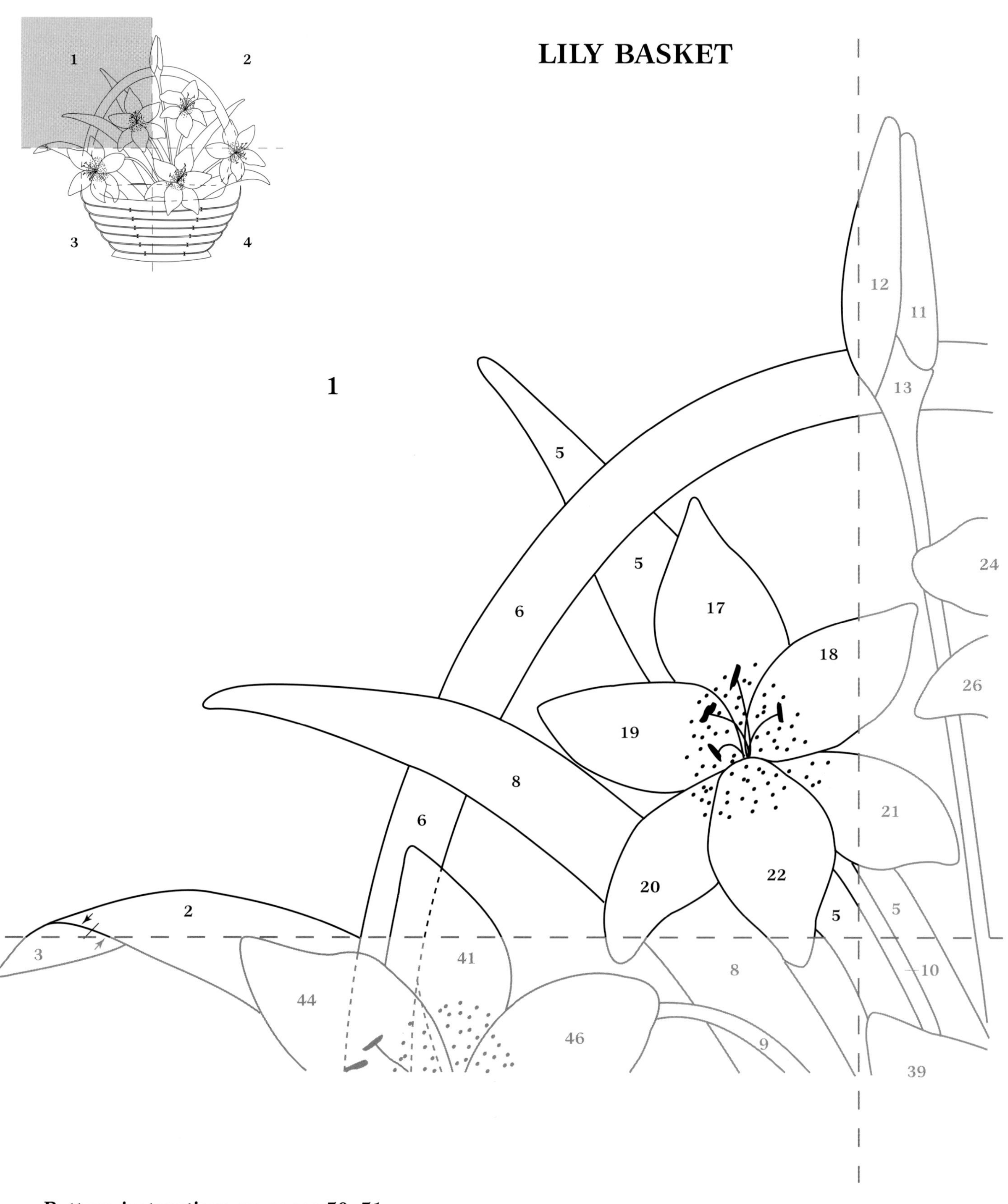

Pattern instructions on pages 50–51.

LILY BASKET

1
2
3
4
12
11
13
6
2
23
24
25
26
27
28
6
4
18
21
22
5
5
13
14
4
30
32
34
8
10
35
29
9
39

LILY BASKET

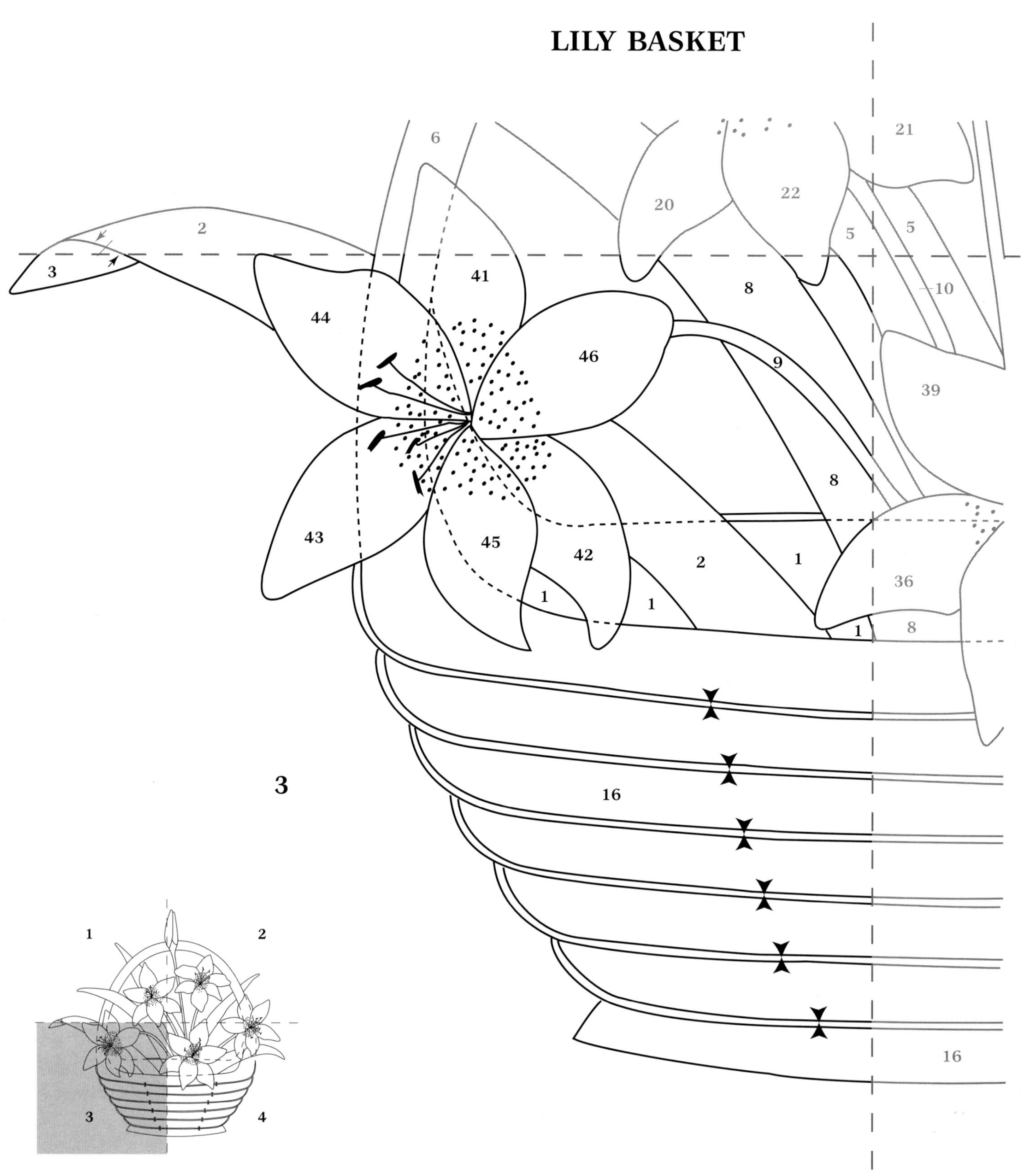

Pattern instructions on pages 50–51.

LILY BASKET

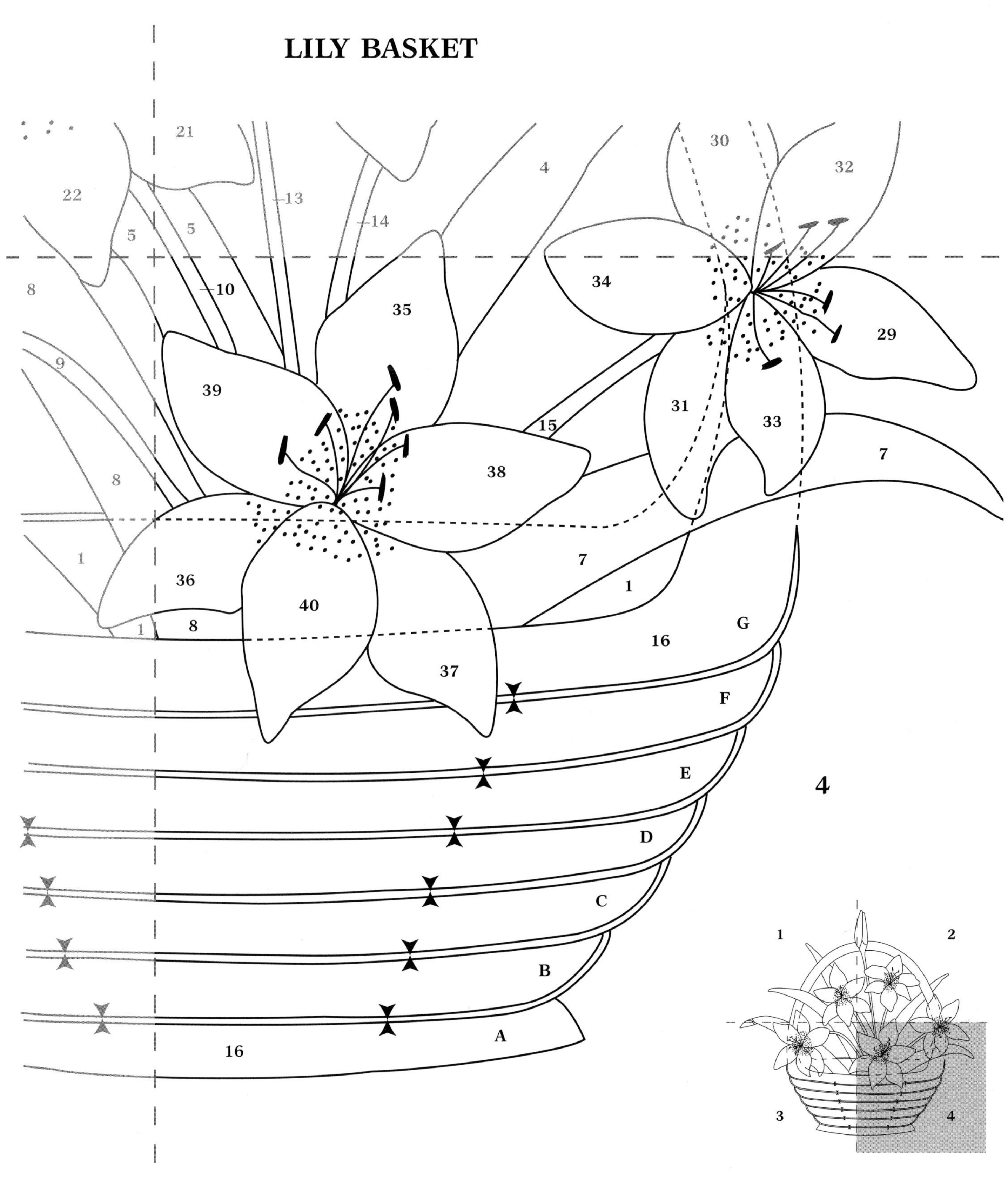
21
22
5
5
13
14
4
30
32
8
10
34
35
29
39
9
31
33
15
38
7
8
1
36
7
40
1
1
8
16
G
37
F
E
4
D
C
1
2
B
A
16
3
4

DAFFODIL BASKET

Pattern instructions on pages 52–53.

DAFFODIL BASKET

DAFFODIL BASKET

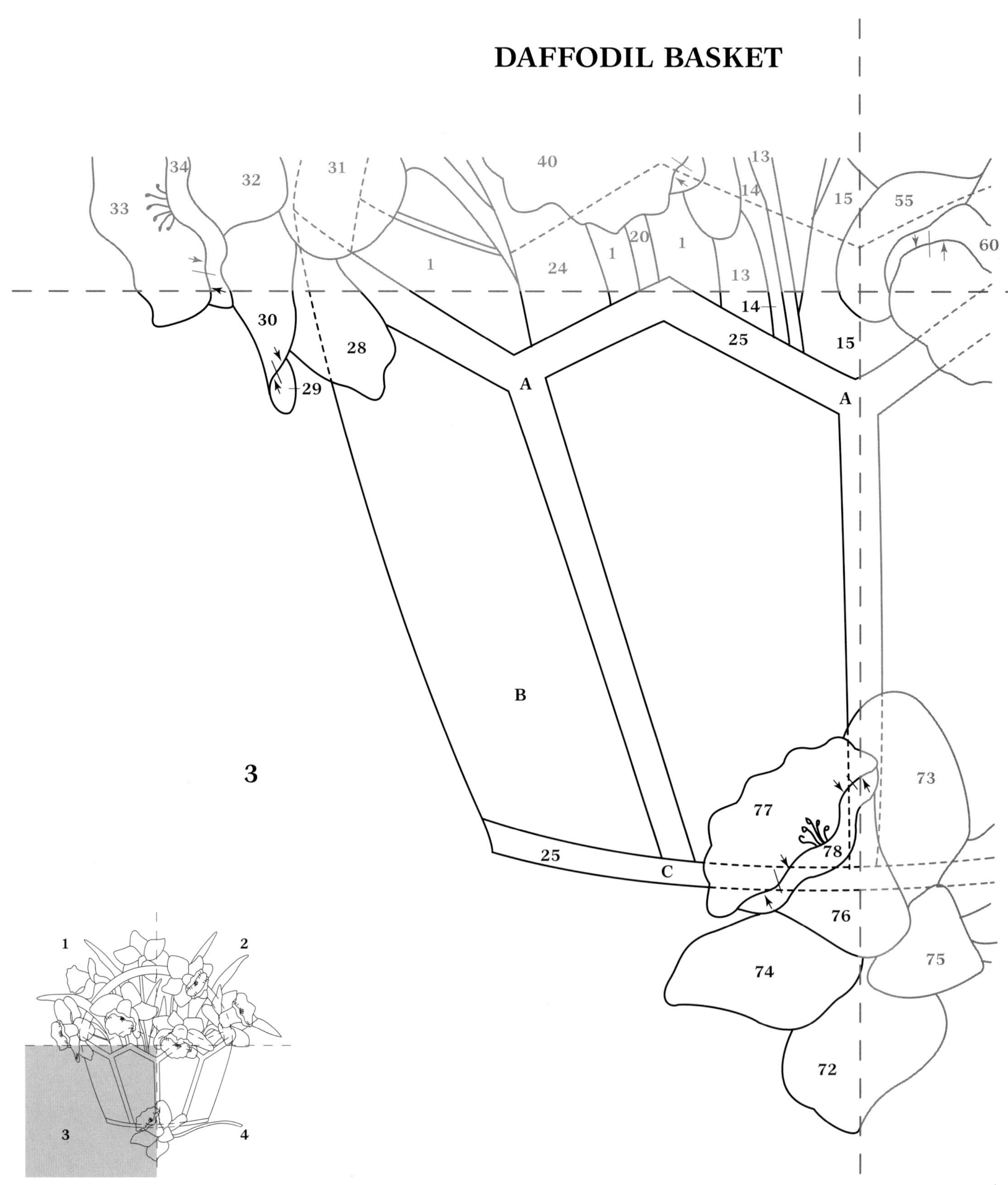

Pattern instructions on pages 52–53.

DAFFODIL BASKET

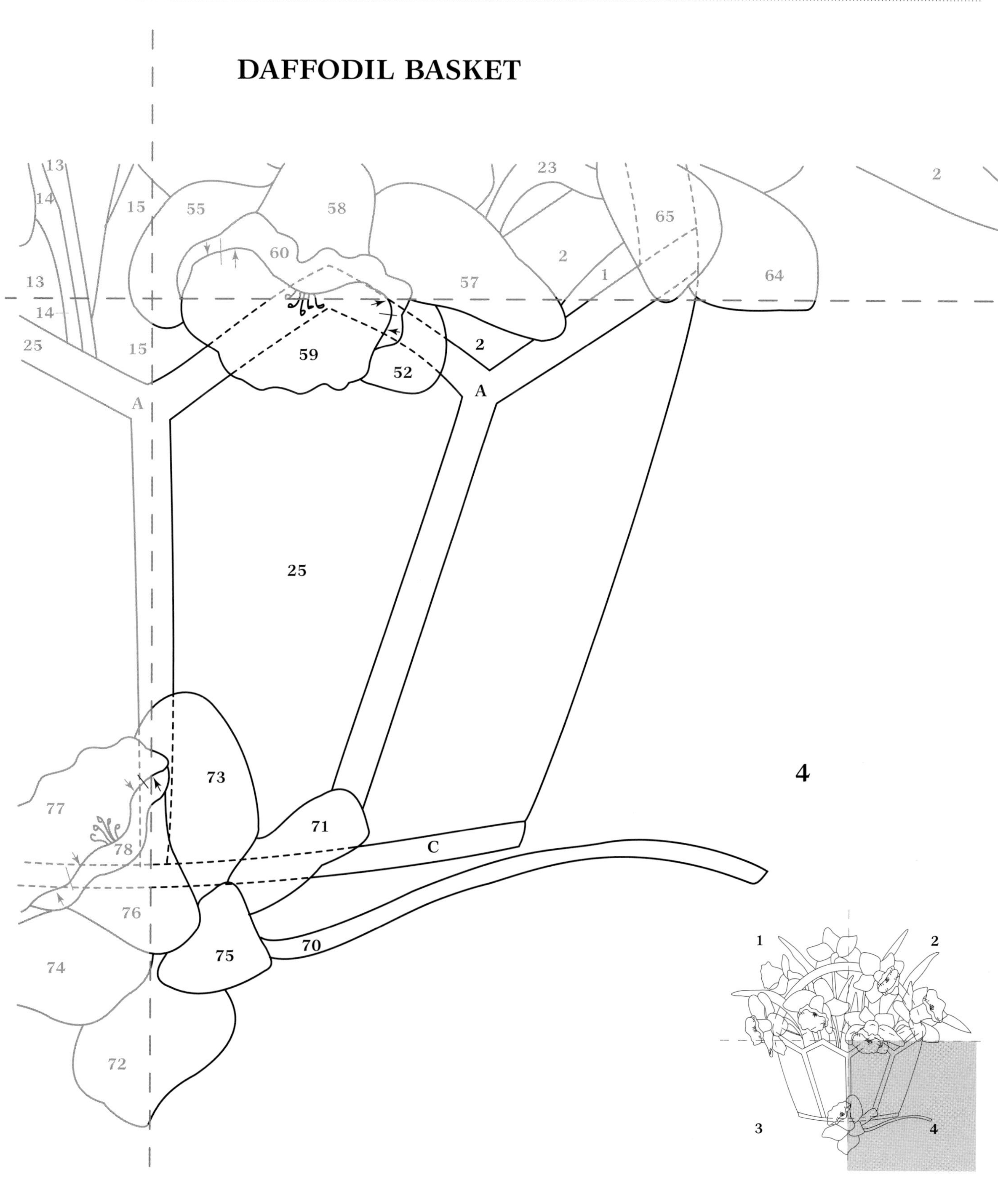

TULIP BASKET

Pattern instructions on pages 54–55.

TULIP BASKET

TULIP BASKET

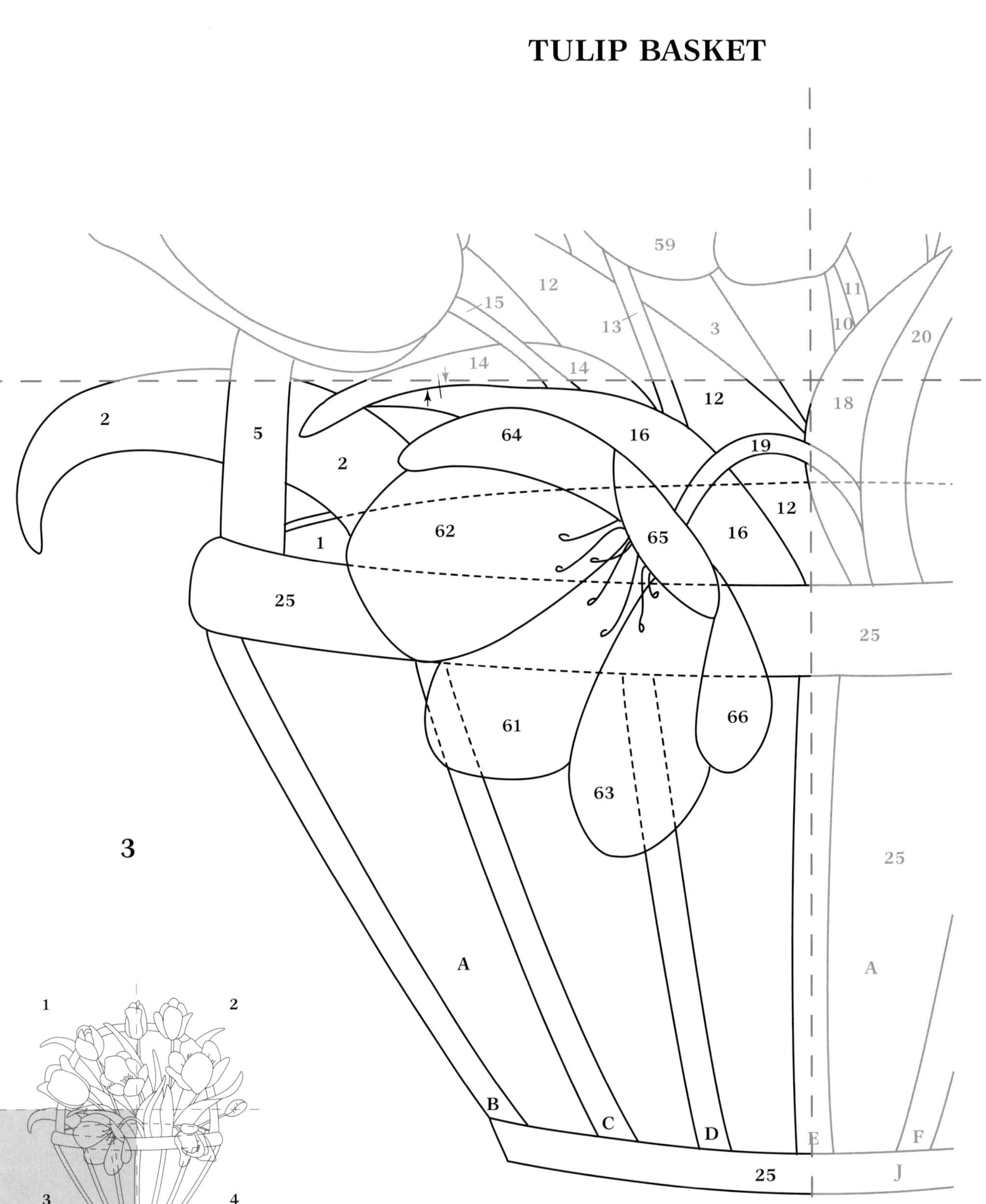

Pattern instructions on pages 54–55.

TULIP BASKET

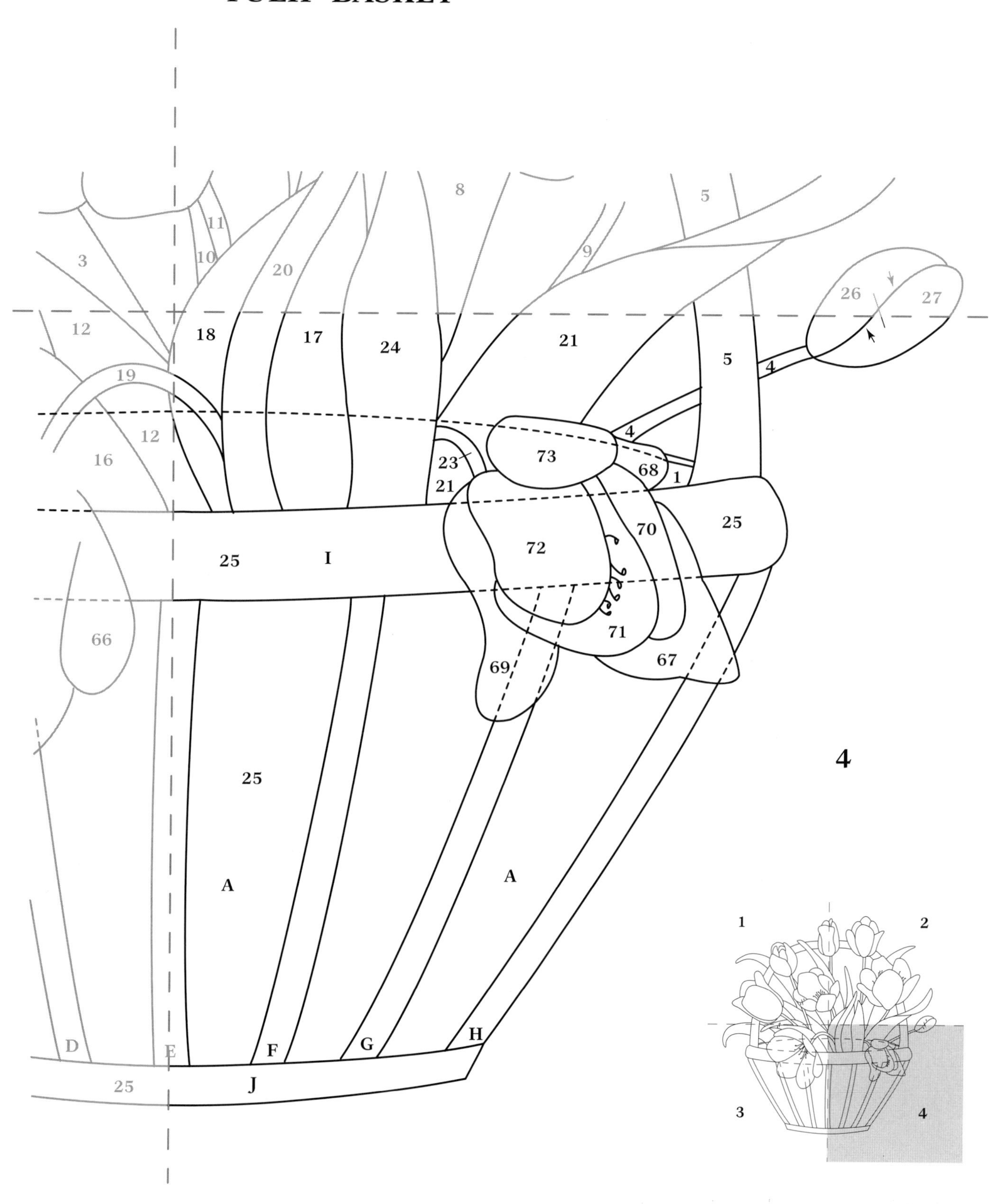

PRIMROSE BASKET

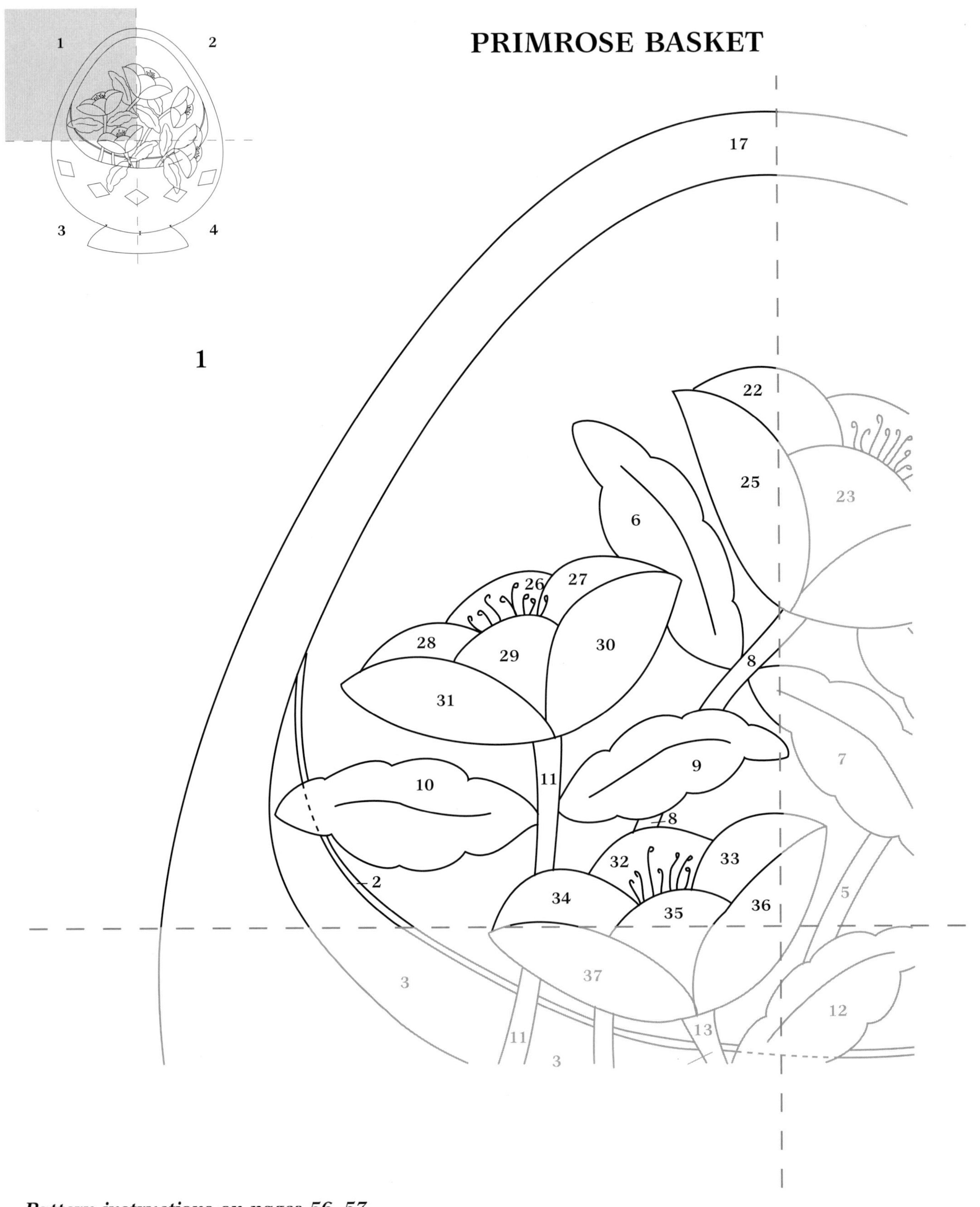

Pattern instructions on pages 56–57.

PRIMROSE BASKET

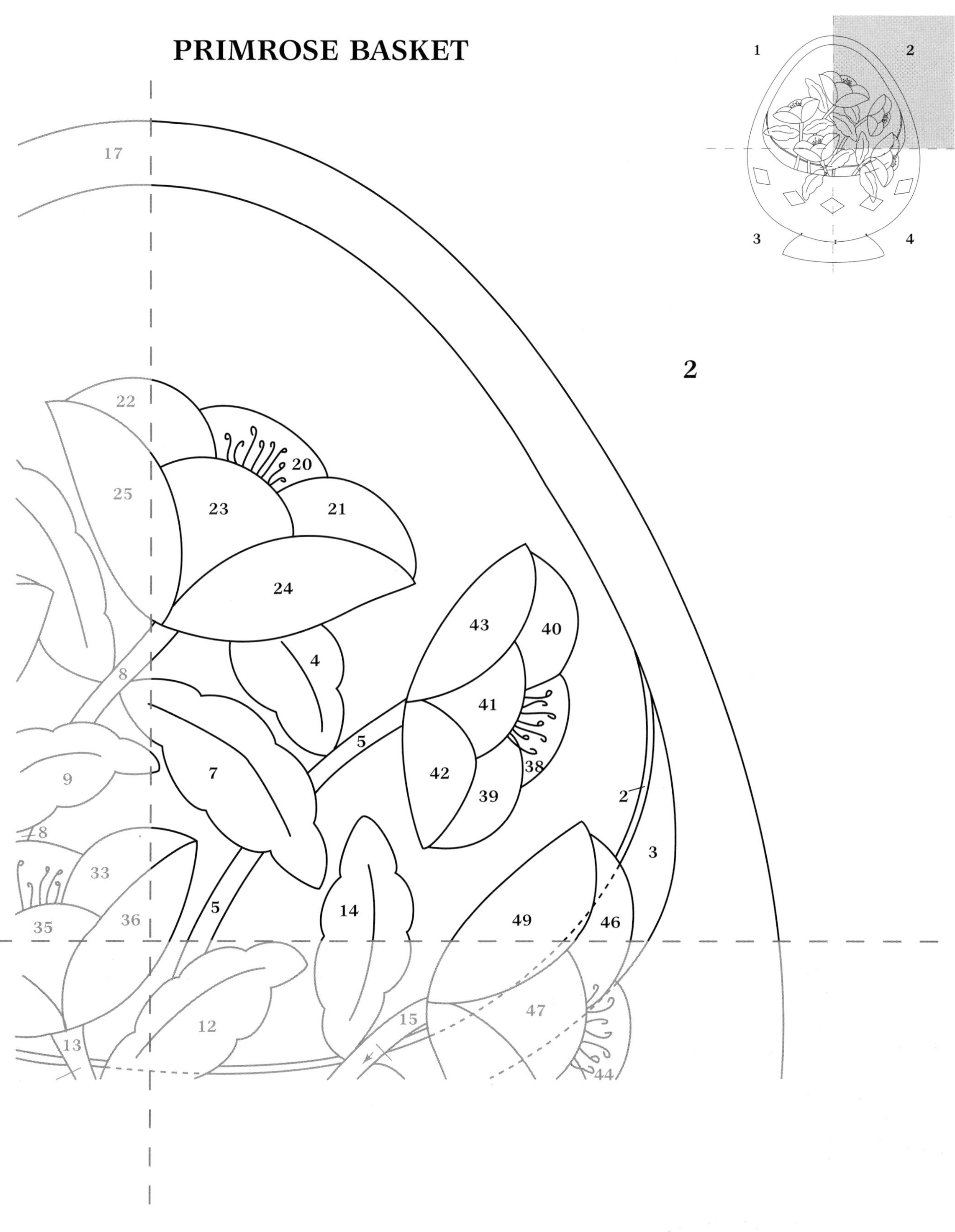

PRIMROSE BASKET

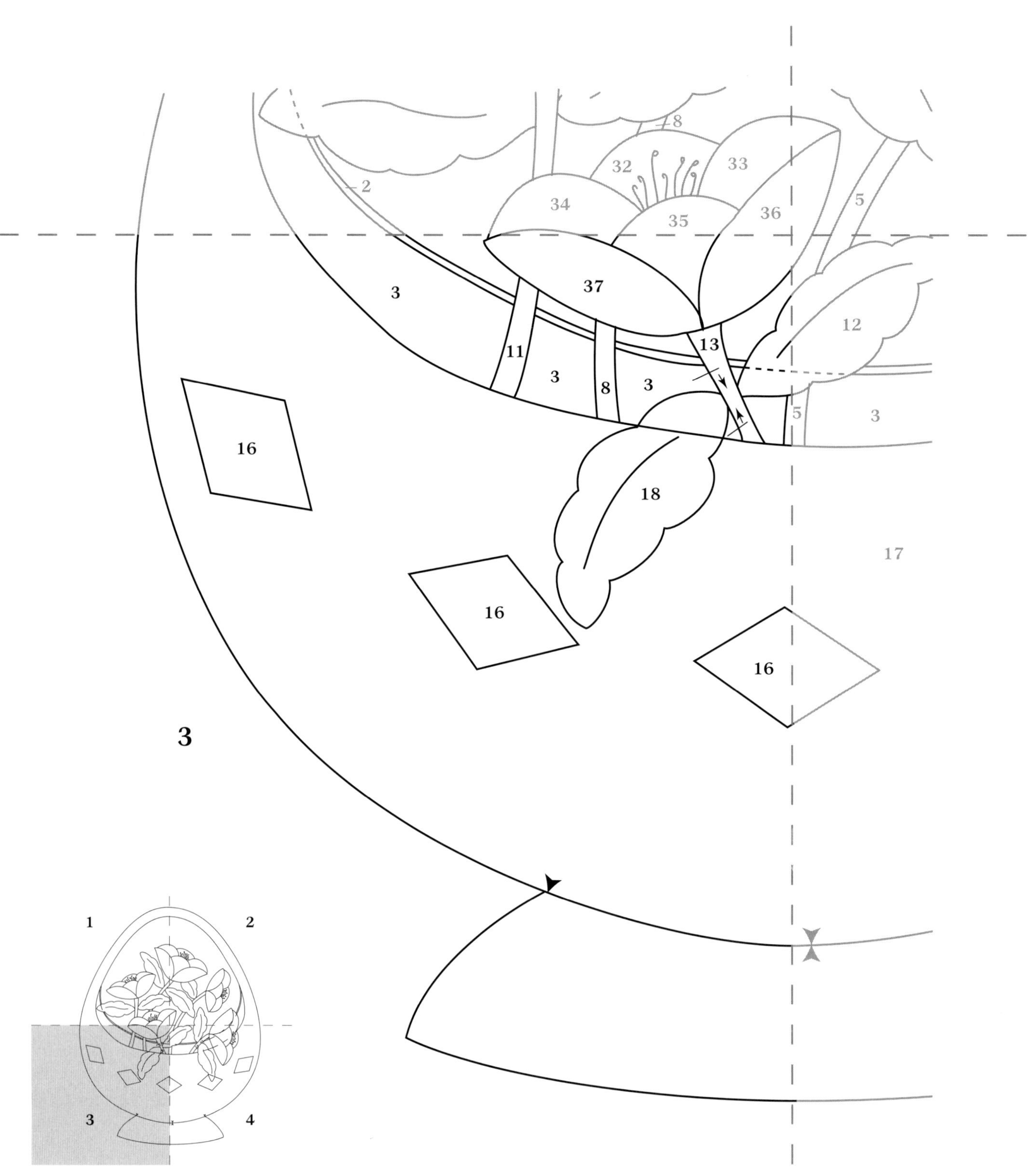

Pattern instructions on pages 56–57.

PRIMROSE BASKET

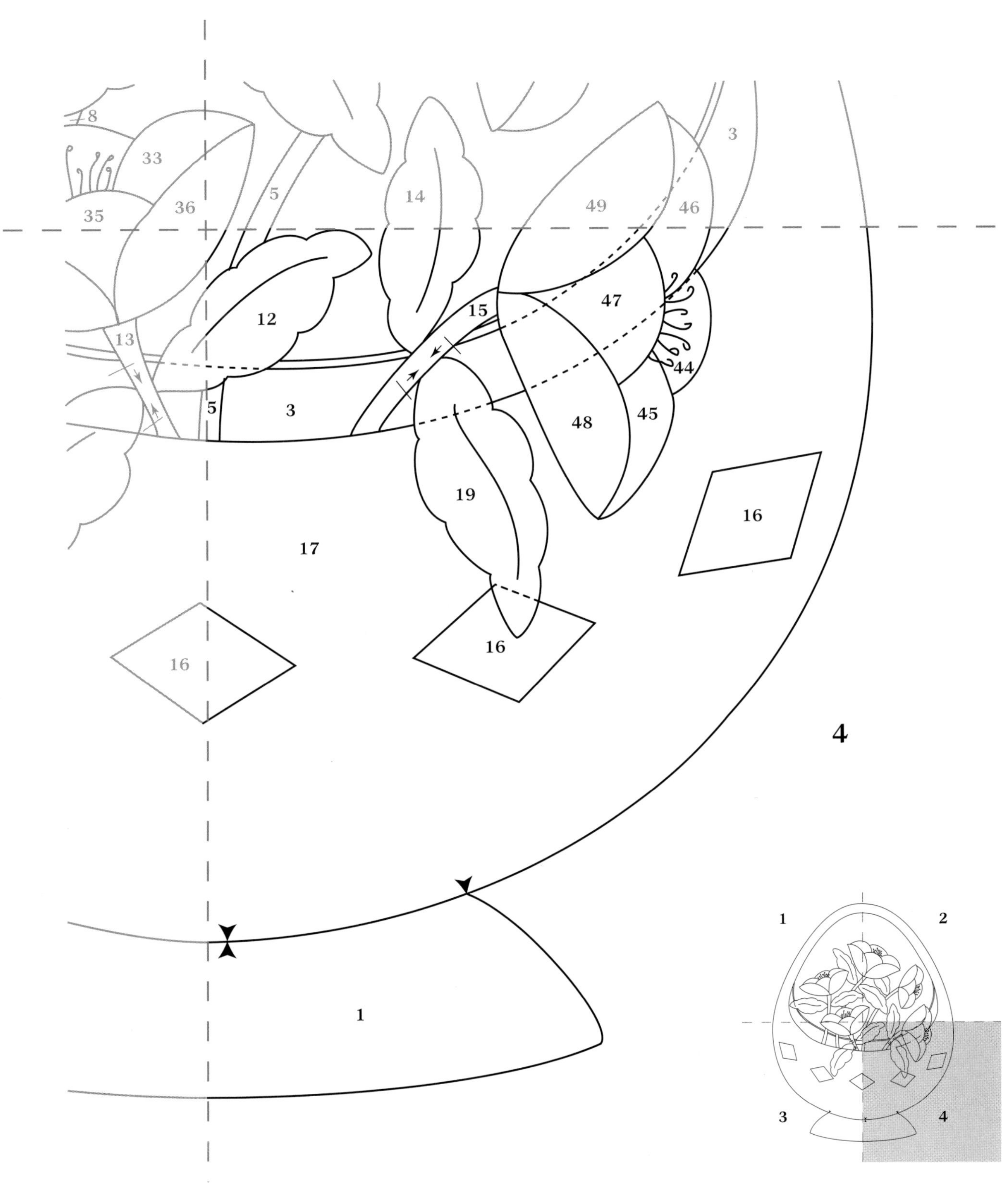

IRIS BASKET

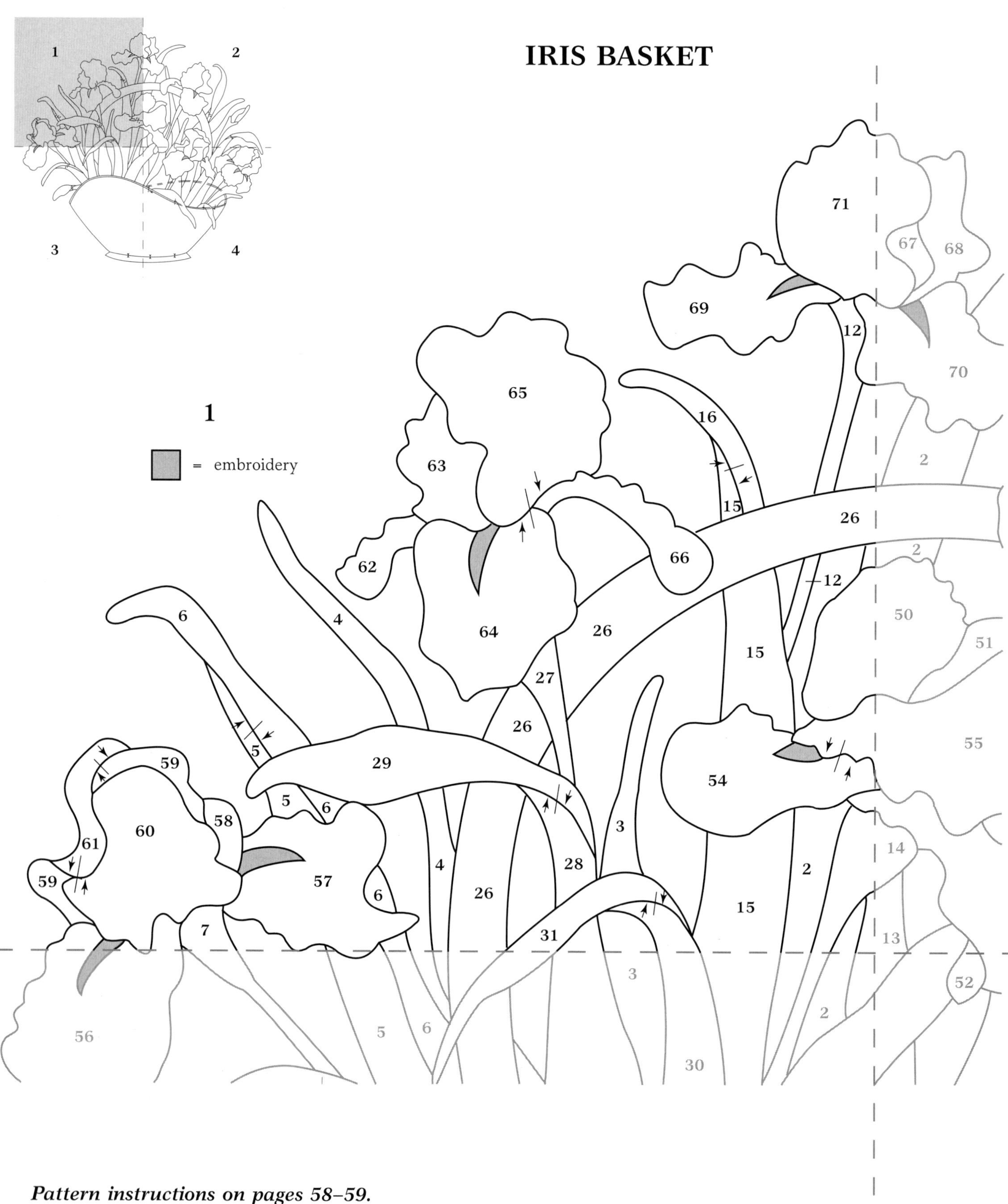

Pattern instructions on pages 58–59.

IRIS BASKET

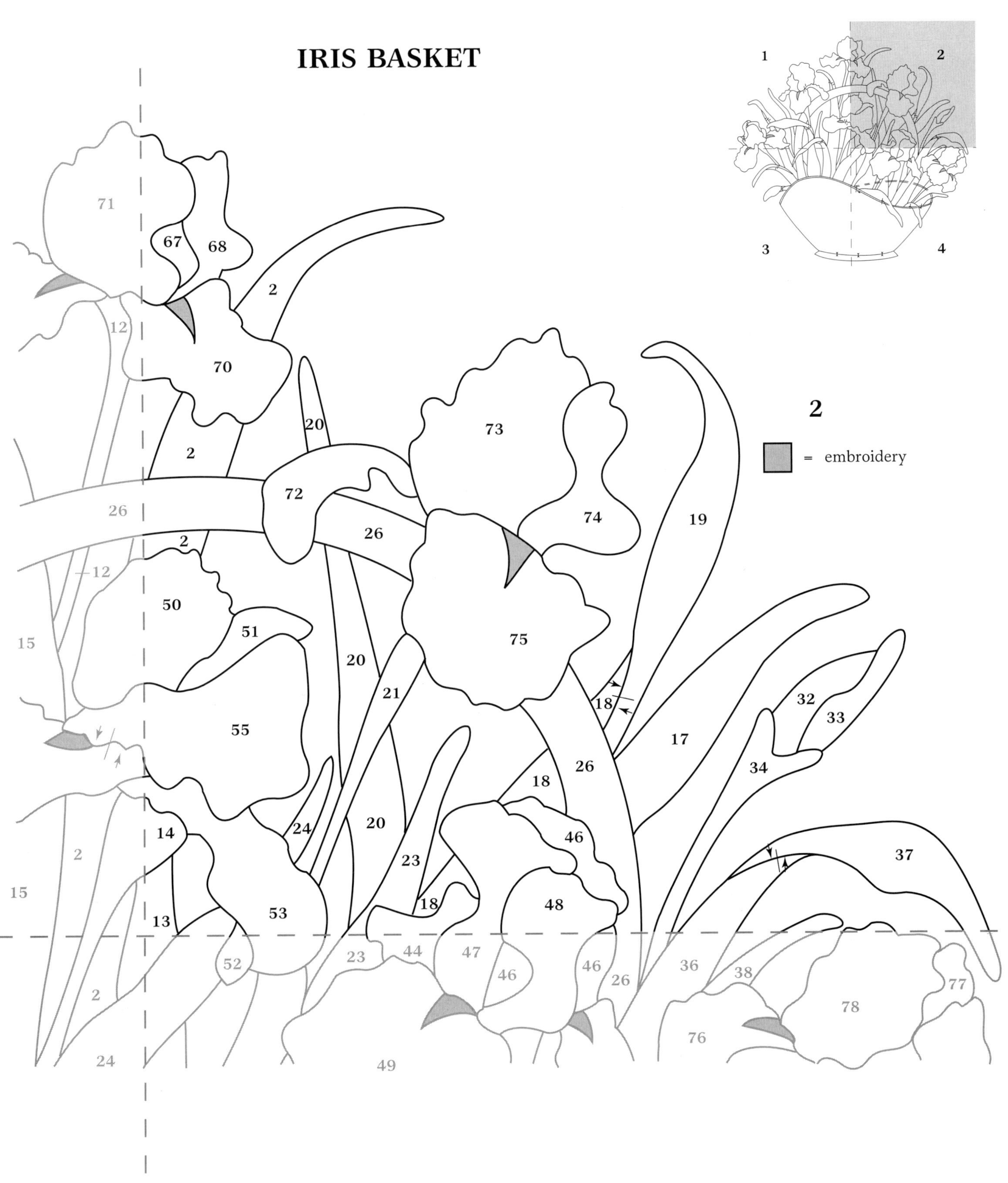

IRIS BASKET

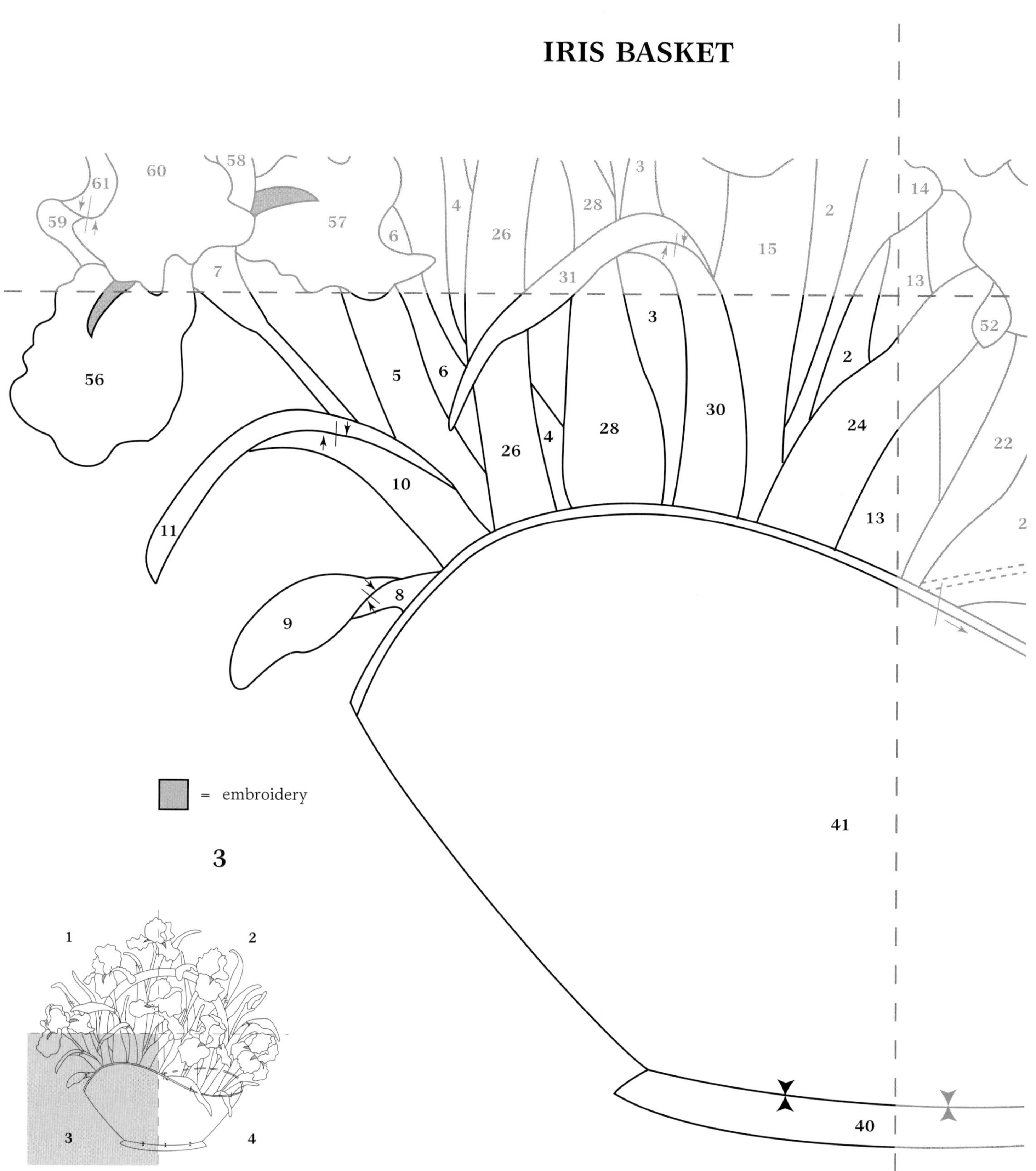

Pattern instructions on pages 58–59.

IRIS BASKET

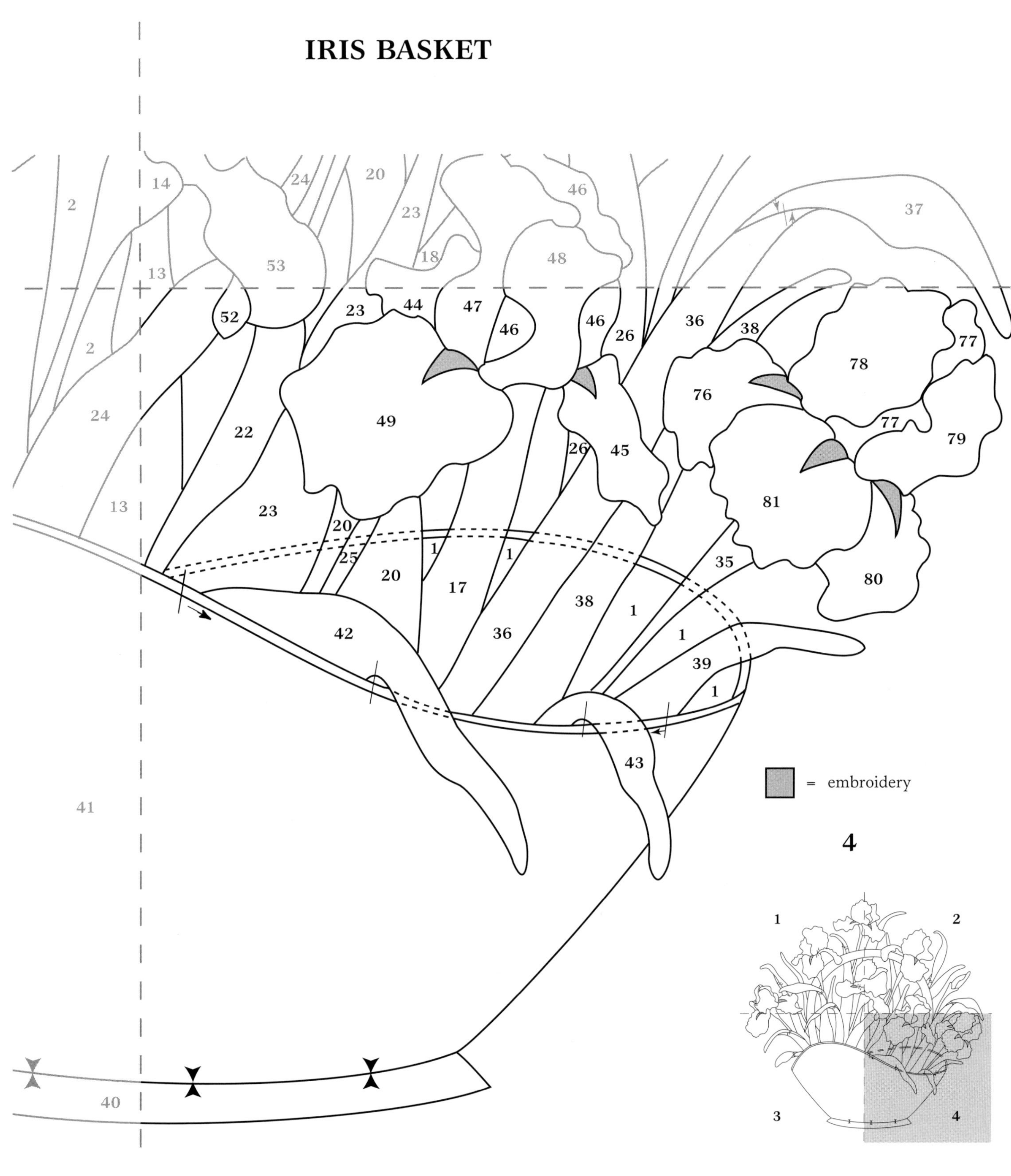
2
14
24
20
23
46
37
13
53
18
48
2
52
23
44
47
46
46
26
36
38
77
78
24
22
49
76
77
79
26
45
13
23
81
20
25
1
1
35
20
17
80
38
1
42
36
1
39
1
43
41
= embroidery
4
1
2
3
4
40

AFRICAN VIOLET BASKET

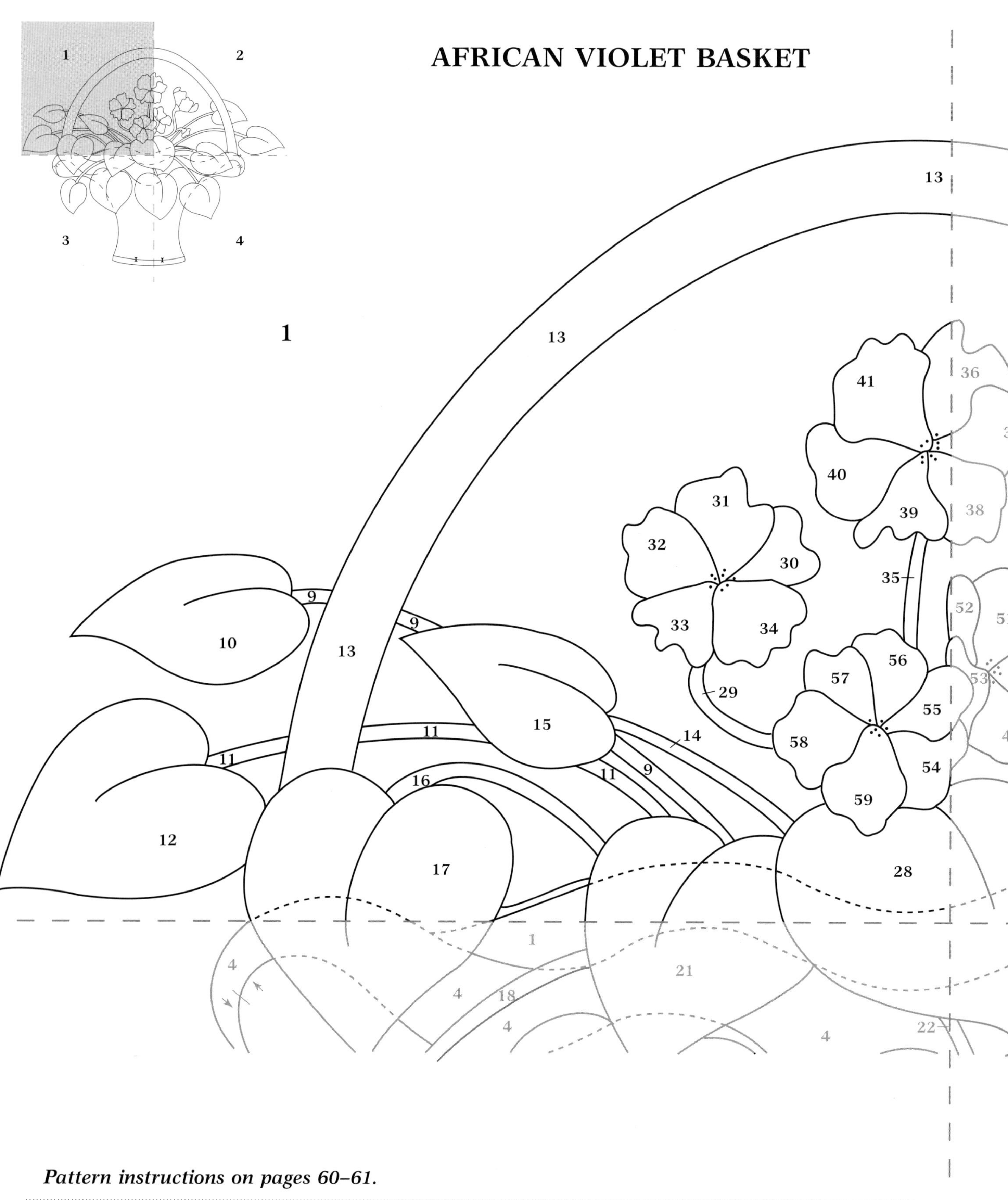

Pattern instructions on pages 60–61.

AFRICAN VIOLET BASKET

AFRICAN VIOLET BASKET

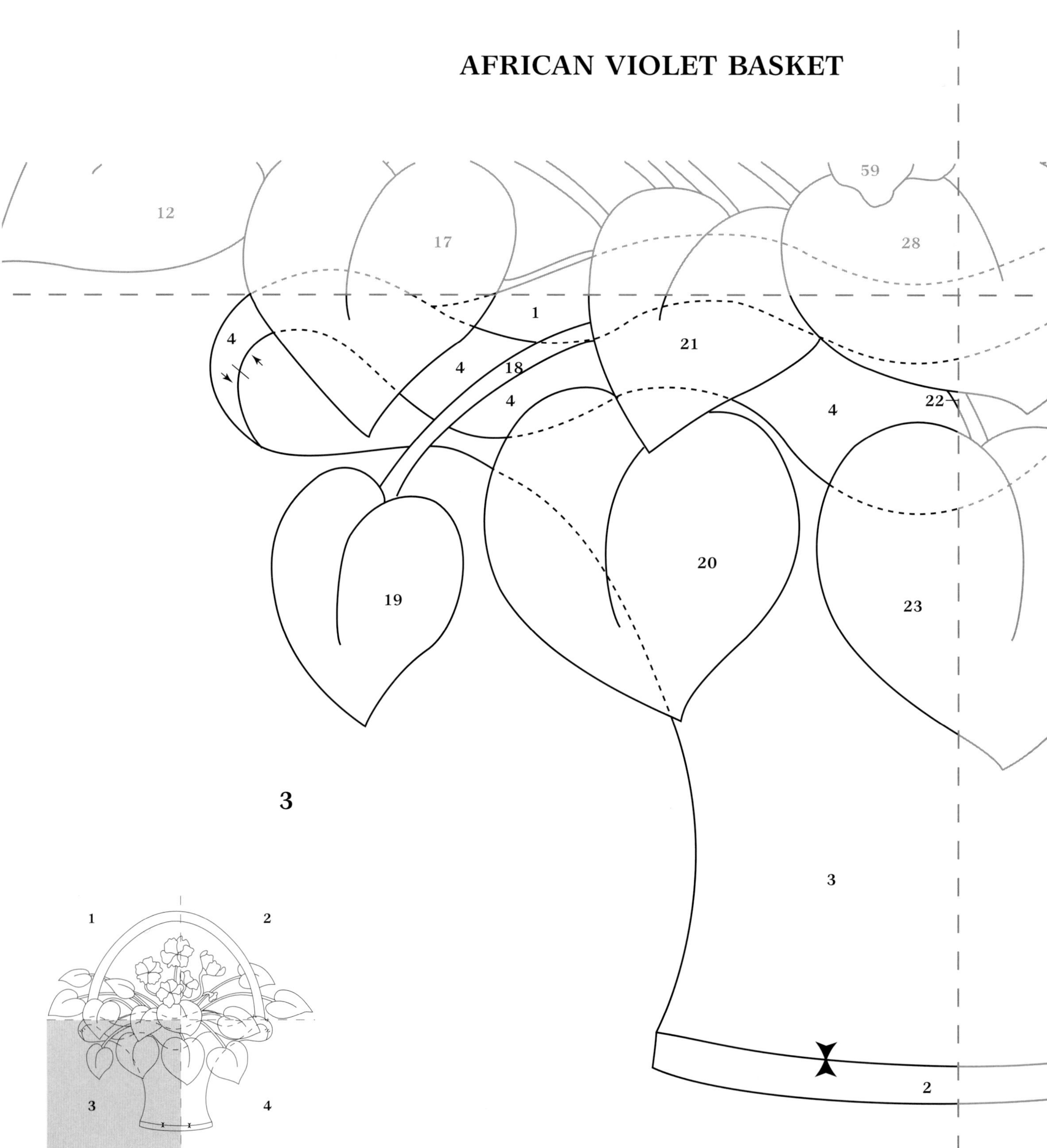

Pattern instructions on pages 60–61.

AFRICAN VIOLET BASKET

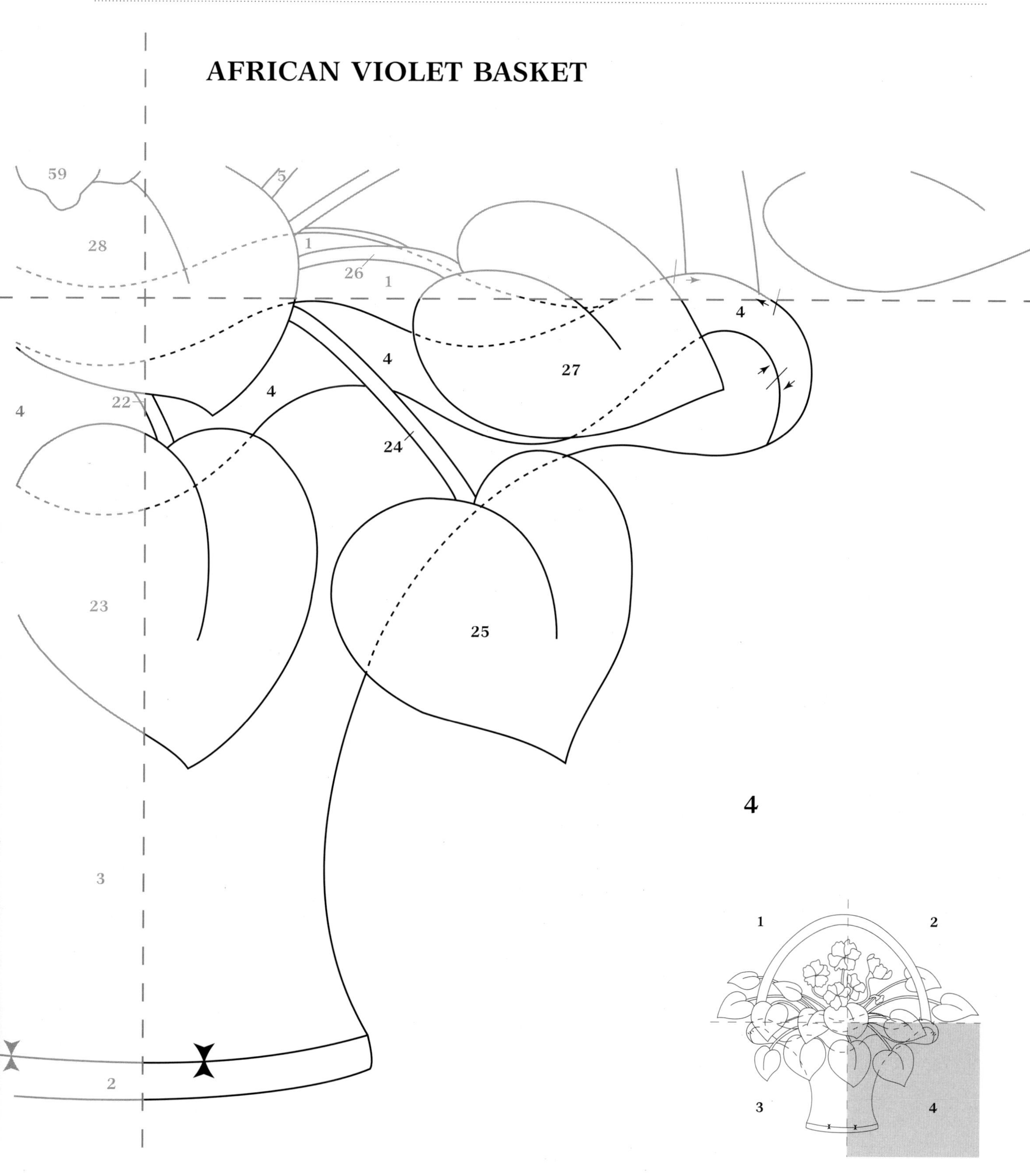

AMARYLLIS BASKET

Pattern instructions on pages 62–63.

AMARYLLIS BASKET

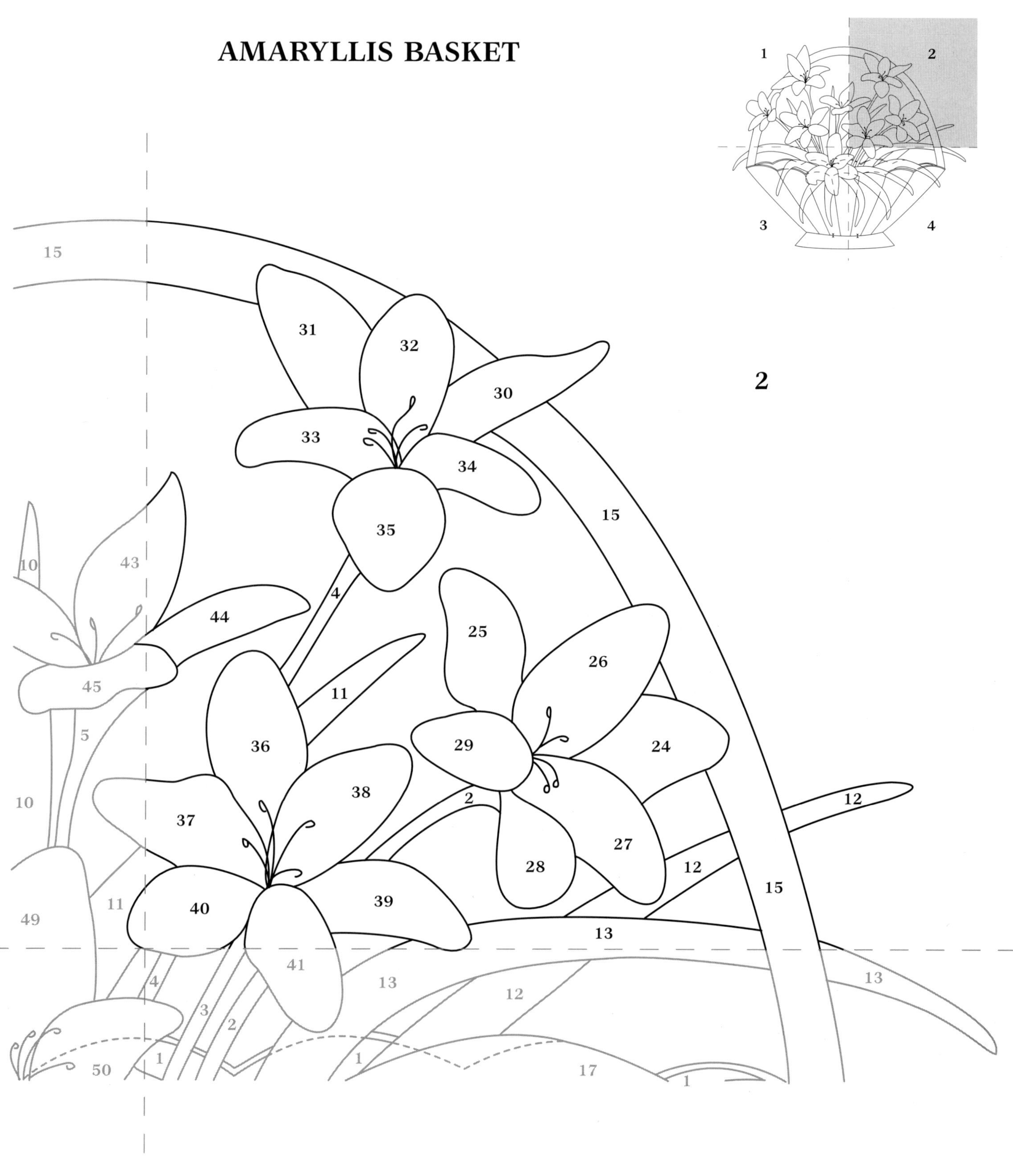

AMARYLLIS BASKET

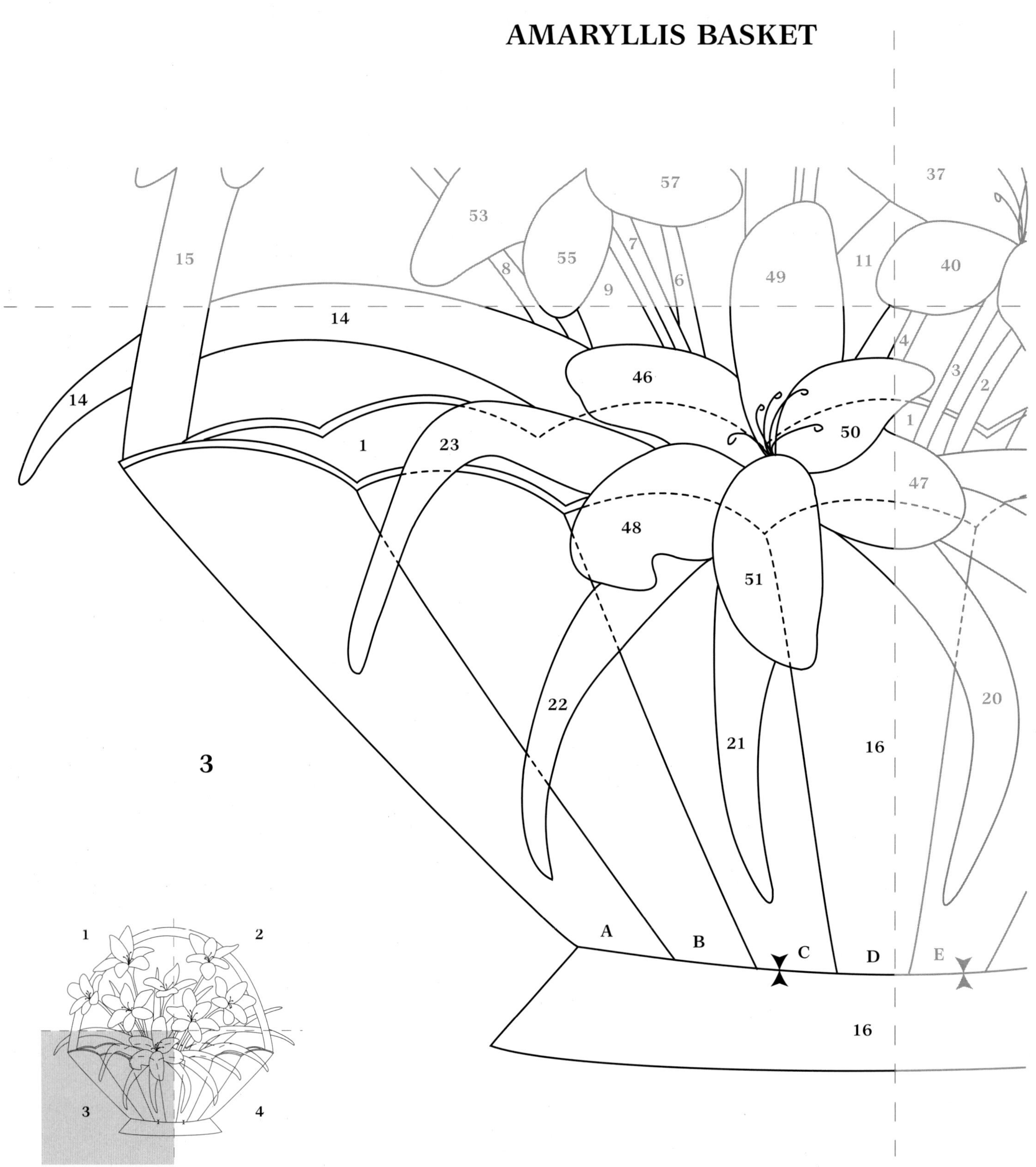

Pattern instructions on pages 62–63.

AMARYLLIS BASKET

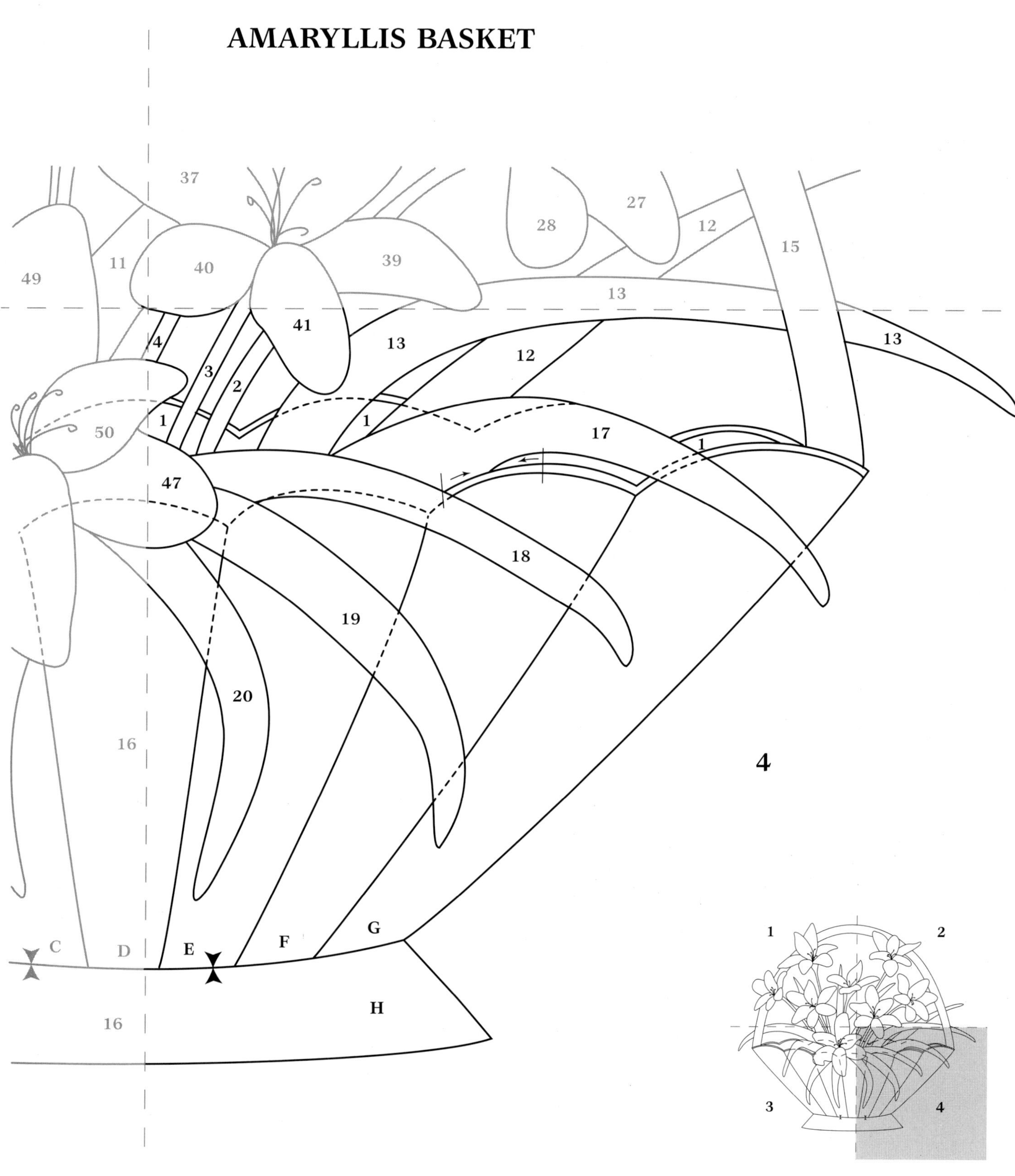

ROSE BASKET

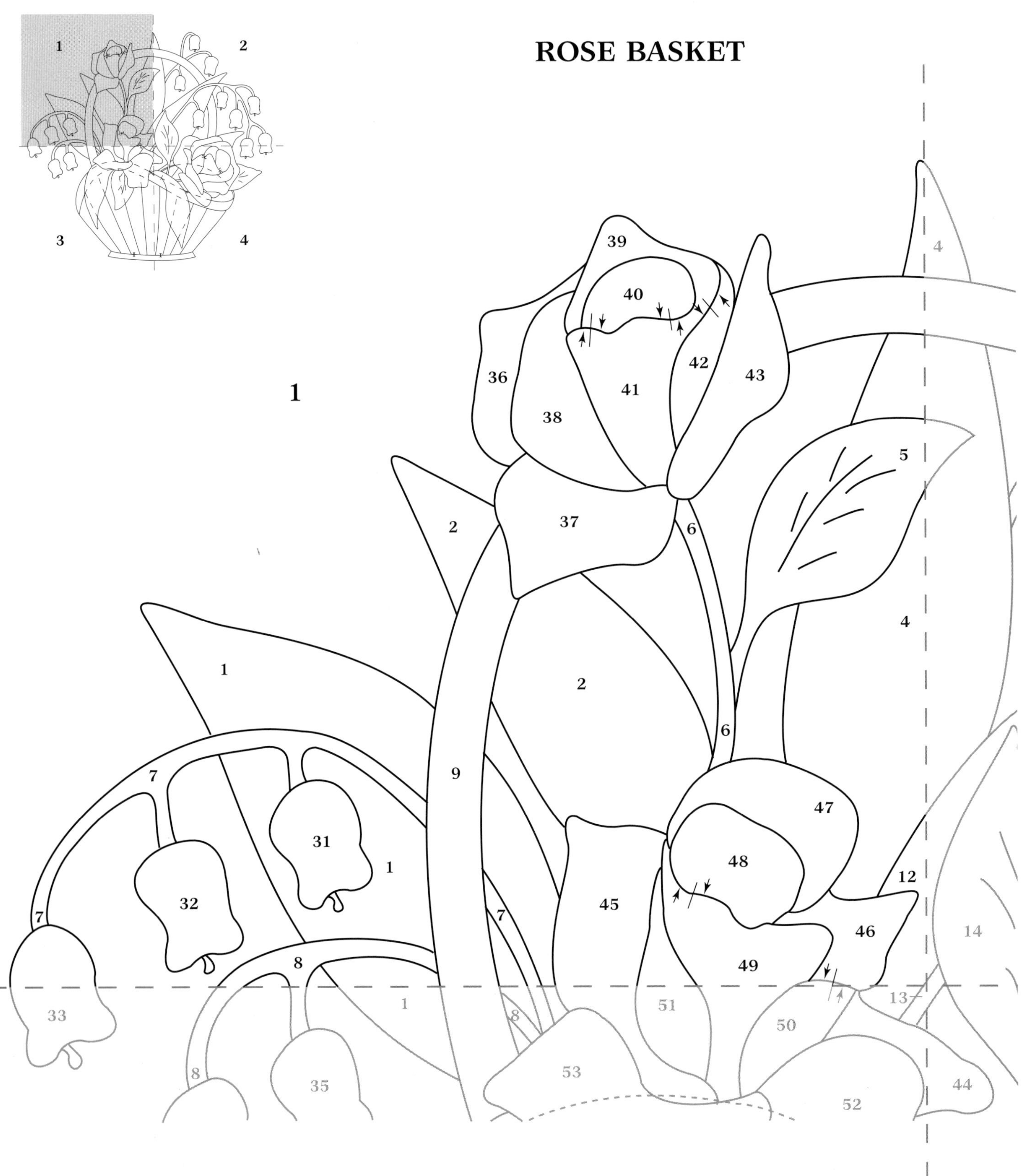

Pattern instructions on pages 64–65.

ROSE BASKET

1
2
3
4
2
4
9
3
30
3
28
3
29
5
12
4
13
12
26
13
25
12
12
27
9
24
47
12
13
12
23
46
14
15
56
22
13
58
60
54
44
63
61
52
62

ROSE BASKET

Pattern instructions on pages 64–65.

ROSE BASKET

12
46
14
15
56
23
13
58
60
22
44
54
52
63
61
62
12
11
64
59
16
15
18
17
K
15
55
58
57
10 (optional)
11
18
K
4
18
19
D
E
F
G
H
I
18
J
1
2
3
4

WILD ROSE BASKET

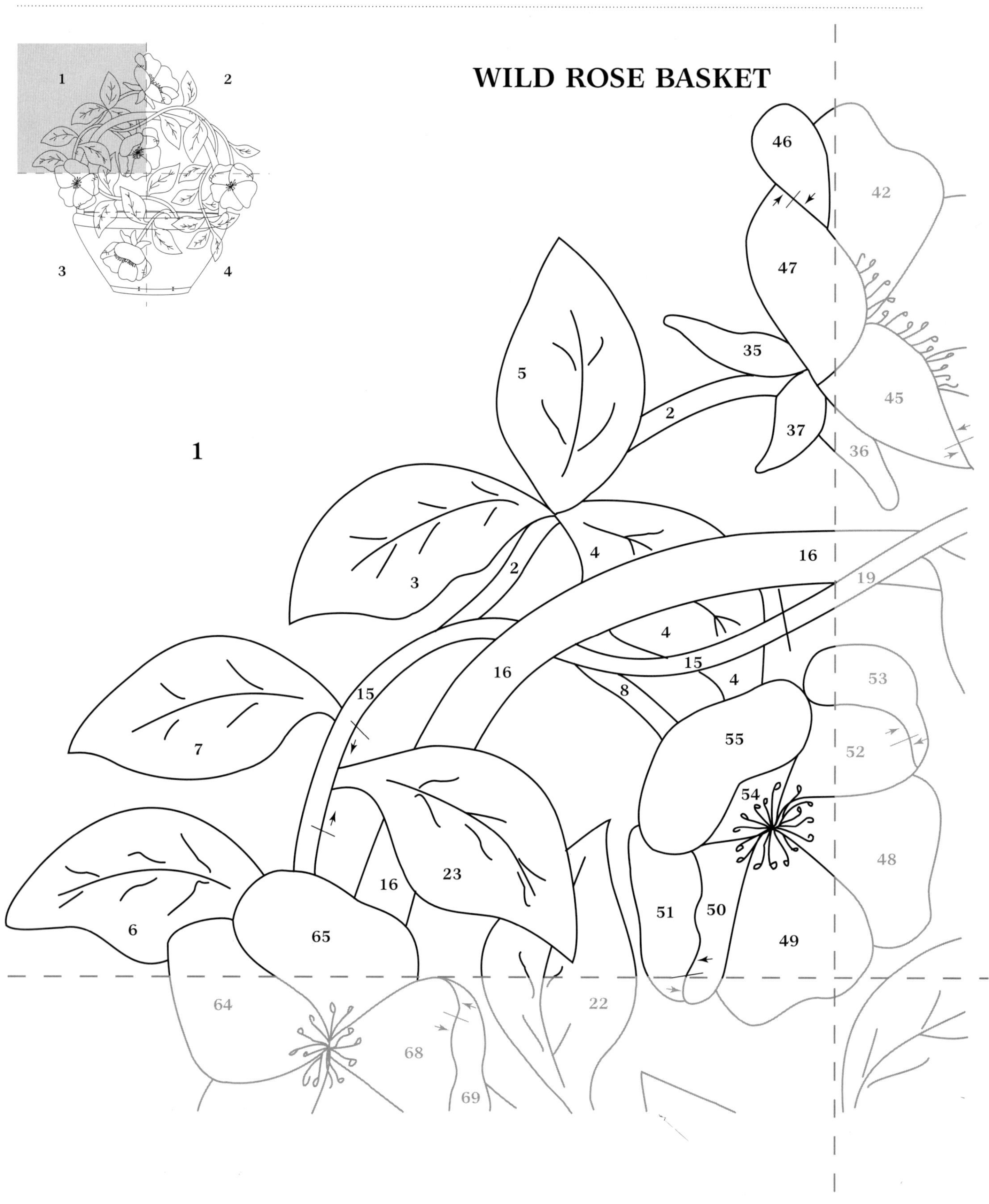

Pattern instructions on pages 66–67.

WILD ROSE BASKET

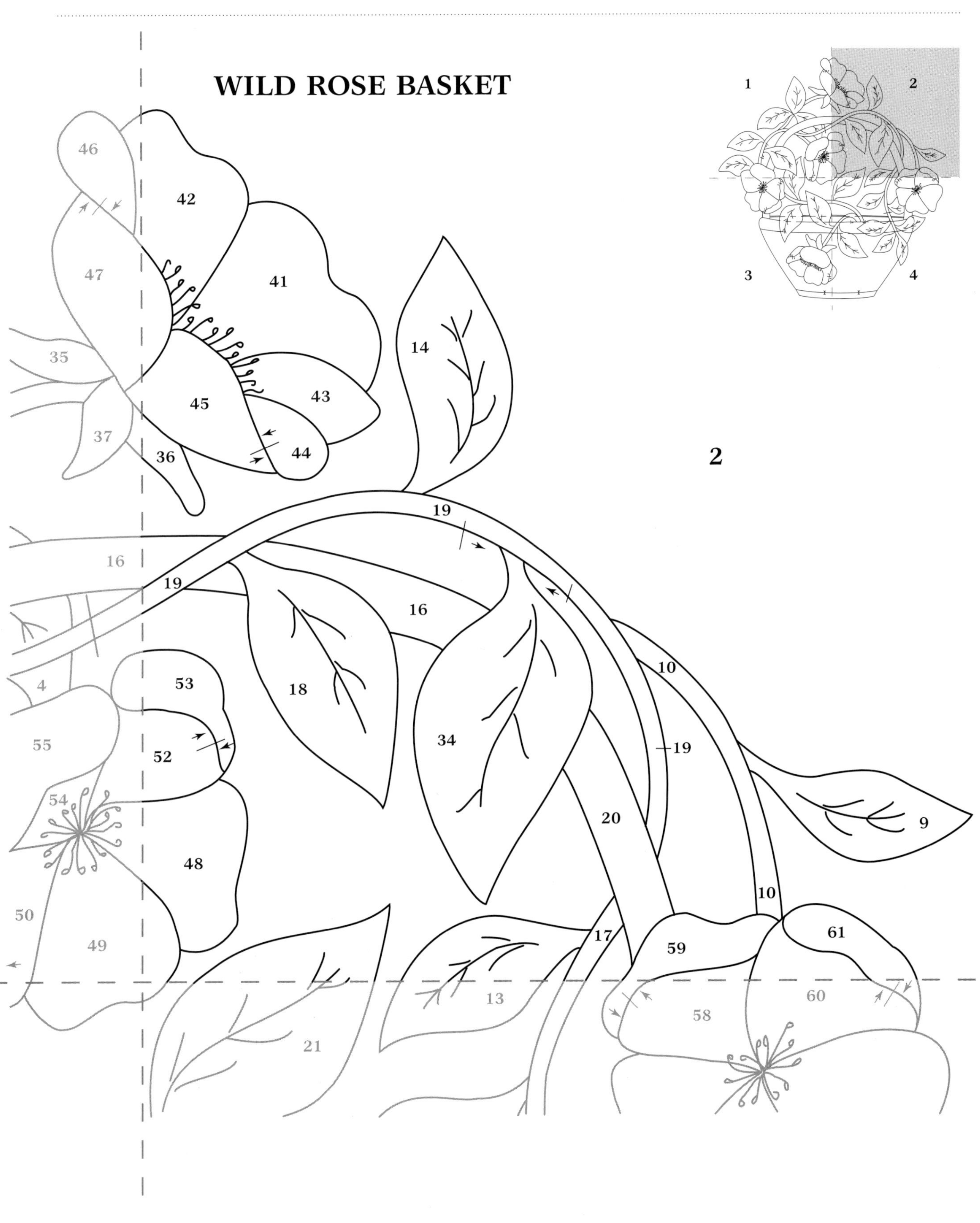

WILD ROSE BASKET

Pattern instructions on pages 66–67.

WILD ROSE BASKET

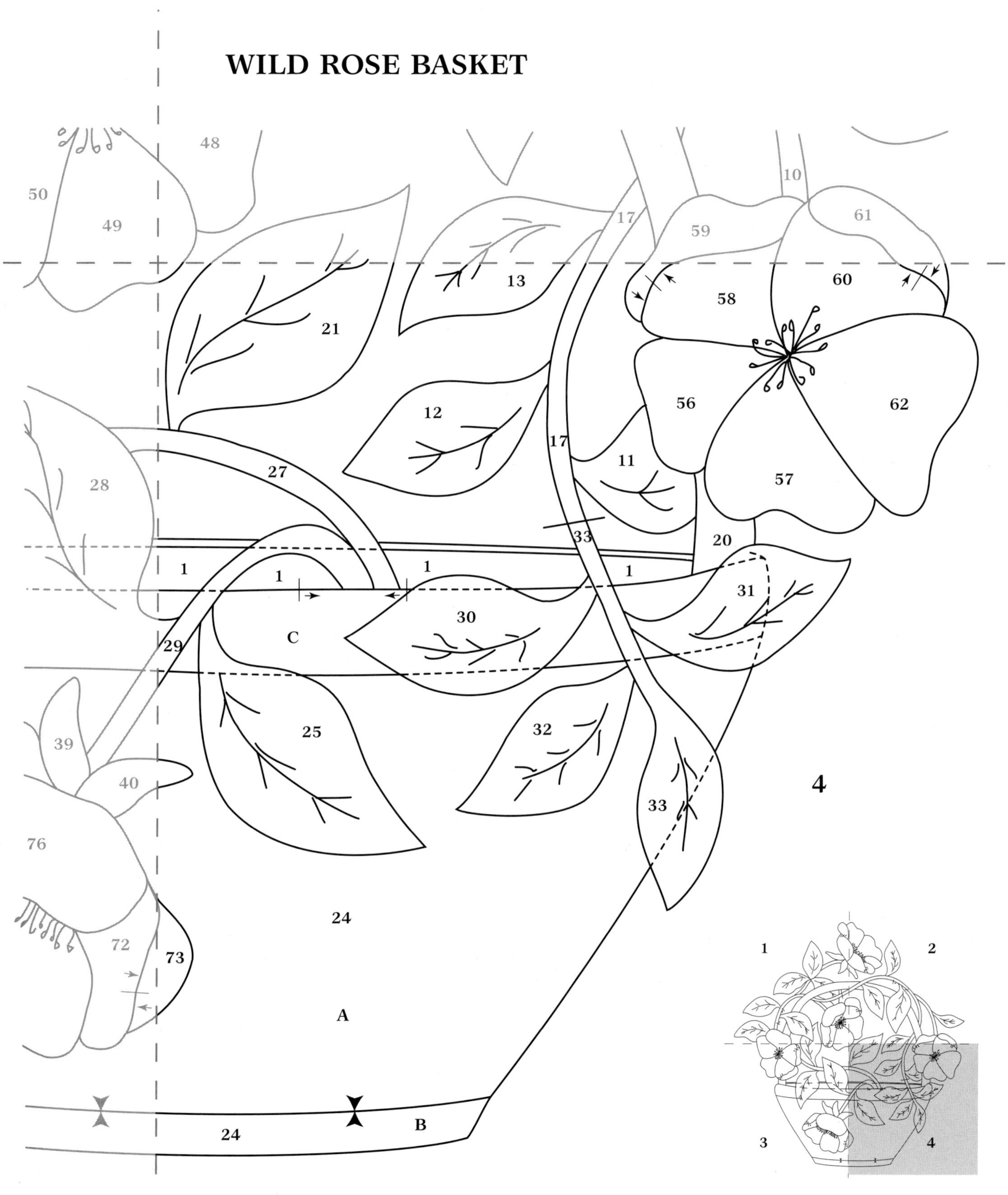

DAISY BASKET

Pattern instructions on pages 68–69.

DAISY BASKET

DAISY BASKET

Pattern instructions on pages 68–69.

DAISY BASKET

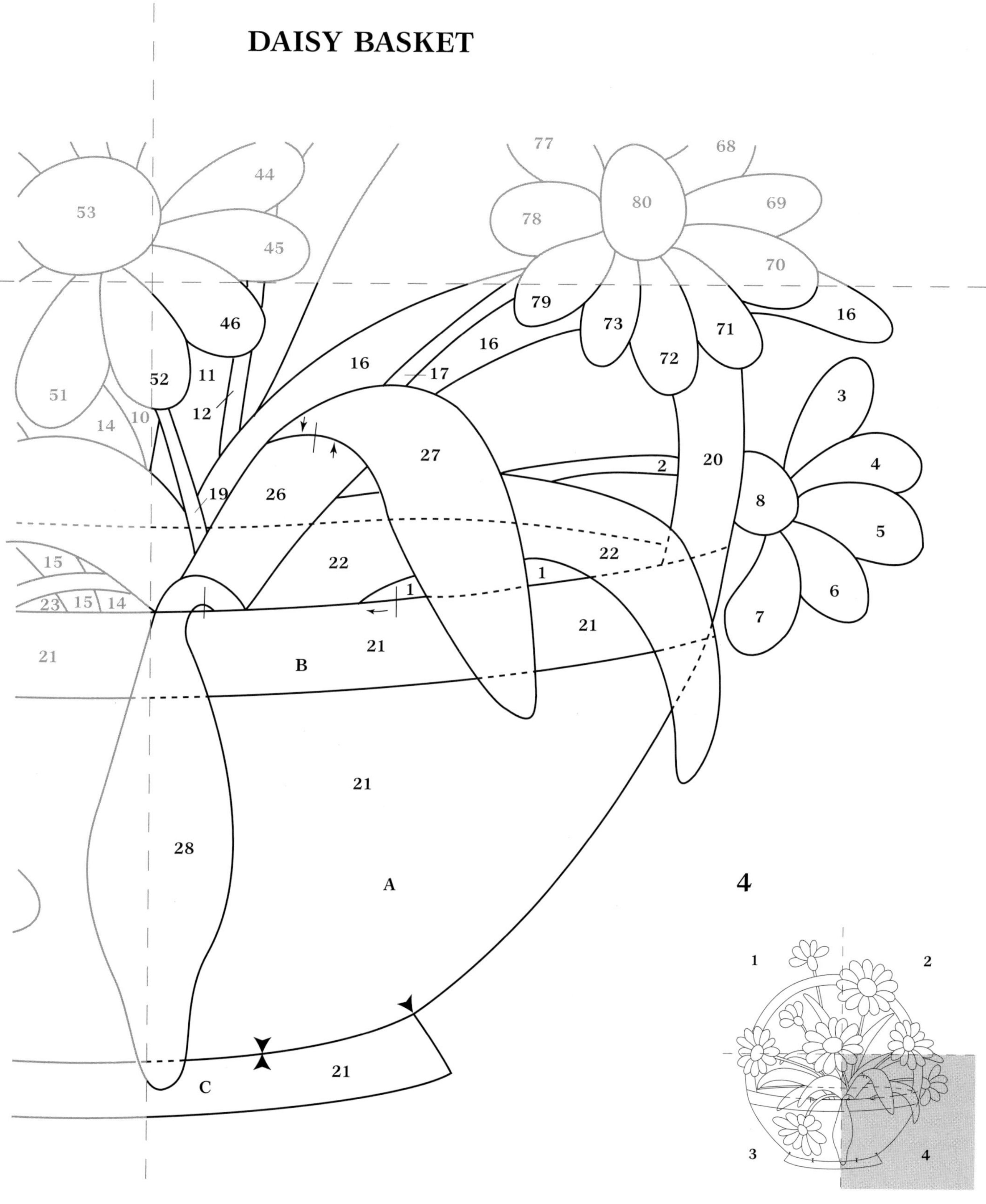

CLEMATIS BASKET

Pattern instructions on pages 70–72.

CLEMATIS BASKET

CLEMATIS BASKET

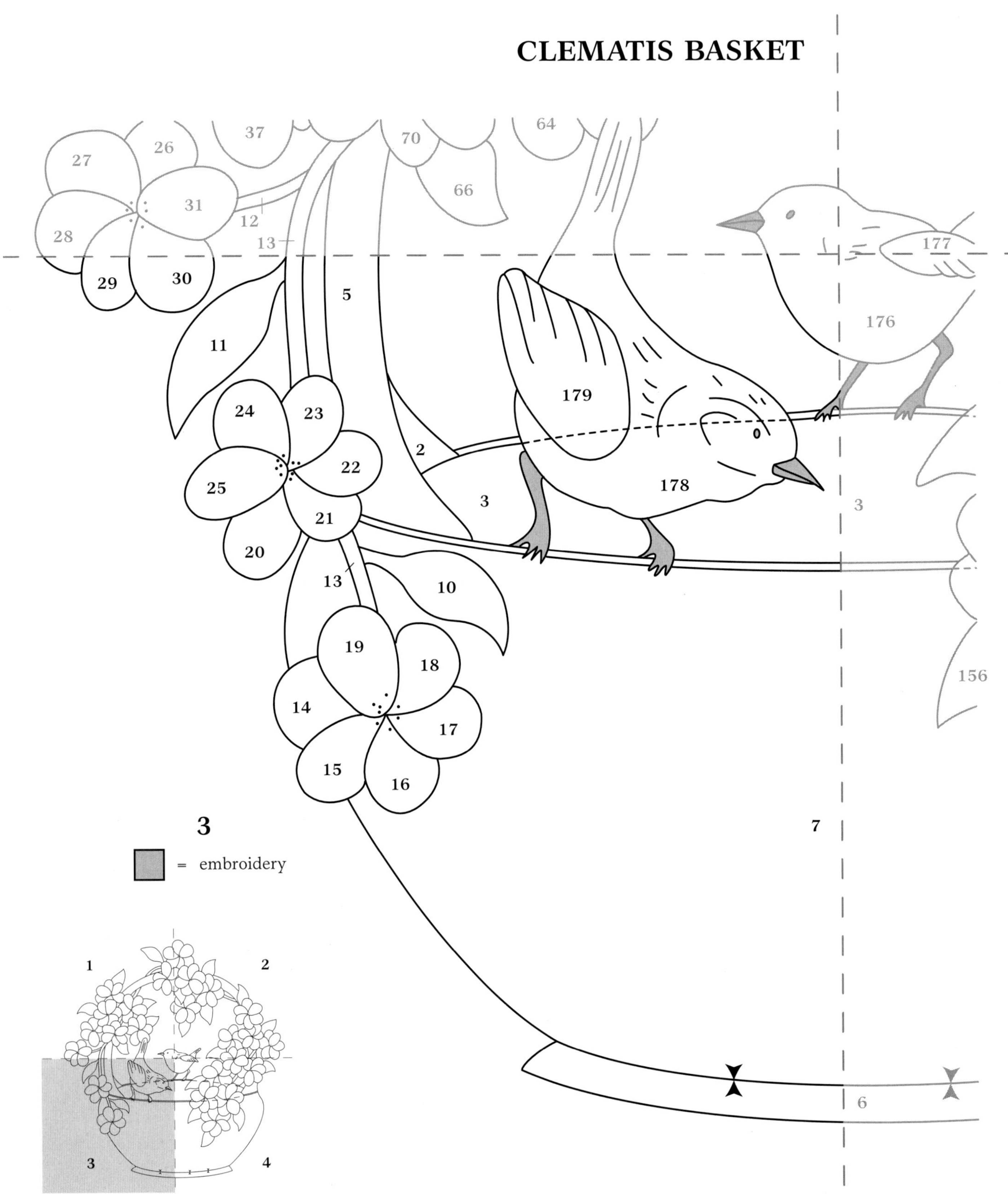

Pattern instructions on pages 70–72.

CLEMATIS BASKET

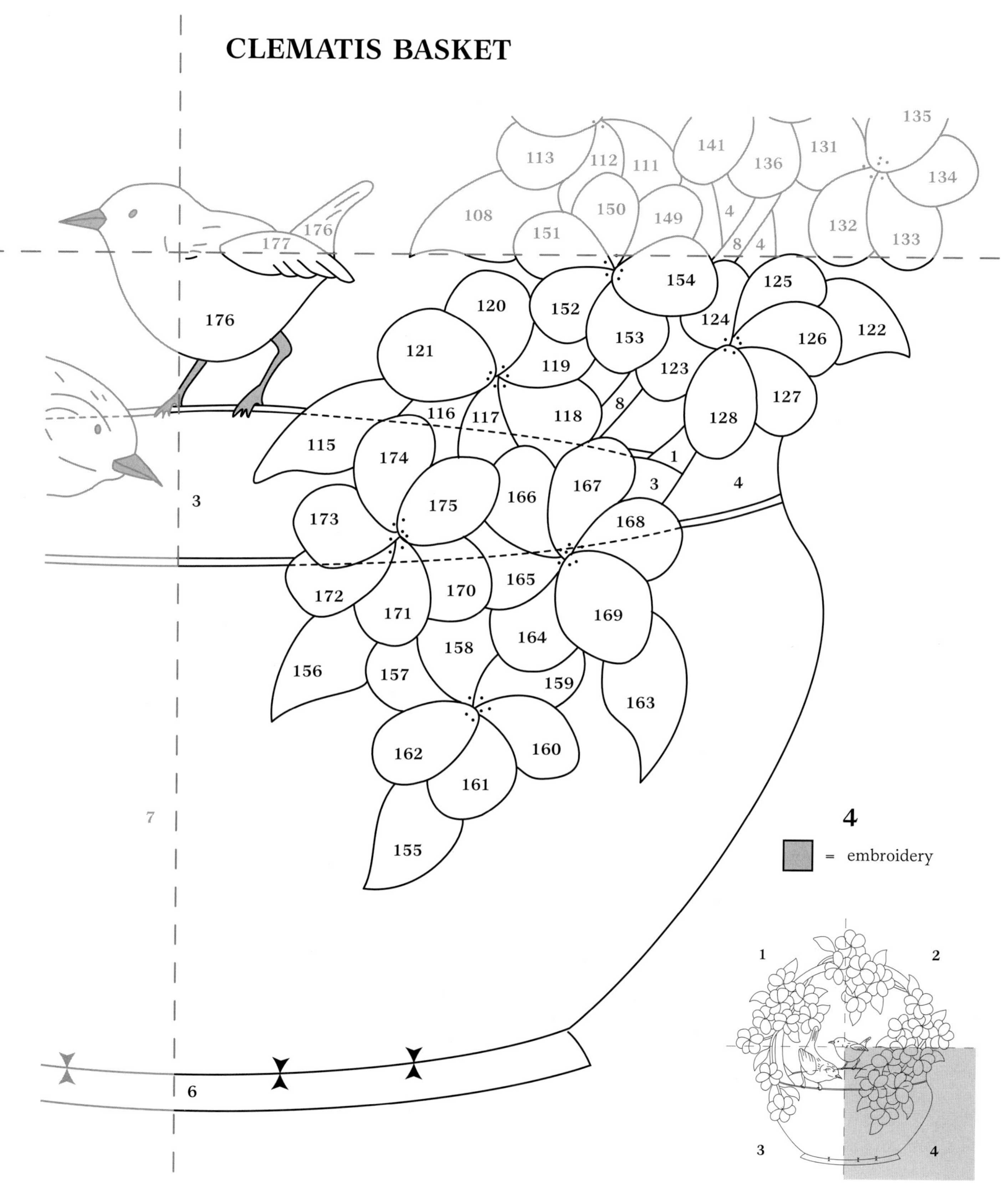

CANNA BASKET

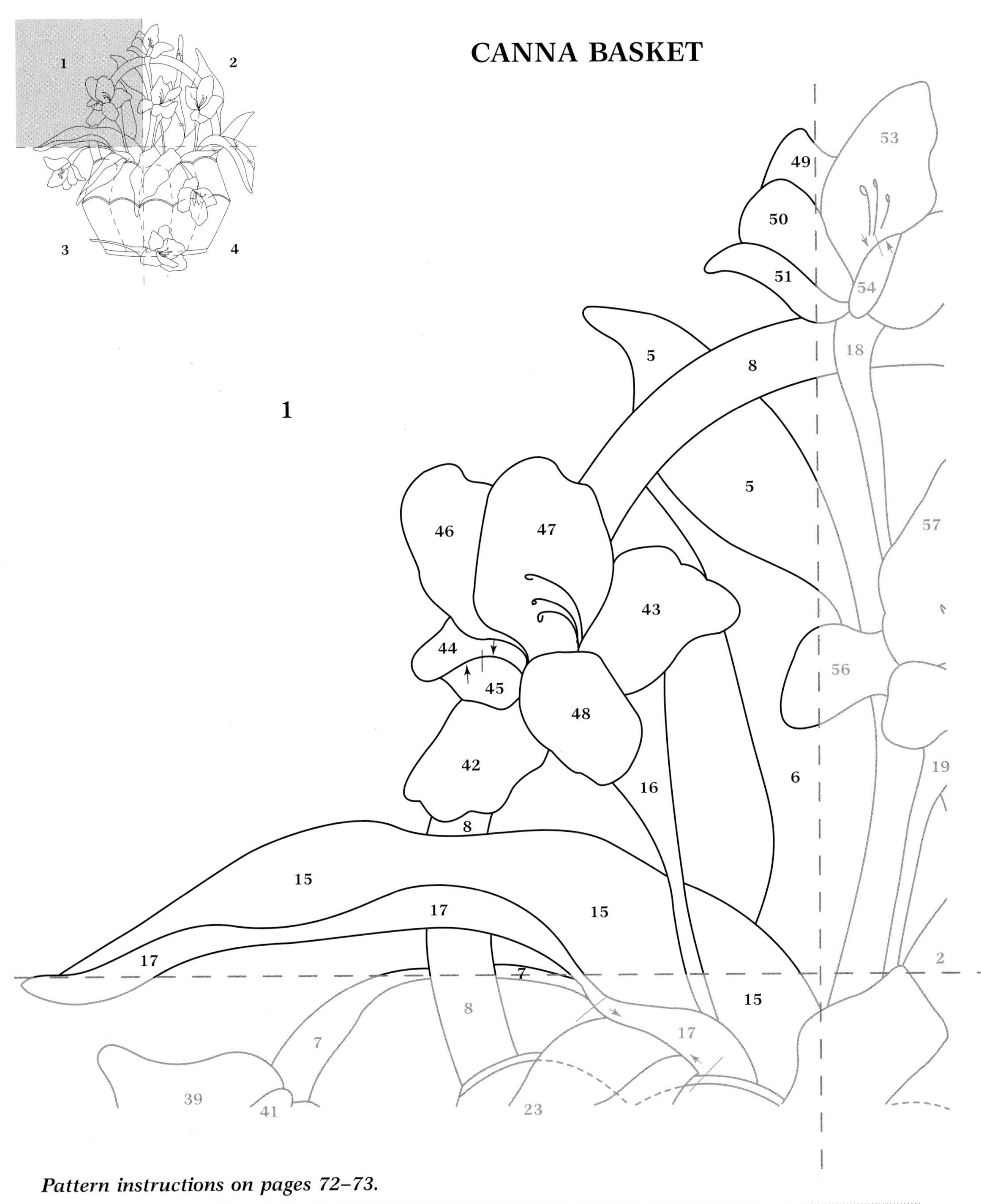

Pattern instructions on pages 72–73.

CANNA BASKET

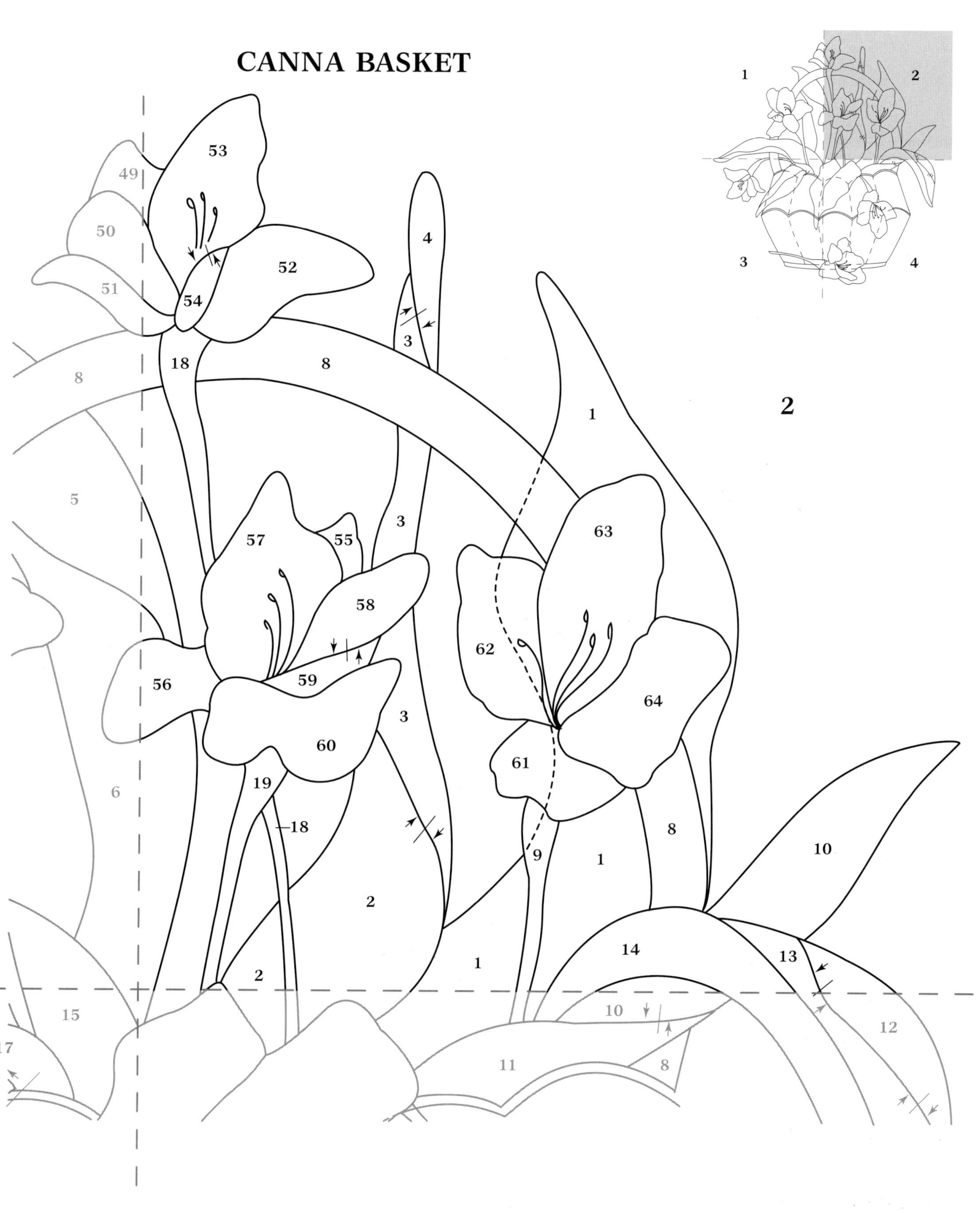

CANNA BASKET

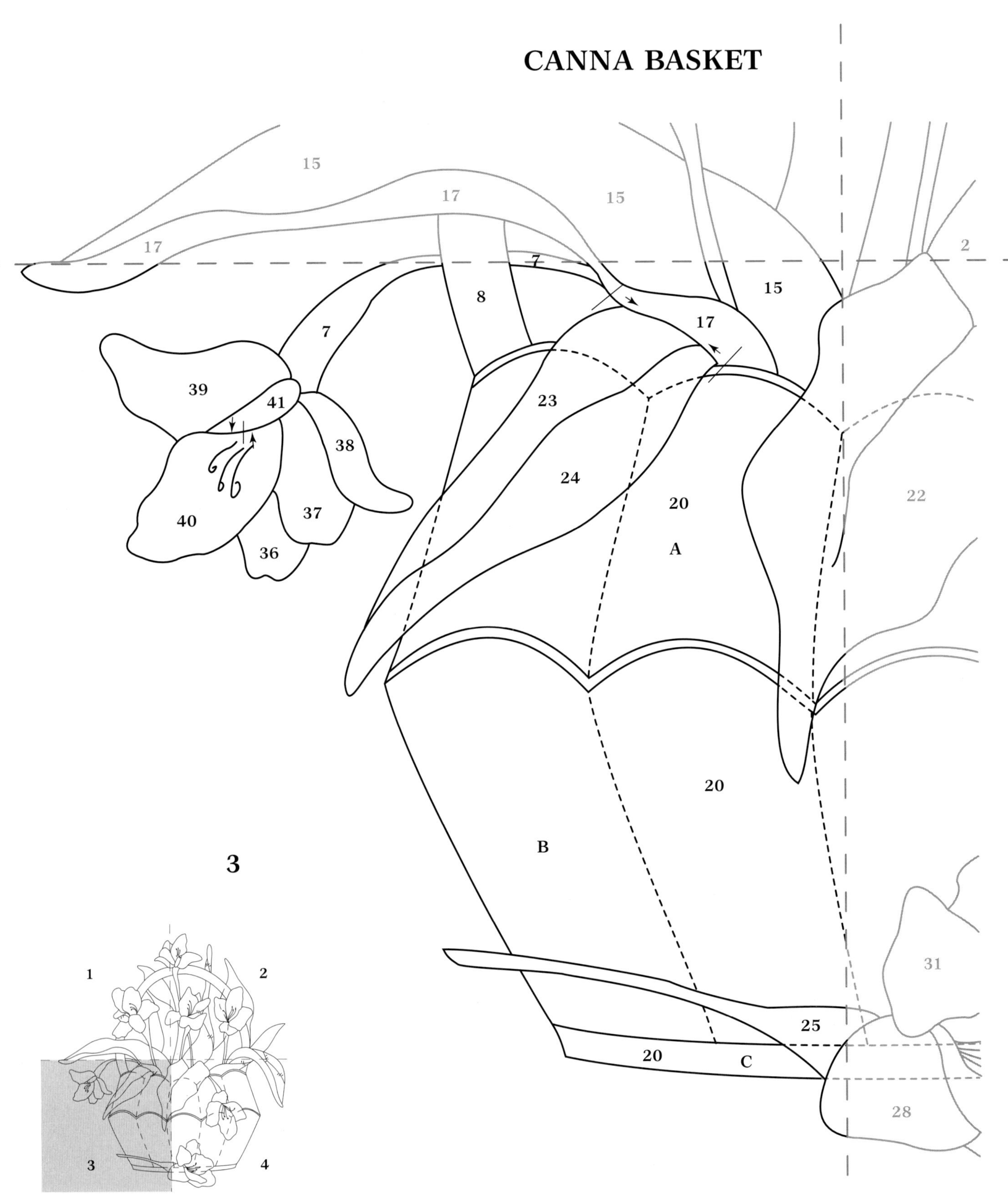

Pattern instructions on pages 72–73.

CANNA BASKET

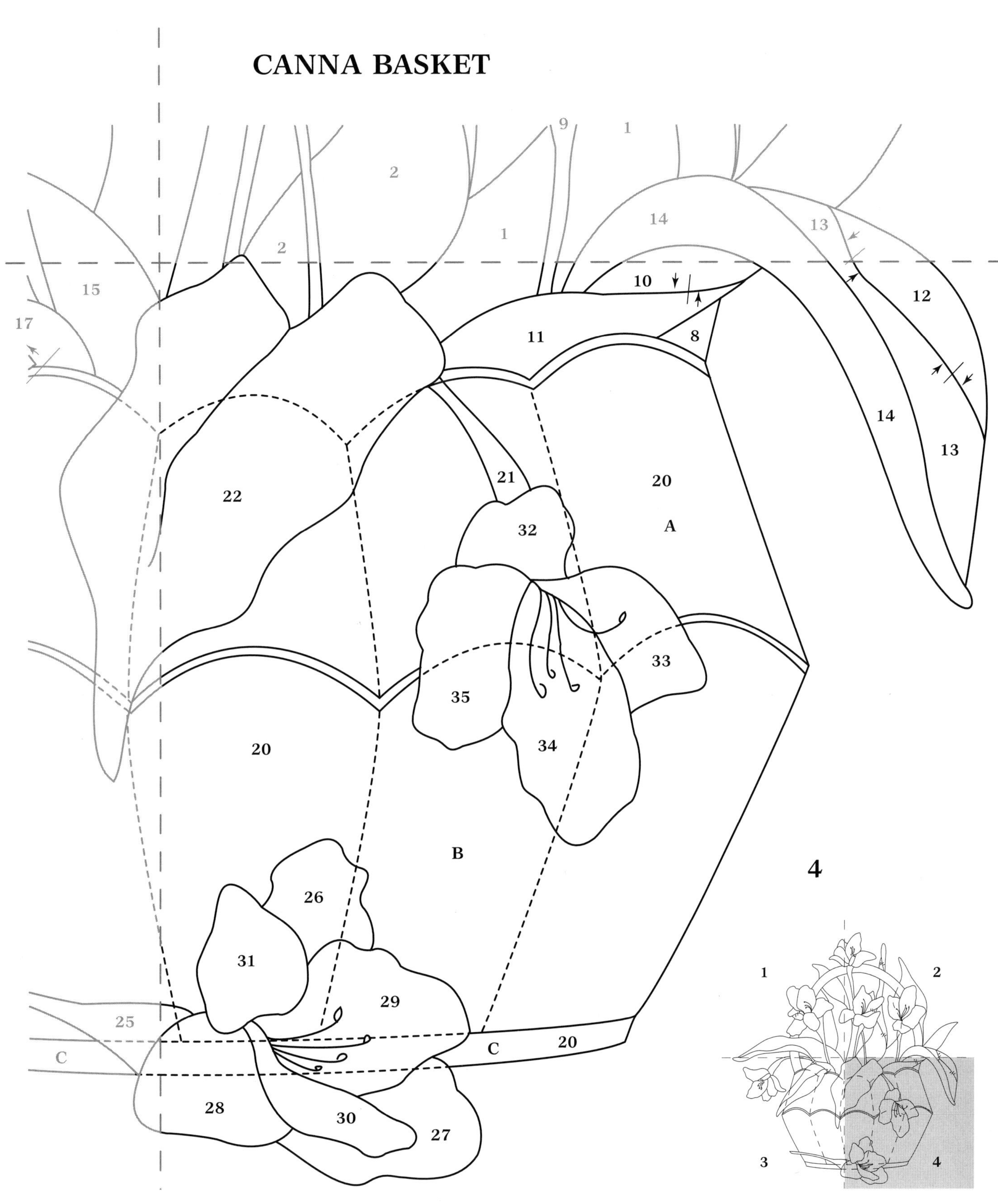

LILY

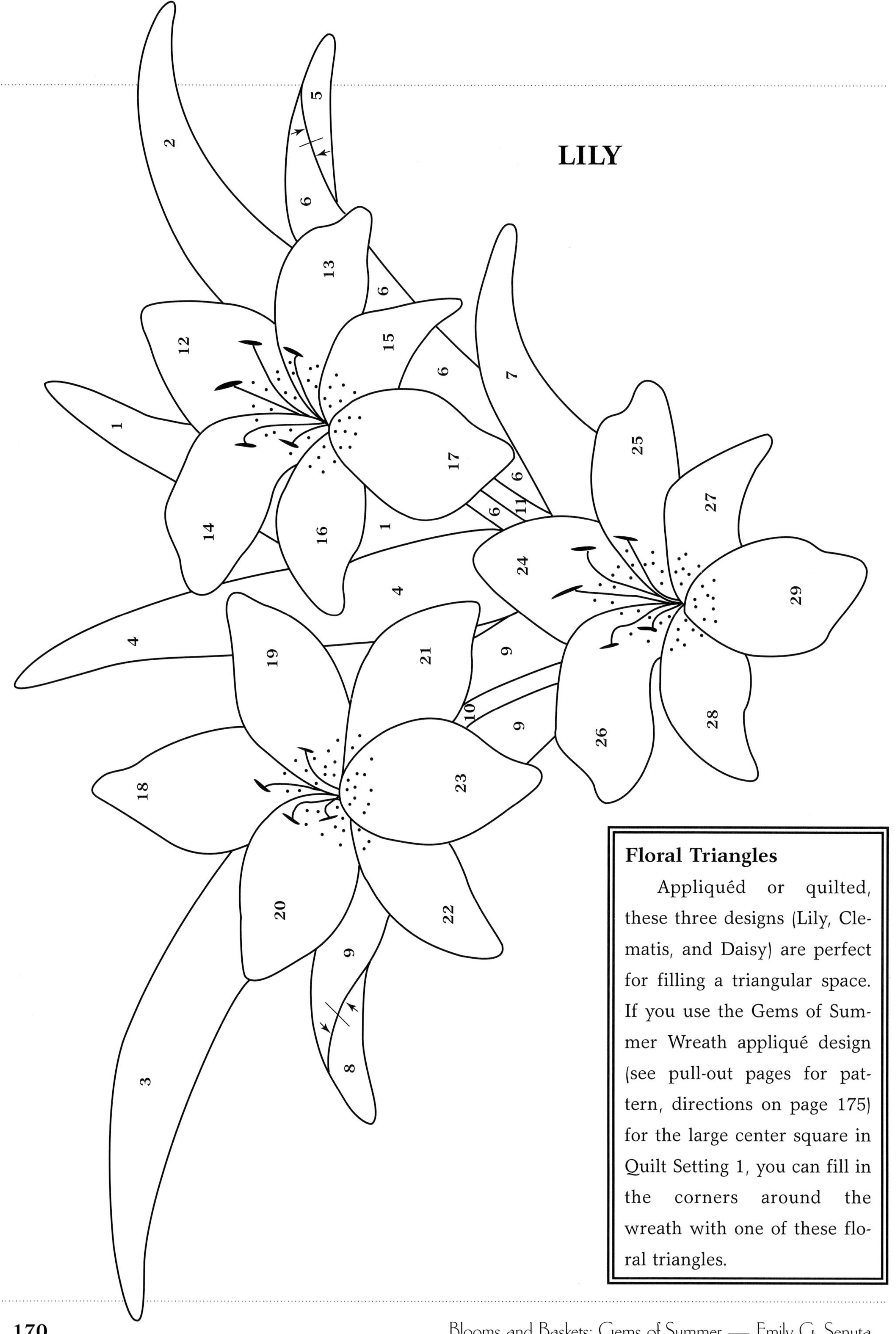

Floral Triangles

Appliquéd or quilted, these three designs (Lily, Clematis, and Daisy) are perfect for filling a triangular space. If you use the Gems of Summer Wreath appliqué design (see pull-out pages for pattern, directions on page 175) for the large center square in Quilt Setting 1, you can fill in the corners around the wreath with one of these floral triangles.

CLEMATIS

1
2
3
4
5
6
7
8
9
10
11
12
13
14
15
16
17
18
19
20
21
22
23
24
25
26
27
28
29
30
31
32
33
34
35
36
37
38
39
40
41
42
43
44
45
46
47
48
49
50
51
52

DAISY

TRAILING ROSE

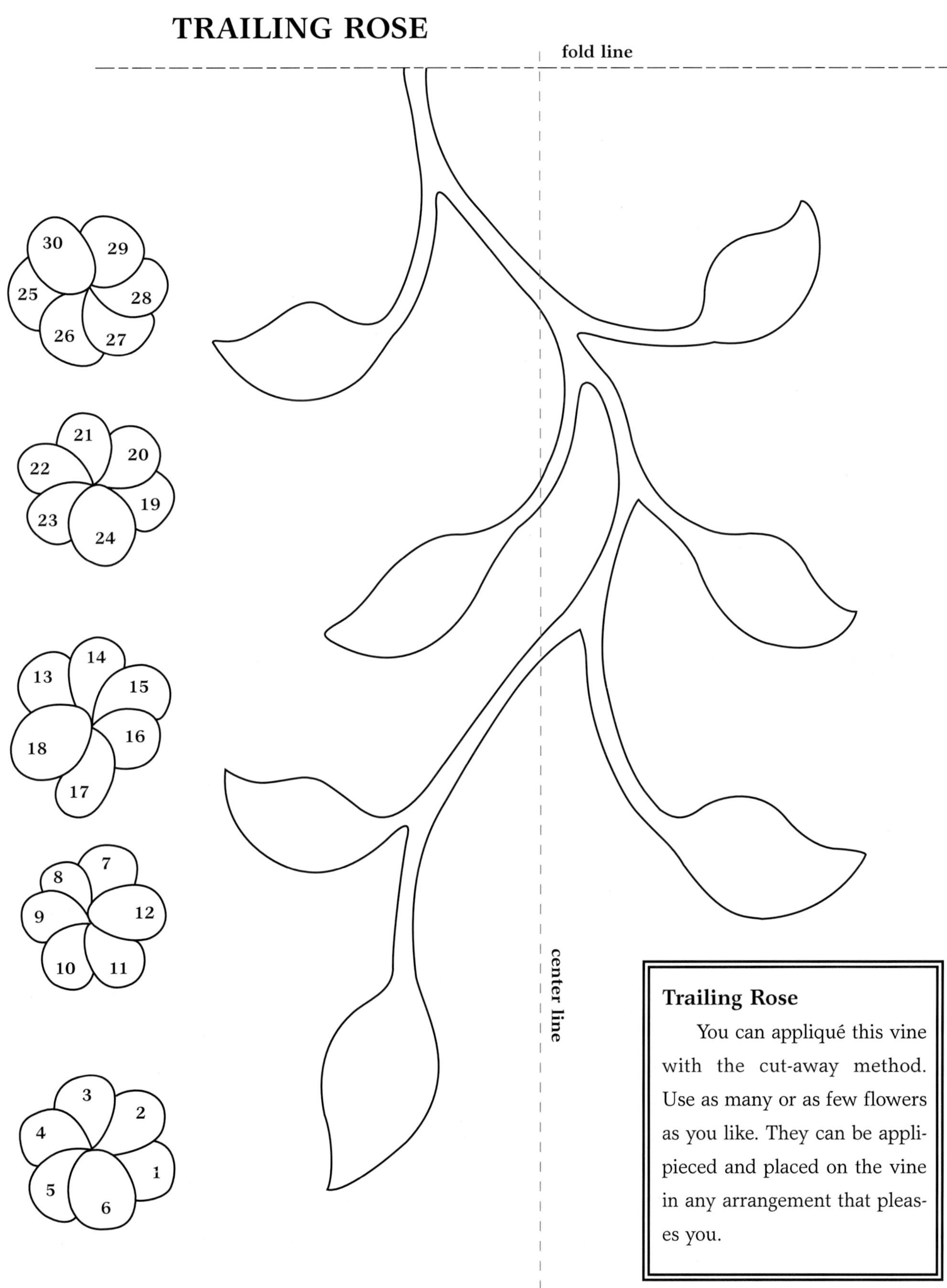

Trailing Rose

You can appliqué this vine with the cut-away method. Use as many or as few flowers as you like. They can be appli-pieced and placed on the vine in any arrangement that pleases you.

WILD ROSE CORNER GARLAND

(Full-size pattern on pull-out sheet.)

This appliqué design is very versatile. It can be used to decorate clothing, or it can be used to form a beautiful center medallion square if you place two of the designs facing each other. Place four designs facing out for a stunning larger center square (Fig. 7–1).

1 For four corner triangles, cut two 29" squares. This is the smallest triangle that can be used for this pattern, but the pattern can be placed in a larger area if needed. In each square, mark a dividing line from one corner to its opposite corner to form two right triangles. To prevent stretching the long bias edge, do not cut the triangles apart until you are ready to set them in a quilt. If you must separate them, stay-stitch the bias edges before cutting them apart, (see page 85 for instructions).

2 To transfer the design to the fabric, use a marker that will wash out. First mark the center line on your background fabric by either folding the triangle in half and creasing it or by lightly marking it with a straight edge and a wash-out marker. Trace the design on one half of the triangle and use the reverse pattern to trace the design on the other half of the triangle. If your fabrics are dark and you need to use the carbon paper method of tracing, which ruins the pattern, you may want to make duplicate patterns before transferring the design to your fabric.

3 Make templates out of freezer paper or contact paper for all numbered pieces and attach the templates to the right side of your selected fabrics. Make a long, narrow bias strip for piece #36. Appliqué pieces onto the background in numerical order.

4 Cut away backs of flowers if desired and add embroidery details.

Fig 7–1. Four Wild Rose corners can be used together for a large medallion center square.

GEMS OF SUMMER WREATH

(Full-size pattern on pull-out sheet.)

When I promised my students a center medallion, I had no idea what it would turn out to be. A wreath incorporating flowers from some of the baskets seemed like a logical and compatible choice. The asymmetrical design in wreaths has always been my favorite. This pattern can stand alone or be combined with patterns in this book for a variety of settings.

1 Cut a background square 27" or larger, depending on the setting you have chosen. You can orient the square either on point or straight. With a wash-out marker, transfer the design to your background, using the "north, south, east, and west" marks. North is the top of the wreath. These marks, along with the center placement mark, will help you align the wreath properly in the square.

2 Cut four bias strips ¾" x 40" (¼" wide finished) for the intertwined wreath structure, plus approximately 2 yards more of bias strips cut ¾" wide (can be short lengths) to complete the structure under the flowers. All bias strips should be cut from one fabric. Consider the possibility of using your basket fabric to unify the center medallion with the basket blocks. Use a different fabric for the stems so the eye can find the wreath structure under the floral arrangement.

3 Make templates for the flowers and leaves, including all instructional marks, and attach them to your selected fabrics.

4 The short bias sections that are part of the wreath structure under the flowers are all marked #1. Appliqué them in place first.

5 The long bias strips for the wreath intertwine. You can baste them all in place, being careful to lace them as shown. Appliqué them to the background and remove the basting thread. Or, if you can manage the loose ends, you can pin and sew as you go. Start at the lower right segment of the wreath, pin and sew bias #3 to the place that bias #5 passes under it. Stop sewing #3 at that point. Pin and sew #2 until you reach the place #5 passes under it and stop. Sew #4 until #5 passes under it. Continue in this manner until you have sewn the entire wreath structure.

6 Appliqué all the stems and leaves in place.

7 Appli-piece the flowers and butterfly and appliqué them in place.

8 Cut away excess fabric layers from the back, if you like, and add embroidery details.

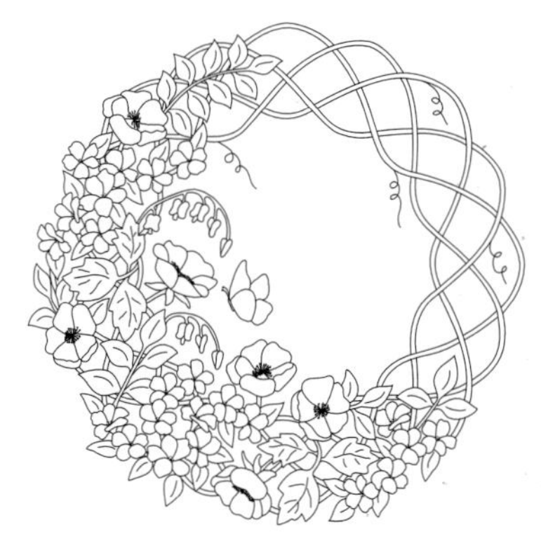

AQS Books on Quilts

This is only a partial listing of the books on quilts that are available from the American Quilter's Society. AQS books are known the world over for their timely topics, clear writing, beautiful color photographs, and accurate illustrations and patterns. The following books are available from your local bookseller, quilt shop, or public library. If you are unable to locate certain titles in your area, you may order by mail from the AMERICAN QUILTER'S SOCIETY, P.O. Box 3290, Paducah, KY 42002-3290. Add $2.00 for postage for the first book ordered and 40¢ for each additional book. Include item number, title, and price when ordering. Allow 14 to 21 days for delivery. Customers with Visa, MasterCard, or Discover may phone in orders from 7:00–5:00 CST, Monday–Friday, Toll Free 1-800-626-5420.

4595 **Above & Beyond Basics,** Karen Kay Buckley $18.95
2282 **Adapting Architectural Details for Quilts,** Carol Wagner $12.95
4813 **Addresses & Birthdays,** compiled by Klaudeen Hansen **(HB)** $14.95
4543 **American Quilt Blocks: 50 Patterns for 50 States,** Beth Summers $16.95
4696 **Amish Kinder Komforts,** Bettina Havig $14.95
4829 **Anita Shackelford: Surface Textures,** Anita Shackelford **(HB)** $24.95
4899 **Appliqué Paper Greetings,** Elly Sienkiewicz **(HB)** $24.95
3790 **Appliqué Patterns from Native American Beadwork Designs,** Dr. Joyce Mori $14.95
2099 **Ask Helen: More About Quilting Designs,** Helen Squire $14.95
2207 **Award-Winning Quilts: 1985-1987** $24.95
2354 **Award-Winning Quilts: 1988-1989** $24.95
3425 **Award-Winning Quilts: 1990-1991** $24.95
3791 **Award-Winning Quilts: 1992-1993** $24.95
4830 **Baskets: Celtic Style,** Scarlett Rose $19.95
4832 **A Batch of Patchwork,** May T. Miller & Susan B. Burton $18.95
4593 **Blossoms by the Sea: Making Ribbon Flowers for Quilts,** Faye Labanaris $24.95
4898 **Borders & Finishing Touches,** Bonnie K. Browning $16.95
4697 **Caryl Bryer Fallert: A Spectrum of Quilts, 1983-1995,** Caryl Bryer Fallert $24.95
4626 **Celtic Geometric Quilts,** Camille Remme $16.95
3926 **Celtic Style Floral Appliqué,** Scarlett Rose $14.95
2208 **Classic Basket Quilts,** Elizabeth Porter & Marianne Fons $16.95
2355 **Creative Machine Art,** Sharee Dawn Roberts $24.95
4818 **Dear Helen, Can You Tell Me?** Helen Squire $15.95
3399 **Dye Painting!** Ann Johnston $19.95
4814 **Encyclopedia of Designs for Quilting,** Phyllis D. Miller **(HB)** $34.95
3468 **Encyclopedia of Pieced Quilt Patterns,** compiled by Barbara Brackman ...$34.95
3846 **Fabric Postcards,** Judi Warren $22.95
4594 **Firm Foundations,** Jane Hall & Dixie Haywood $18.95
4900 **Four Blocks Continued...,** Linda Giesler Carlson $16.95
2381 **From Basics to Binding,** Karen Kay Buckley $16.95
4526 **Gatherings: America's Quilt Heritage,** Kathlyn F. Sullivan $34.95
2097 **Heirloom Miniatures,** Tina M. Gravatt $9.95
4628 **Helen's Guide to quilting in the 21st century,** Helen Squire $16.95
1906 **Irish Chain Quilts: A Workbook of Irish Chains,** Joyce B. Peaden $14.95
3784 **Jacobean Appliqué: Book I, "Exotica,"** Campbell & Ayars $18.95
4544 **Jacobean Appliqué: Book II, "Romantica,"** Campbell & Ayars $18.95
3904 **The Judge's Task,** Patricia J. Morris $19.95
4751 **Liberated Quiltmaking,** Gwen Marston **(HB)** $24.95
4897 **Lois Smith's Machine Quiltmaking,** Lois Smith $19.95
4523 **Log Cabin Quilts: New Quilts from an Old Favorite** $14.95
4545 **Log Cabin with a Twist,** Barbara T. Kaempfer $18.95
4815 ***Love to Quilt:* Bears, Bears, Bears,** Karen Kay Buckley $14.95
4833 ***Love to Quilt:* Broderie Perse: The Elegant Quilt,** Barbara W. Barber $14.95
4890 ***Love to Quilt:* Dye & Discharge,** Sara Newberg King $14.95
4598 ***Love to Quilt:* Men's Vests,** Alexandra Capadalis Dupré $14.95
4816 ***Love to Quilt:* Necktie Sampler Blocks,** Janet B. Elwin $14.95
4753 ***Love to Quilt:* Penny Squares,** Willa Baranowski $12.95
4995 **Magic Stack-n-Whack Quilts,** Bethany S. Reynolds $19.95
4911 **Mariner's Compass Quilts: New Quilts from an Old Favorite** $16.95
4752 **Miniature Quilts: Connecting New & Old Worlds,** Tina M. Gravatt $14.95
4514 **Mola Techniques for Today's Quilters,** Charlotte Patera $18.95
3330 **More Projects and Patterns,** Judy Florence $18.95
1981 **Nancy Crow: Quilts and Influences,** Nancy Crow $29.95
3331 **Nancy Crow: Work in Transition,** Nancy Crow $12.95
4828 **Nature, Design & Silk Ribbons,** Cathy Grafton $18.95
3332 **New Jersey Quilts,**The Heritage Quilt Project of New Jersey $29.95
3927 **New Patterns from Old Architecture,** Carol Wagner $12.95
2153 **No Dragons on My Quilt,** Jean Ray Laury $12.95
4627 **Ohio Star Quilts: New Quilts from an Old Favorite** $16.95
3469 **Old Favorites in Miniature,** Tina Gravatt $15.95
4831` **Optical Illusions for Quilters,** Karen Combs $22.95
4515 **Paint and Patches: Painting on Fabrics with Pigment,** Vicki L. Johnson ..$18.95
5098 **Pineapple Quilts, New Quilts from an Old Favorite** $16.95
4513 **Plaited Patchwork,** Shari Cole $19.95
3928 **Precision Patchwork for Scrap Quilts,** Jeannette Tousley Muir $12.95
4779 **Protecting Your Quilts: A Guide for Quilt Owners, Second Edition** $6.95
4542 **A Quilted Christmas,** edited by Bonnie Browning $18.95
2380 **Quilter's Registry,** Lynne Fritz $9.95
3467 **Quilting Patterns from Native American Designs,** Dr. Joyce Mori $12.95
3470 **Quilting with Style,** Gwen Marston & Joe Cunningham $24.95
2284 **Quiltmaker's Guide: Basics & Beyond,** Carol Doak $19.95
4918 **Quilts by Paul D. Pilgrim: Blending the Old & the New,** Gerald E. Roy $16.95
2257 ***Quilts:* The Permanent Collection – MAQS** $9.95
3793 ***Quilts:* The Permanent Collection – MAQS Volume II** $9.95
3789 **Roots, Feathers & Blooms,** Linda Giesler Carlson $16.95
4512 **Sampler Quilt Blocks from Native American Designs,** Dr. Joyce Mori $14.95
3796 **Seasons of the Heart & Home: Quilts for a Winter's Day,** Jan Patek $18.95
3761 **Seasons of the Heart & Home: Quilts for Summer Days,** Jan Patek $18.95
2357 **Sensational Scrap Quilts,** Darra Duffy Williamson $24.95
4783 **Silk Ribbons by Machine,** Jeanie Sexton $15.95
3929 **The Stori Book of Embellishing,** Mary Stori $16.95
3903 **Straight Stitch Machine Appliqué,** Letty Martin $16.95
3792 **Striplate Piecing,** Debra Wagner $24.95
5012 **Take-Away Appliqué,** Suzanne Marshall $22.95
3930 **Tessellations & Variations,** Barbara Ann Caron $14.95
3788 **Three-Dimensional Appliqué,** Anita Shackelford $24.95
4596 **Ties, Ties, Ties: Traditional Quilts from Neckties,** Janet B. Elwin $19.95
3931 **Time-Span Quilts: New Quilts from Old Tops,** Becky Herdle $16.95
4919 **Transforming Fabric,** Carolyn Dahl $29.95
2029 **A Treasury of Quilting Designs,** Linda Goodmon Emery $14.95
3847 **Tricks with Chintz,** Nancy S. Breland $14.95
5014 **The Wholecloth Garment Stori,** Mary Stori $19.95
2286 **Wonderful Wearables: A Celebration of Creative Clothing,** Virginia Avery $24.95
4812 **Who's Who in American Quilting,** edited by Bonnie Browning **(HB)** $49.95
4956 **Variegreat! New Dimensions in Traditional Quilts,** Linda Glantz $19.95
4972 **20th Century Quilts,** Cuesta Benberry and Joyce Gross ....$ 9.95